Suicide in East German Literature

Studies in German Literature, Linguistics, and Culture

Suicide in East German Literature

Fiction, Rhetoric, and the Self-Destruction of Literary Heritage

Robert Blankenship

CAMDEN HOUSE
Rochester, New York

First published 2017
by Camden House

Camden House is an imprint of Boydell & Brewer Inc.
668 Mt. Hope Avenue, Rochester, NY 14620, USA
www.camden-house.com
and of Boydell & Brewer Limited
PO Box 9, Woodbridge, Suffolk IP12 3DF, UK
www.boydellandbrewer.com

ISBN-13: 978-1-57113-574-2
ISBN-10: 1-57113-574-X

Library of Congress Cataloging-in-Publication Data

Names: Blankenship, Robert, 1980– author.
Title: Suicide in East German literature : fiction, rhetoric, and the self-destruction of literary heritage / Robert Blankenship.
Description: Rochester, New York : Camden House, 2017. | Series: Studies in German literature, linguistics, and culture | Includes bibliographical references and index.
Identifiers: LCCN 2017022531| ISBN 9781571135742 (hardcover : alk. paper) | ISBN 157113574X (hardcover : alk. paper)
Subjects: LCSH: Suicide in literature. | German literature—Germany (East)—History and criticism.
Classification: LCC PT3710.S85 B53 2017 | DDC 830.93548—dc23 LC record available at https://lccn.loc.gov/2017022531

This publication is printed on acid-free paper.
Printed in the United States of America.

Contents

Acknowledgments

Many people have helped me with this project, so many, in fact, that it would be impossible to list them all here. I am truly grateful to all of them. I must, however, expressly mention a few people who have helped in extraordinary and enduring ways. Richard Langston has long been a key mentor for me and was crucially helpful in the formative stages of this project. He deserves special thanks. I am grateful to the Berlin-based graphic designer, muralist, and general guru of all things visual, Alexis Laskaris, for creating the image on the cover of this book, an image that I believe supports the underlying claim of this monograph. I thank my colleagues and students at California State University, Long Beach, for providing me with a welcoming and energetic place to read, write, teach, learn, and productively argue about German literature and cinema. In the parlance of our institution, Go Beach! The entire team at Camden House has been fantastic. Jim Walker has been particularly helpful. He has been a reliable and enthusiastic champion of this project for a long time. I am also grateful to the two anonymous reviewers for providing thoroughly helpful reviews. A few brief passages in chapter 6 are adapted from my chapter "Hamlet as Unmarked Intertext: The Imperative of Remembrance in Horn's End" in *The Hamlet Zone: Reworking Hamlet for European Cultures*, edited by Ruth J. Owen (Newcastle upon Tyne: Cambridge Scholars, 2012), 189–96. As always, I am grateful for the support and love I receive daily from Courtney and Jeremiah.

Robert Blankenship
Long Beach, California
April 2017

Introduction: The Rhetoric of Suicide in East Germany

FICTIONAL SUICIDES FROM the German Democratic Republic have been greatly misunderstood. One assumption seems to be that suicide in GDR fiction was primarily a direct reflection of real suicides in GDR society. Several scholars and critics who have dealt with this issue have maintained that view.[1] Further, conversations I have had while working on this project, both with scholars of German literature and with interested non-academics, have revealed that many people assume that suicide in GDR literature must represent some realistic reflection of politically motivated suicide in the GDR. Such assumptions seem fair on the surface. It might seem that suicide was rampant in the GDR, given the regime's attempt to hide suicide rates. The quantity of major works of GDR literature, especially in the 1970s and 1980s, with suicide as a major theme might also cause one to surmise that suicide rates in the GDR were anomalously high. It might seem too that writers used literature as a secret code to communicate about the real problem of suicide. And Florian Maria Georg Christian Graf Henckel von Donnersmarck's 2006 film *Das Leben der Anderen* only reinforces these assumptions. However, such assumptions about the nature of suicide in GDR literature are mostly false. While suicide was a taboo topic in the GDR, the fictional suicides do not primarily reflect a problem of suicide in GDR society, perceived or real. These fictional suicides are much more complex. Above all, they are literary. Read closely, they reveal a wealth of literary devices and theorizations of literary problems. Taken together, they form an interesting literary history, one that is situated among other developments in GDR literature, including, for example, the movement from socialist realism toward a belated modernism, the toying with taboos following Erich Honecker's 1971 assertion that there were to be no taboos in GDR literature (with the problematic caveat that the writer must write as a socialist), and the movement of intertextuality from the notion of cultural and literary heritage (*Kulturerbe*) as an antidote to fascist aesthetics toward the use of intertextuality as a method of reevaluating and eventually eroding literary heritage.

The story of intertextuality in GDR literature is a particularly important parallel to the story of suicide in that literature. Most suicides in GDR literature, at least in the 1970s and 1980s, are intertwined with stark intertextual elements. Further, suicide worked in tandem with intertextuality in GDR literature over time to unravel the literary heritage of the GDR, highlighting the self-destructive nature inherent in the notion of literary heritage. Part of the reason for the relationship between suicide and intertextuality has to do with the fact that one of the first major works to deal explicitly with suicide—Ulrich Plenzdorf's *Die neuen Leiden des jungen W.* (The New Sufferings of Young W.)[2]—also deals overwhelmingly explicitly with intertextuality; it offers a reworking of Goethe's *Die Leiden des jungen Werther* (The Sorrows of Young Werther),[3] in which the main character argues in defense of suicide and later kills himself. There are also later works of fiction that deal with suicide and allude to Plenzdorf's novel. Further, virtually all the major works of literature in the GDR following *Die neuen Leiden des jungen W.* that have suicide as one of their major themes also offer intertexts and theorizations of intertextuality. Understanding the nature of suicide in GDR fiction, then, requires some knowledge of the central role of cultural and literary heritage in the GDR.

The cultural and literary heritage of the German Democratic Republic was constructed. Some degree of cultural heritage had to be established in 1949 for the GDR as a new country, but also for the purposes of establishing a heritage antithetical to that which had been invented by German fascists and different from the literary heritage claimed by the Federal Republic of Germany. Officially, the process of inventing heritage was part of the "Programm der antifaschistisch-demokratischen Erneuerung" (Program of Antifascist-Democratic Revitalization, 1945–49). Debates concerning German cultural heritage had already occurred in the 1930s and early 1940s among Germans in exile, but ideas about cultural heritage were turned into policy in 1946. As early as June 11, 1945, barely a month after the National Socialists capitulated, the German Communist Party (KPD) called for a "Weg der Aufrichtung eines antifaschistischen, demokratischen Regimes, einer parlamentarisch-demokratischen Republik mit allen demokratischen Rechten und Freiheiten für das Volk"[4] (path to the construction of an antifascist, democratic regime, a parliamentary-democratic republic with all democratic rights and freedoms for the people). Not long thereafter, the cultural equivalent of this process was proposed, when Wilhelm Pieck declared: "Nun wirklich einmal [werden] die erhabenen Ideen der besten unseres Volkes . . . zu den beherrschenden Mächten in unserem Kulturleben und ebenso zu lebendigen Kräften, die unser gesamtes politisches und gesellschaftliches Leben richtunggebend gestalten"[5] (that now for once the sublime ideas of the best of our people will really become the ruling powers in our cultural life as well as the living forces that shape our entire political and societal life). In his speech at the Erste Zentrale Kulturtagung (First Central Cultural Congress) on February 3, 1946, Anton Ackermann stated:

> Die Erneuerung des deutschen Kultur- und Geisteslebens nach zwölfjähriger Nazibarbarbei und Knechtschaft gebietet stärker denn je die restlose Verwirklichung einer der grundlegendsten humanistischen Forderungen, nämlich der Forderung nach Freiheit der wissenschaftlichen Forschung und der künstlerischen Gestaltung.[6]
>
> [The revitalization of German cultural and intellectual life after twelve years of Nazi barbarism and servitude demands the complete realization of one of the most basic humanistic requirements now more than ever, namely the requirement of scientific and artistic freedom.]

Although Ackermann's use of words such as "humanism" and "freedom" may ring false for many Western readers, such key words nevertheless played a large role in the creation of GDR cultural heritage. GDR literary heritage, furthermore, consisted largely of a dichotomous conception of literary history, with romanticism, modernism, and expressionism, for example, condemned as unhealthy and dangerous, while humanism, classicism, and realism were lauded as healthy and useful. This conception of literary history, called, among other things, the *Vollstreckertheorie* (executor theory), meaning that it saw socialist realism as inheriting a lineage of literary development stretching from the ancient Greeks to Luther and Shakespeare to classicism to bourgeois realism and, finally, to socialist realism. Adherence to these original policies regarding the invented cultural heritage in the GDR held fast until the early 1970s.

In the early 1970s, however, the cultural heritage of the German Democratic Republic (GDR) experienced a crisis that was never resolved.[7] On December 17, 1971, First Secretary of the Socialist Unity Party (SED) Erich Honecker, who had just ascended to power in May 1971, announced that there were to be no taboos in the literature and art of the GDR, as long as the author or artist started firmly from the standpoint of socialism. Seemingly overnight, the role of literary heritage in the literary production of the GDR was disrupted. One of the early ways that writers tested the murky waters of Honecker's rhetoric was by subverting literary heritage in their own literary works. Such subversion by way of literary productions allowed for new interpretations of canonical works and a reevaluation of the literary heritage, both by scholars and by lay readers. In 1972, Horst Haase, a scholar of German literature and a member of the SED, admitted that the officially sanctioned literary heritage was not easily accessible to workers in the GDR and that they saw it as having little to do with their daily lives.[8] On July 6 of the same year Kurt Hager, who was "Chefideologe" (chief ideologist) of the SED and largely responsible for cultural matters, maintained in his speech at the Sixth Meeting of the Central Committee of the

Socialist Unity Party that the literary heritage was important but that it should be engaged critically and not fossilized as an archive.[9] He also declared the socialist project to be more than a simple continuation of the humanist-bourgeois trajectory.[10] He thereby downgraded the value of the bourgeois tradition and transformed the Party's approach to its literary heritage. New discussions about the literary heritage culminated around the publication of Ulrich Plenzdorf's *Die neuen Leiden des jungen W.* in 1972/1973. After the early 1970s, critical engagement with the official literary heritage as well as with works that did not belong to it became commonplace in GDR literature. For example, Christa Wolf reevaluates German Romanticism, Goethe, and the ancient Greeks. Werner Heiduczek alludes to thinkers as varied as Kant, Schopenhauer, Goethe, Thomas Mann, and even Josef Stalin. Christoph Hein is influenced by William Faulkner and Walter Benjamin. Heiner Müller engages with writers as varied as Shakespeare, Brecht, Lessing, the ancient Greeks, and Fyodor Gladkov. Two trends can be seen here. On the one hand, writers began to engage with works that had been previously off limits, such as those by Faulkner and the romantics. On the other hand, writers began to engage previously acceptable figures, such as Goethe and the ancient Greeks, in previously unacceptable ways.

Apparent in the crisis of GDR literary heritage of the early 1970s was the always already ambiguous nature of literary heritage. This ambiguity was obvious, for example, in the fact that it was referred to by various names—all of which implied different sources, ideologies, and intended outcomes—such as: kulturelles Erbe (cultural heritage), klassisches Erbe (classical heritage), humanistisches Erbe (humanist heritage), nationales Erbe (national heritage), realistisches Erbe (realist heritage), sozialistisches Erbe (socialist heritage), and revolutionäres Erbe (revolutionary heritage).[11] The problem of heritage, furthermore, applied not only to literature but also to music, visual art, and philosophy from several centuries. The various names required to describe it indicate its splintered nature. Given both its different names and referents, it represented an imagined totality, a constructed cultural currency established by East German and Soviet communists in order to combat the feared effects of what they perceived as fascist and capitalist aesthetics. In part as a result of such fear, the communists planned their aesthetics just as they planned their economy. While the goal of preventing the reemergence of the fascist aesthetic would seem admirable, aesthetic planning inadvertently brought with it aesthetic resistance. The multifaceted literary heritage naturally invited dissent, as there were inevitably different ways to read texts and traditions. The fragile nature of literary heritage in the GDR was, indeed, received in varying ways by both readers and writers. These writers illuminated the fact that the literary heritage was invented and ambiguous, stifling and fragile, perhaps helpful in 1945 but ultimately doomed to failure. Their engagement with literary heritage revealed that such heritage was a double-edged sword.

One topical vehicle through which literary heritage in the GDR was subverted was suicide. Indeed, suicide was a taboo topic in the GDR, in both journalism and literature.[12] As the topic of suicide emerged in GDR literature, the literary heritage of the GDR began to unravel. Rather than describing suicide in GDR literature as an indicator that life in the GDR was unbearable, this study questions the notion that suicides in GDR fiction constitute a realistic, sociological reflection of GDR society, as is commonly assumed. Instead, these fictional suicides engage and erode the literary heritage of the GDR. These disruptive, fictional suicides, more so than real suicides, are a site of dissent in the GDR.

Although I see the problem of suicide in GDR literature as something largely specific to GDR literature, one challenge facing this study is the state of research on suicide in general; most of it is focused on empirical data. Suicidology, as it is often called, asks who, when, where, how, and, most often, why people kill themselves.[13] It is concerned with statistics that reflect objectively under what circumstances—whether psychological, sociological, or historical—suicides take place. Apart from this statistical orientation, there are also studies with legalistic, theological, or philosophical arguments regarding if and when one ever has the right to commit suicide. There are, however, relatively few studies that query the *meaning* of suicide, the *semiotics* of suicide, or the *rhetorical* or *metaphorical* nature of suicide. This lack of attention to the meaning of suicide is similar to the lack of attention to the literariness of GDR literature.

In 2006 Udo Grashoff published a monograph that constitutes the first comprehensive history of suicide in the GDR.[14] Querying the commonly held belief that suicide rates increased during the period of communist rule in East Germany (which arose in part since the authorities in the GDR stopped publishing GDR suicide rates in 1962), Grashoff comes to the conclusion that the territory that became the Soviet Occupation Zone (SBZ) and later the GDR (previously known as *Mitteldeutschland*) has had relatively constant suicide rates since at least the early nineteenth century. Because of factors such as climate and the responsibility placed on the individual in Protestant theology (50–54)—factors that have been shown to increase suicide rates in other places as well—suicide rates in that territory have historically been higher than in the territory that became West Germany. Grashoff goes on to explain that about half of the cases of suicide in the GDR involved senior citizens and that many other cases involved the chronically ill (50–54). The majority of cases of suicide in the GDR were only peripherally political (50–54). The notion many people have about widespread suicide as political protest in the GDR is mostly the result of the SED's inflated and polarizing fear that such might be the case (265–68, 470–74). (Of course, the case of Protestant Pastor Oskar

Brüsewitz must be mentioned as a counterexample. Brüsewitz set himself on fire in 1976 in protest against the SED's push toward secularization and policies affecting churches. However, his case is a rare one in the GDR, and self-immolation was a global phenomenon. In 1963, Buddhist monk Thích Quảng Đức set himself on fire to protest against the pro-Catholic South Vietnamese government. In 1965, Norman Morrison set himself on fire to protest against US involvement in the Vietnam War. In 1969, Czech student Jan Palach set himself on fire to protest against the suppression of the Prague Spring movement by Warsaw Pact troops.) Grashoff's historical research largely disqualifies real suicides in the GDR as a realistic theme for East German literature, which raises the question: If the fictional suicides in GDR literature are not a realistic reflection of real, widespread suicide enacted as political protest, what else might be at work in those literary works?

Before pursuing that question, it is worthwhile to view suicide rates in the GDR from another angle. Before Grashoff, Matthias Matussek published a small journalistic volume in 1992 that set out to explore the phenomenon of the "Wende" suicide, that is, suicide as a melancholy reaction to the disappearance of the GDR and the collapse of the Eastern European communist project. Matussek speculated that suicide rates in East Germany actually declined slightly with the "Wende" of 1989/1990.[15] The change that Matussek detects, however, is very slight and largely confirms that real suicides in East Germany have little to do directly with politics. Although most of the book is concerned with empirical reality and examines case studies of real suicides, the brief third chapter discusses suicide as a possible metaphor for the self-destructive nature of the GDR, a matter that often emerged in his correspondence with family and friends of those who killed themselves. This metaphor is also implicit in a few of the literary works that deal with suicide in the GDR, and it emerges on several occasions in this study.

Just as scholarship on historical suicides in the GDR is scant, scholarship on suicide in GDR literature is also lacking. In 1969 Fritz J. Raddatz declared the death of Christa T. in Christa Wolf's 1968 novel *Nachdenken über Christa T.* (The Quest for Christa T.)[16] to be a case of suicide and cited high suicide rates in the GDR as part of what the novel reflects.[17] In 1983, Michael Rohrwasser published an article on the matter, in which he cited Raddatz, as well as numerous literary works, as evidence that cases of suicide have long been abundant in GDR literature.[18] Rohrwasser went on to outline briefly the history of socialist silence regarding suicide, chiefly real suicide but also literary instances. He then briefly posited a limited topography of literary suicide in the GDR and concluded that suicide in GDR literature from the late 1960s onward is not a matter of hope, as Ernst Bloch might have argued in his *Das Prinzip Hoffnung*, but rather is a matter of doubt about the future and a realization of meaninglessness in GDR socialism. Udo Grashoff and Dieter Sevin both briefly discuss literary suicide in the GDR in sections of their monographs. Grashoff, a historian, explores the cultural ramifications of historical suicide. Sevin, a literary scholar, is interested in suicide as one of many possible narrative strategies.[19]

Although Rohrwasser's reading of suicide in GDR literature represents the common assumption that it is a realistic representation of politically motivated suicide in GDR society, seeds of other ideas regarding suicide in GDR literature exist. In a 1988 essay on death and hope (but not specifically on suicide) in GDR prose, Magdalene Mueller lists six literary works from the early to mid-1980s GDR that deal with the theme of death.[20] She alludes to chapter 52 of Ernst Bloch's *Das Prinzip Hoffnung* (The Principle of Hope),[21] the chapter that deals with the theme of death, and, seemingly in contradistinction to Michael Rohrwasser, she posits that a lengthier engagement with Bloch's philosophy could shine much light upon the emergence of death as a frequent theme in GDR literature of the 1980s. Such a project, were it to mine deeply both Bloch's interpretation of Hegel and the reception of Bloch's philosophy in the GDR, might indeed highlight the potential of hope that some GDR writers and readers may have seen in morbidity. Mueller's insightful but brief prolegomena to such a project, however, remains underdeveloped. She does not propose examining works by Christa Wolf, many of whose works deal with death, and who was influenced by Bloch perhaps more so than most GDR authors,[22] nor does she engage in depth with Bloch's philosophy. However, Mueller's article does provide a subtle parallel to the study of fictional suicide in the GDR in the 1970s and 1980s. It uses a similar periodization, and it asks why there is so much fictional death in that period. Michael Douglas Schleihauf Zimmermann claims that GDR novels involving suicide largely constitute a homogenous block, maintaining that they all revolve around the conflict between the individual and GDR society.[23] Zimmermann's argument seems valid only when GDR fictional suicides are contrasted with those of West Germany. Such a view, however, does not illustrate a nuanced picture of the literary history of suicide within the GDR. By examining numerous texts from both Germanys over a period of forty-five years, Zimmermann, furthermore, sacrifices close readings, focusing instead on what the basic plots of those numerous texts indicate about the societies of the two Germanys. Indeed, Zimmermann relies on Edwin Shneidman's suicidology as his primary theoretical tool, thereby slipping back into Rohrwasser's contention that GDR fictional suicides are merely a reflection of the role of historical suicide in GDR society.

What is missing in those studies of suicide in GDR literature is attention to the literariness of the literary works. None of the scholars mentioned examine the fictional suicides as fiction. None of them see the fictional suicides as or in relation to literary devices, whether intertext, metaphor, metonym, or otherwise. The very fictionality of these suicides, however, ought to invite examination of their semiotic, metaphorical, rhetorical, and intertextual nature. Unlike the scholarly claims that repeatedly return to the realm of the historical, my focus is on the relationships these fictional suicides have with other fictional suicides; I examine the subversive character of their intertextuality. Although there are several recent noteworthy studies on East German literature, much work remains to be done on the distinctive role of intertextuality, at least in a way that offers a theoretical model of intertextuality, in GDR literature. While a general theory of intertextuality in GDR literature is largely beyond the scope of this book as well, this study of suicide in GDR literature has developed to offer me more insight into intertextuality in GDR literature than I could ever have expected, as the taboo of suicide in GDR literature and the notion of literary heritage in the GDR unraveled largely in tandem.

In exploring the interaction between fictional suicides and intertextuality in GDR literature, I ask questions such as these: How are the suicides in GDR fiction transformations of other suicide narratives? How do these narratives subvert and transform the literary heritage of the GDR? What is transformed in these narratives of suicide, and how are the transformations narrated? In other words, how does the reworking of classic works in Western literature dealing with suicide, combined with the insistence by GDR cultural authorities on honoring literary heritage, shape a discourse of suicide in the GDR imagination?

Just as historical research engages the archive of political documents, communiqués, speeches, and census records, this study delves into the archive of canonical European literature that would have been read by the writers and readers of the works under examination in this study. I then ask: What are the relationships between such texts and the texts under examination? Such an emphasis on intertextuality allows for an approach to dealing with the role of suicide in the East German literary imagination without ignoring the literariness of literary works.

While what follows is, in part, a history of suicide in GDR literature—a literary historical narrative that is deeply fascinating in its own right—I also have another motive in telling the story of suicide in East German literature: Through close readings of these fictional suicides, I wish to demonstrate the extent to which GDR literature can and should be read *qua* literature, as a body of literary texts that can fruitfully be approached with literary methodology. While Wolfgang Emmerich called for the use of literary methodology in dealing with GDR literature as early as 1992,[24] and while scholars such as David Bathrick,[25] Julia Hell,[26] and Benjamin Robinson[27] have successfully probed GDR literature using sophisticated and intelligent methodology, much work remains to be done in this area. Historical, political, and sociological approaches still seem to be the most intuitive ways of thinking about GDR literature for most people, scholars and laymen alike. There are several probable reasons for this: the fact that the German Democratic Republic was a historical anomaly for many reasons, the fact that cultural authorities in East Germany themselves tended to view literature in terms of a contrived and oversimplified realism, the assumption that East German writers' primary motive was to convey information to the East German populace by way of the *roman-à-clef*, and the assumption on the part of many conservative Cold War warriors in the West that nothing good could come out of a communist country. Historicist approaches can be fruitful, but they often lack attention to literariness. In what follows, I set aside historical, political, and sociological reality temporarily and focus my attention on the literariness of works of East German literature involving suicide. Doing so shows that these texts are not merely simple exercises in literary realism, but that these fictional suicides engage other fictional suicides, thereby disrupting GDR literary heritage. In other words, these intertextual works about suicide are political, and they do interact with history, but not in any simple or straightforward way, as Rohrwasser and Zimmermann imply. Again, the strength of the defiance involved in fictional suicides in the GDR—as with many defiant narratives in the GDR—derives largely from intertextuality. In a literary culture so heavily organized in terms of "kulturelles Erbe," one in which the Lukácsian dichotomy of realism versus modernism was, on the surface, so pervasive, it should come as no surprise that subtle uses of intertextuality provided a weighty source of dissent. Through their relationship to both sanctioned and unsanctioned literary texts, these fictional suicides subverted the official literary heritage of the GDR.

In exploring such literary subversion, my methodological approach makes use of a broad and eclectic set of tools for exploring fictionality, literariness, and intertextuality. I should also state at the outset, however, that my approach is particularly indebted to the French structuralist and father of narratology, Gérard Genette, whose taxonomy of the relationships among texts is broadly called "transtextuality." (From this point on, I shall use Genette's broad term "transtextuality" or his more specific taxonomic terms for types of transtextuality, rather than the more generic term "intertextuality.") Genette's transtextuality expands Julia Kristeva's concept of intertextuality to explicate relationships among texts beyond the scope of intertextuality. While Kristeva's intertextuality correctly illustrates that the textual is always inherently intertextual, Genette's transtextuality allows for the explanation of specific types of transformation in specific texts. Genette distinguishes among five different types of transtextual relationships:

1. "Kristevan" intertextuality (allusion, quotation, plagiarism)
2. paratextuality (matter attached to a text but not part of the text proper, such as: marginalia, dust jacket blurbs, epigraphs, and titles)

3. metatextuality (commentary)
4. hypertextuality (reworkings of texts) (which is further explained below)
5. architextuality (genre, structures)

Of these five forms of transtextuality, it is the fourth category that is most important for this study. Hypertextuality for Genette is complex. Above all, it involves a hypertext (for example, Plenzdorf's *Die neuen Leiden des jungen W.*) that is a reworking of a hypotext (for example, Goethe's *Die Leiden des jungen Werther*). Genette explores the various types of relationships between hypertexts and hypotexts, which include parody, travesty, pastiche, caricature, forgery, and serious transformation, the latter of which is the subject of the second half of *Palimpsests.* Serious (as opposed to humorous) transformation is the primary type of hypertextual relationship that is examined in this study in order to describe fictional, hypertextual suicides in the GDR. Serious transformation is also divided into several subcategories, which I will explain later when they are applied to specific works. Genette's typologies provide a starting point for defining the ways that the texts at hand make use of other texts to explore the defiant possibilities of fictional suicide in the context of the GDR in the 1970s and 1980s. As Genette insightfully points out, "serious transformation, or transposition, is without any doubt the most important of all hypertextual practices, if only because of the historical importance and the aesthetic accomplishment of some of the works that fall under its heading."[28] The works included in this study confirm this statement. In part because of the truth of that statement, Genette's structuralist apparatus can be used to move far beyond structuralism to dig into deeper, more relevant issues of memory, fictionality, and power. In stretching Genette's transtextuality beyond the realm of structuralist taxonomizing, my approach is also greatly informed by Soviet literary historian and semiotician Yuri Lotman's dynamic semiotics, as they are useful for explaining the subversive, political ramifications of what Genette calls serious transformation.

The question remains then: why suicide? Indeed, a broad argument could be made about literariness and transtextuality in GDR literature without engaging the topic of suicide. There are at least four reasons for the pairing of suicide and literariness, specifically the literary quality of transtextuality: First, nearly all the fictional suicides in GDR literature in the 1970s and 1980s have strong transtextual elements. Second, the topic of suicide, along with the discipline of suicidology, tends unnecessarily to conjure concrete sociological paradigms, a mistake I hope to counter with this study. Third, there is a common assumption (masterfully dispelled by the historian Udo Grashoff) that suicides in East Germany were most often politically motivated, a matter that I wish to dispel further by showing that GDR literature, like historical evidence, does not support it. Fourth, the explosion of fictional suicides in East German literature closely parallels the unraveling of the official East German cultural and literary heritage—both developments being set into motion in the early 1970s and moving forward into the 1980s. Suicide in East German literature offers an ideal thematic case study in the development of GDR literature, because suicide in East German historical reality and suicide in East German literature are so different. While the former was a concrete, sociological and medical phenomenon, the latter is heavily laden with literary devices and deeply embedded in a centuries-old, literary discourse.

Despite this study's methodological resistance to historicism, the chapters are organized more or less historically. Indeed, the book is a literary history, but one that insists on emphasizing the *literary* in literary history. Chapter 1 provides the literary history of suicide in the GDR roughly from the end of the Second World War to Honecker's "No Taboos" Speech of 1971. It shows how fictional suicides, from the Soviet Occupation Zone and then in the GDR of the 1940s, 1950s, and 1960s, moved from anti-fascist suicides, in which characters kill themselves out of motives related to the rise of fascism and the horrors of the Holocaust, to workers' suicides, in which working-class socialist heroes ironically work themselves to death, to fictional suicides that progressively become more and more imaginative.

Chapter 2 examines Ulrich Plenzdorf's novel *Die neuen Leiden des jungen W.* (1973), which emerged two years after Honecker's "No Taboos" speech. It was the first major instance of fictional suicide in East German literature, responding to Honecker's speech as well as to other aspects of the transformation of power from Ulbricht to Honecker. It tells the story of seventeen-year-old Edgar Wibeau, who after quarreling with his boss, leaves his apprenticeship and moves into his friend's gardenhouse (*Wohnlaube*) where he finds a copy of Goethe's *Die Leiden des jungen Werther* (1774), spends a great deal of time reading it, and later, like Werther, kills himself. Edgar tells his story—with the help of several documents and several people who knew him—from beyond the grave. Edgar's reading of Goethe and other texts, as well as Werther's own readings, reveal the fluidity of literary heritage. The end of chapter 2 also outlines works of GDR literature that allude specifically and explicitly to *Die neuen Leiden des jungen W.*

Chapter 3 contends that Werner Heiduczek's 1977 novel *Tod am Meer* (Death on the Sea)[29] is largely a reworking of Thomas Mann's *Der Tod in Venedig*. It is imperative, I argue, to read the main character Jablonski's refusal to follow his doctor's orders or to leave the Black Sea coast alongside Mann's protagonist Aschenbach's vainglorious insistence upon staying in Venice despite the epidemic outbreak of Asiatic cholera, in order to be around the boy with whom he has fallen in love but whom he knows he cannot have. Jablonski, like Aschenbach, is a writer who travels to the beach for vacation and recuperation. Jablonski's reluctance to leave the hospital, combined with his painful life story, then, becomes a metaphor for the dogmatic and suicidal path of Marxism-Leninism in the GDR. Furthermore, Jablonski is trained as a biographer of Stalin, whose life, much like that of Jablonski, has much to say about the self-destructive nature of the Party.

Chapter 4 examines the radical reappraisal of literary values in Christa Wolf's *Kein Ort. Nirgends* (No Place on Earth),[30] in which Heinrich von Kleist and Karoline von Günderrode, in a fictional meeting, reevaluate Goethe's classicism and also discuss *Werther* and suicide. The narrator finally informs the reader at the end of the book, "Wir wissen, was kommt" (151). This event that the reader knows is to come is the fictional double suicide of Kleist and Günderrode. (Historically, they killed themselves separately—she in 1806, he in 1811. In Wolf's novel they do it together.) Both in their conversations about literature and in the suicide, these two semi-fictional characters provide a model for reevaluating literary heritage, a model that parallels Wolf's own reevaluation of GDR literary heritage.

Chapter 5 disrupts the chronological order of the other chapters and productively puts to the test my argument that fictional suicides in GDR literature have little to do with historical suicides in the GDR. It juxtaposes an unlikely pair of texts: Heiner Müller's unorthodox play *Hamletmaschine* (Hamlet Machine) and Sibylle Muthesius's *Flucht in die Wolken* (Flight into the Clouds),[31] a creative co-opting of her daughter's diary. Both these texts are, on some level, inspired by real suicides. Müller's wife killed herself, and his play also alludes to Ulrike Meinhof's alleged suicide. Muthesius's daughter killed herself, and the text, much more than that of Müller, really does consist of a coming-to-terms with a real suicide. Both texts, however, utilize an astonishing wealth of literary allusions that resist interpretation or simplification. Taken together, these two texts complicate, but also enrich, the literary history that I have established.

Chapter 6 examines Christoph Hein's 1985 novel *Horns Ende* (Horn's End),[32] in which a historian named Horn hangs himself after he was reprimanded by the regime for both his scholarship and a museum exhibit. The key to reading *Horns Ende* is the interspersed dialogue between the long-dead Horn (who speaks from the dead) and the now aging Thomas, who, as a boy, found Horn's corpse hanging in the woods. A focus on this dialogue reveals that Horn's suicide instigates the conversation between Thomas and Horn's ghost and ultimately propels change. Reading Horn's ghost's statements requires inquiry into the nature of haunting. Horn's ghost's haunting is remarkably similar to that of the ghost of Hamlet's father. "Erinnere dich," the ghost of Horn commands Thomas in the first two words of the novel. Both ghosts command someone to remember. My reading of the novel thus sees Horn's ghost as a vessel of subversive, intergenerational memory, a way of disturbing, not dissimilar to the ghost of Hamlet's father.

By investigating the role suicide played in GDR literature, I have come to realize that these fictional suicides, rather than being mere historicist reflections of suicides in GDR society, transformed and disrupted the official literary heritage and prescriptive literary values of that country. As such, the story of suicide in East German literature is not so much about real suicides. Instead, it is a story about the complexity and power of the literary imagination.

1: Suicide as an Antifascist Literary Trope: 1945–71

While this study is primarily about fictional suicides and the crisis of literary heritage beginning with Honecker's "No Taboos" Speech in 1971, this first chapter briefly outlines the representations of suicide in East German literature before 1971. In a sense, this chapter is a summary of a book that I did not write but could have written had this study been a two-volume set. In short, the fictional suicides in East German literature before the 1970s do not primarily struggle with literary heritage, as those of the 1970s and 1980s do. Further, they tend not to be central to the work in which they appear, and some of them are not clear cases of suicide. Working more or less chronologically, I subdivide the fictional suicides in East German literature of the 1940s, 1950s, and 1960s into four sections: antifascist suicides, workers' suicides, hints of suicide in the works of Christa Wolf before *Kein Ort. Nirgends*, and one cleverly literary suicide in Rolf Schneider's 1968 short story "Imagination."[1]

This progression from antifascist suicides to workers' suicides through Wolf's works of the 1960s and Schneider's "Imagination," leading toward the caesura of the early 1970s, also moves by and large from fictional suicides as relatively realistic representations of society (although they were never quite that simple) to fictional suicides that are many steps removed from being mere reflections of society. This chapter, then, recounts the prehistory of the story I tell beginning in chapter 2. While chapters 2–6 offer analysis of transtextual relationships and their relations to representations of suicide, this chapter is a relatively straightforward literary historical overview of suicide in East German literature in the 1940s, 1950, and 1960s. I should add the disclaimer that fictional suicides can be difficult to identify as such. I make no promise that I have included all fictional suicides in GDR literature.

Antifascist Suicides

While most of the fictional suicides described in this book are not primarily realistic representations of real suicides, some of the fictional antifascist suicides—suicides related in some way to the horrors of fascism, the portrayal of which is antifascist, regardless of whether the character who kills himself is fascist or antifascist—may to some degree be inspired by real suicides that took place in the context of the Second World War and the Holocaust. Indeed, the horrors of fascism and the Holocaust instigated both real and fictional suicides. Some, such as Walter Benjamin, committed suicide to avoid capture by the Nazis. Some killed themselves in exile. Some killed themselves in concentration camps and ghettos. Numerous Holocaust survivors have killed themselves years, even decades, after the end of the Second World War.[2] Both the young government of the German Democratic Republic, which saw itself as an antifascist state, and writers returning from exile and immigrating to the GDR, freely acknowledged the horrors of Nazi Germany and the Holocaust and sought to establish an antifascist culture that remembered and memorialized the Holocaust as atrocity. Methods of memorializing the Holocaust in the GDR, however, eventually became scripted, a phenomenon for which Thomas Fox coined the pun "stated memory."[3] Still, antifascist tropes were important in early GDR literature. There are several fictional suicides, both in GDR literature and in works written in the late 1930s and early 1940s by writers who later lived in the Soviet Occupation Zone or the GDR, works that were important for the early GDR. Because of their antifascist nature, most of these works were not heavily censored in the GDR. That does not mean, however, that they are necessarily simplistic. Rather, the suicides in these works function as a literary trope to express the atrocity of fascism. In other words, these fictional antifascist suicides are not necessarily acts that combat fascism in the narrative; rather, the fact that they occur in the narratives in the ways they do represents a literary antifascist statement by the writer and for the reader.

The phenomenon of the antifascist suicide in GDR literature begins perhaps in the works of Anna Seghers (born Netty Reiling), a writer who spent the Second World War in exile, mostly in Mexico. She immigrated to West Berlin in 1947 and then to East Berlin in 1950, where she lived until her death in 1983. Although there are other antifascist suicides in the fiction of communist writers, Seghers was the primary author to shape this trope. Part of the reason why she is such an early developer of the trope is because she, a Jewish communist, was writing in exile during the war as a committed antifascist. Although some of Seghers's works were written and published before the founding of the German Democratic Republic, they were warmly received in the GDR, to such an extent that they may even be considered East German literature. *Das siebte Kreuz* (The Seventh Cross),[4] for example, became required reading in GDR schools starting in 1950. Further, Seghers later became president of the East German Writers' Union (Schriftstellerverband), an office she held from 1952 until 1978. Certainly, the works of Seghers are an important piece of the story of suicide in East German literature, even if some of them predate the GDR.

The first antifascist suicide in Seghers's works appears in her novel *Das siebte Kreuz*, which she began writing in 1938 in exile in France and published both in the United States (in English) and in Mexico (in German) in 1942. There is one clear suicide in the novel and a second case in which the narrator notes a rumor of suicide. Seven men escape from a concentration camp, and a Nazi commander named Fahrenberg orders the construction of seven crosses so that each of the escaped men can be bound to a cross once recaptured. Six of the men either die while fleeing or are captured and bound to a cross. One man, however, Georg Heisler, the protagonist of the novel, escapes to freedom. The novel's title comes from the cross that was intended for Heisler. One of the seven escapees, an artist named Anton Meier, who goes by the pseudonym Belloni, kills himself by jumping off the roof of a building just as he is about to be recaptured by the Nazis. He dies later that day in a hospital. While Heisler is the novel's hero, Belloni cannot be censured for his suicide, as the alternative—allowing himself to be recaptured by Fahrenberg's men—would also have been suicide. Belloni, then, uses suicide as a final act of freedom (81–83). But Belloni may not be the only character in the novel who kills himself. The narrator states at the end of the novel that is rumored that Fahrenberg may have killed himself: "Er soll sich im Fürstenberger Hof einquartiert haben. Er soll sich dann eine Kugel in den Kopf geschossen haben. Das ist nur ein Gerücht. Es paßt auch nicht recht zu Fahrenberg" (312; he was said to have taken lodgings at the Fürstenberger Hof and to have put a bullet through his brain—but that was only rumor. It didn't quite fit him, 394). The narrator further notes that Fahrenberg might have been murdered, as several people had varying motives, or he might have survived and climbed the postwar political ranks, a warning in the spirit of Wolfgang Staudte's 1946 film *Die Mörder sind unter uns*. Either way, Fahrenberg is a brutal character with an inferiority complex, and his suicide would not have bothered the communist authorities later in the GDR, as he was condemnable anyway.

Seghers's novel *Transit*[5] also contains a suicide. *Transit* was written in exile in 1941 and 1942, was published in English and Spanish in 1944, and finally appeared in German in serialized form in the *Berliner Zeitung*—an East Berlin-based newspaper, which was founded almost immediately after the end of the Second World War—in 1947 and then as a book in 1948. In this novel, the narrator and protagonist has escaped from a concentration camp and, now in occupied Paris, meets a man he knows from the camp, who has also escaped. This man asks the narrator to deliver a letter to a writer named Weidel, who is fleeing Germany. It turns out, however, that Weidel has killed himself. The narrator then assumes Weidel's name and identity as a way of not being recaptured by the authorities. He takes Weidel's briefcase and discovers in it an incomplete book manuscript and other papers, a detail that may recall Walter

Benjamin's suicide, as well as paperwork for a visa that allows the narrator to emigrate. As Friedrich Albrecht points out, it is Weidel's suicide that allows the narrative to unfold as it does.[6] Weidel's suicide sets in motion what turns out to be a complex process of identity construction.

Seghers's short story "Der Ausflug der toten Mädchen"[7] (The Dead Girls' Outing) also contains a suicide. The story, written in exile in Mexico in 1943–44 and published in 1946 in New York (in German), involves a German narrator in exile during the Second World War wandering through the desert in Mexico, who experiences a hallucination in which she thinks she is on a school field trip in 1913. The narrator simultaneously remembers the field trip and what has become of her classmates and teacher in the years between that field trip and the narrative present. Some of her classmates collaborated with the Nazis and some of them became their victims. A classmate named Gerda killed herself using a gas oven when her husband flew the Nazi flag from their apartment against her will. Gerda's suicide gives the narrator the chance to recount how Gerda's husband had flown the Nazi flag not out of much conviction but rather because he feared the consequences of not doing so.

Finally, Seghers's novel *Die Toten bleiben jung*,[8] (The Dead Stay Young) which she began writing in Mexico, finished after she returned to Germany, and published in 1949 in East Germany, contains a murder-suicide. The novel is a multi-perspectival study of political developments in the Weimar Republic and the rise of fascism. It opens with the murder of a Sparticist named Erwin by the Freikorps, an event that sparks several interrelated narratives, one of which is the story of Klemm and Becker, the former an army officer, the latter his chauffeur. Klemm gives the order to kill Erwin. Becker is especially loyal to Klemm because of their shared combat experiences in the First World War, but when Klemm fires Becker because Klemm's new bride wants them to keep her chauffeur, Becker drives the car off a bridge into the Rhein, killing both of them (160–64). While Becker is no antifascist, the murder-suicide he commits does occur in the context of the rise of fascism, and the deaths of these two characters still function, loosely, as an antifascist literary trope. Further, Seghers insisted that Becker and Klemm die in this way, as her correspondence with Rolf Schneider shows. In preparation for creating a DEFA film adaptation of the novel, Schneider, the screenwriter, wrote a letter to Seghers outlining some proposed changes to the plot. Among these changes he proposed that Becker should not die in the car crash. However, Becker's suicide, and not just his murder of Klemm, was an important element in the story for Seghers. She replied to Schneider that "Chauffeur muß mit Klemm umkommen. Andere Lösung Quatsch."[9] (Chauffeur must die with Klemm. Other solution nonsense.)

Like the works by Anna Seghers with antifascist suicides, Hans Fallada's novel *Jeder stirbt für sich allein*[10] (Every Man Dies Alone) was written before there was a country called the GDR. Fallada (born Rudolf Wilhelm Friedrich Ditzen), who remained in Germany during both the war and the Soviet occupation, composed the novel quickly in 1946, and it was published in 1947 in the Soviet Occupation Zone. Like Seghers's work, *Jeder stirbt für sich allein* deals with the rise of fascism and the horrors of Nazi Germany, and it also contains antifascist suicides. In short, it is a realist novel that portrays acts of resistance in Nazi Germany. The work contains a large number of characters, and several of them kill themselves. Frau Rosenthal, a Jewish woman who is in hiding and whose husband has already been taken away, leaps from a window to her death (157). Enno Kluge, who is wrongfully accused by Commissar Escherich of distributing antifascist propaganda, shoots himself with Escherich's pistol in an especially frightening scene. Escherich convinces him to commit suicide and instructs him how to use the pistol. Kluge, an aquaphobe, agrees to kill himself as long as there is no water involved. Once Kluge has the pistol, he tries to shoot Escherich but misses. Escherich then grabs Kluge to throw him in the water, and Kluge then shoots himself (367–71). Escherich throws the corpse in the water. The novel refers to Kluge's death as a "Selbstmord" in quotation marks (397). Later, Escherich kills himself with his pistol (506). Furthermore, a character named Trudel kills herself by leaping head first off the top of an iron grating ("Eisengitter des Ganges") in a prison (582).

Jurek Becker's *Jakob der Lügner*[11] (Jakob the Liar, 1969) was published twenty years after the works of Seghers and Fallada depicting antifascist suicides. However, it also contains such suicides. *Jakob der Lügner* takes place in a ghetto, and the main character of the novel, Jakob, creates a false sense of hope among others in the ghetto by telling them that he has a radio, on which he has heard that the Soviets are nearby and will soon liberate them. The radio, however, does not exist. The first suicide occurs as an act of resistance. A character named Kirschbaum, a physician, is asked to provide medical services to a Nazi officer. Kirschbaum poisons himself rather than helping the Nazi. At the end of the novel, the narrator offers two separate endings for the story, both of which would occur in tension with the false hope represented by the lie that is Jakob's radio. Either Jakob never tells the truth, feels increasingly guilty, and kills himself, or he tells the truth, and his friend Kowalski loses the sense of hope that Jakob had given him and kills *him*self. The narrator then reveals that the second ending is the true one. Kowalski hangs himself.

The trope of the antifascist suicide has a last hurrah in GDR literature in the character of Horst Binder, who appears in two separate novels by Christa Wolf: *Nachdenken über Christa T.* (1968) and *Kindheitsmuster* (Patterns of Childhood, 1976).[12] Horst Binder is a troop leader in the Hitler Youth, who is obsessed with Hitler's day-to-day activities. When the Soviet Army is approaching in the spring of 1945, at the age of sixteen, he kills his parents and then himself, in order not to be captured by the Soviets. He is mentioned only briefly in chapter 3 of *Nachdenken über Christa T.*, as someone the narrator remembers as being commended for denouncing his father for listening to foreign radio stations and who later shot his mother and then himself as the Soviets are approaching. In chapter 9 of *Kindheitsmuster*, more of his story is revealed as he courts the protagonist Nelly. It is here that his obsession with Hitler and with self-sacrifice is recounted. Further, whereas the narrator of *Nachdenken über Christa T.* remembers that he shot his mother and then himself, the narrator in *Kindheitsmuster* recalls that he shot both of his parents before shooting himself. Other suicides in the works of Wolf are described later in this chapter, but the suicide of the fascist Horst Binder, recounted in the spirit of antifascism, is in the vein of the antifascist suicides in the works of Seghers, Fallada, and Becker.

Workers' Suicides

The other category of suicide in GDR literature of the pre-Honecker era is that of the workers' suicide. Given the emphasis on both workers and production in GDR rhetoric—and the conundrum that workers' rights and ever-increasing production quotas were in tension with one another—it should come as no surprise that writers composed works of fiction in which workers kill themselves. I know of no historical cases, however, in which workers in the GDR killed themselves out of protest against working conditions or worked themselves to death. But the tension between the rhetoric of the GDR as a workers' and peasants' state, on the one hand, and the real employment of production norms that affected workers negatively, on the other hand, did not go unnoticed. In 1949 the bricklayer Hans Garbe repaired a brick oven while it was still burning in order to save the factory money, and the Party began using the legend of Garbe as a way to motivate workers. In the late 1950s, however, Heiner and Inge Müller composed and produced a play called *Der Lohndrücker*[13] (The Scab), in which they illustrate the problem inherent in the stories of such superstar workers: that—besides the fact that working on a burning oven is dangerous—the superstar worker functions in opposition to workers' solidarity. However, neither Garbe nor the character based on Garbe in *Der Lohndrücker* kill themselves. There are, however, works of literature written by East Germans in which workers die on the job, work themselves to death, or commit suicide as a result of work that they have done. While these deaths may be interpreted as suicides, some of them are not clear cases. And even so, not all of them could be published in the GDR.

Uwe Johnson's *Mutmaßungen über Jakob*[14] (Speculations about Jacob, 1959) seeks to understand Jakob's death through multiple voices and unorthodox narrative strategies. Jakob is killed by a train, although he had worked for the railway for seven years and knew his way around trains and train tracks. The narrator then attempts to determine whether Jakob's death was suicide, murder, or an accident. Because of both its implication that Jakob's death may have been a suicide and its unorthodox narrative strategies, *Mutmaßungen über Jakob* was never published in the GDR. However, because much of it takes places in Mecklenburg, it has a distinct East German quality about it. The work was published in West Germany in 1959, and in the same year Johnson fled to the West. Between 1970 and 1983 he published a nearly two-thousand page novel called *Jahrestage*[15] (Anniversaries), in which Jakob's lover Gesine, whose mother is suicidal, contemplates the fact that there is no explicit prohibition on suicide mentioned in the Bible, and eventually kills herself.

In Erwin Strittmatter's *Ole Bienkopp*[16] (1963), the eponymous main character works himself to death. The farmer Ole Hansen, known as Ole Bienkopp, used to fancy himself as apolitical. A certain constellation of events, however, has motivated him to become especially politically engaged. He helped found a local agricultural collective (LPG), and throughout the novel he works to develop and maintain socialism in his village, largely through the LPG. However, socialist collaboration becomes increasingly difficult, as a result of bureaucracy, dogma, and incompetence. He works night and day with a shovel to dig up marlstone, which the LPG needs. After days of digging, Bienkopp dies, shovel in hand, trying to dig up the marl. Thus he digs his own grave. The day after he dies, the backhoe that he needed for the job, and had vociferously requested,[17] arrives. While the cause of Jakob's death in *Mutmaßungen über Jakob* is mysterious, it is clear that Bienkopp works himself to death trying to acquire materials for his village's LPG. Nonetheless, some villagers claim that he died of obstinacy, an altruistic kind of obstinacy.

> "An seinem Eigensinn ist er zugrunde gegangen," schimpft Emma. "Anton hätte das nicht geduldet."
> Karl Krüger zupft am Schilfbett des toten Genossen. "Eigensinn ohne Eigennutz—dafür gibts noch kein Wort."[18]
>
> ["He died of stubbornness," cursed Emma. "Anton would never have tolerated that."
> Karl Krüger picked at the dead comrade's bed of reeds. "Stubbornness without selfishness—there's not yet a word for that."]

The fact that Karl Krüger says that there is not yet a word for the kind of obstinacy that caused Bienkopp's death suggests that the phenomenon is increasing to the extent that there may one day be a word for it. Such a suggestion, like much else in the book, was a powerful condemnation.

Indeed, as most critics point out, Bienkopp's persistent digging not only killed him; it also created the first major literary work in the GDR to subvert explicitly the doctrine of socialist realism. Not only is the novel not fully socialist realist, but it represents a kind of realism that seems like socialist realism at first but then goes on to undermine aspects of that doctrine. In particular, the story of Bienkopp subverts the expectation of the positive hero. Typically, in socialist realism, the protagonist is a worker-hero, who functions as a savior to help bring about socialist progress. Bienkopp, however, is a worker who fails despite his best efforts—indeed, one whose best efforts toward socialist progress kill him.

Hints of Suicide in Christa Wolf's Works of the 1960s

While Christa Wolf's 1979 work *Kein Ort. Nirgends*, which is the topic of chapter 4, has a double suicide at the center of its narrative, several other works in Wolf's oeuvre point toward suicide. This should come as no great surprise, since she was heavily influenced by the two great crafters of the antifascist suicide: Anna Seghers and Hans Fallada. Seghers and Wolf maintained frequent correspondence, and Wolf cited Seghers as a major influence on multiple occasions. It could be argued, in fact, that Seghers was the single greatest literary influence on the work of Wolf. Like Seghers, Hans Fallada also had a great influence on Wolf, as her university Diplomarbeit, or thesis, which she wrote under the direction of the famous Germanist Hans Mayer, was entitled "Probleme des Realismus im Werk Hans Falladas" (Problems of Realism in the Works of Hans Fallada).

Rita Seidel's accident in the *Der geteilte Himmel*[19] (Divided Heaven, 1963) is typically read as a suicide attempt. Rita is a student who, in the spirit of the Bitterfelder Weg—the movement beginning in 1959 to encourage factory workers to write and writers to work in factories—is working in a locomotive factory. Her boyfriend flees to West Berlin. She visits him but realizes that she cannot live in a consumerist society such as West Germany and returns to the GDR. But shortly thereafter she collapses on the railroad tracks between two trains. Her doctor puzzles over what might have caused her condition. She is not sure what happened either and begins to recollect, which is the source of the narrative. In the end, Rita herself thinks that the accident may have been a suicide attempt, one that she averted somehow at the last minute. Julia Hell describes the incident perhaps most accurately with the phrase "this 'unconscious' suicide attempt."[20] However, regardless of Rita's conscious or unconscious intentions, she does not die.

The death of Christa T. in *Nachdenken über Christa T.*, who leads a somewhat mysterious life and dies young of leukemia, has been read as a suicide. West German critic Fritz J. Raddatz declares the death of Christa T. to be a case of suicide and cited high suicide rates in the GDR as part of what the novel reflects.[21] Raddatz, rushing to condemn the GDR of causing real suicides, also compares *Nachdenken über Christa T.* to Strittmatter's *Ole Bienkopp*. In particular, Raddatz writes, "was hier beschrieben wird, ist ja nicht der Tod durch Leukämie—es ist die Geschichte eines Selbstmords"[22] (What is described here is not death through leukemia—it is the story of a suicide). However, the narrator never provides much detail about Christa T.'s death. While Christa T. certainly suffered in the GDR for several reasons, she ultimately dies of leukemia, at least medically speaking. Raddatz's argument, then, is not entirely convincing.

A Transitional Case: Rolf Schneider's "Imagination"

Rolf Schneider's 1968 short story titled "Imagination" (which is visually interpreted on the cover of this volume by Berlin-based artist Alexis Laskaris) provides an appropriate segue between the suicidal workers and the unraveling of literary heritage begun by Honecker's "No Taboos" speech and the appearance of Plenzdorf's *Die neuen Leiden des jungen W.* Schneider's story theorizes the interaction between fiction and history in the form of a short work of fiction in which a retired colonel is shot by his imaginary friend, a case that the police file as suicide. The colonel, Oberst G. H. F. L. M. Rock, returns home after being stationed abroad for thirty-four years, leaving his mistress and their children behind. Now that he is living alone, his perception of reality begins to slip: "Es gab reizvolle Übergänge von der Wirklichkeit der Wirklichkeit zur Wirklichkeit der Vorstellung"[23] (There were delightful transitions from the reality of reality to the reality of imagination). He meets a man with the pseudonym Harry Tube, which causes him to remember a childhood friend with the exact same first and last name. Overtaken by loneliness and boredom, he invents an imaginary friend named Harry, who is a young enlisted man. Long conversations with Harry convince the colonel to promote him to lieutenant. One day, while reenacting a historical battle, Harry, representing the side that historically lost that battle, leads that army to victory over the forces that historically won the battle, represented by the colonel. The colonel cannot understand how this is possible, and Harry convinces him that, having caused the deaths of so many soldiers, he should kill himself. The colonel puts the gun to his head but cannot follow through with the act and asks Harry to do it for him. The conversation follows:

> Harry, arrogant: Sie glauben, als eine von Ihnen erfundene Figur könne ich Sie nicht wirklich töten?
> Oberst G. H. F. L. M. Rock: Ich glaube nichts dergleichen.[24]

> [Harry, arrogantly: You believe that I, as a character that you made up, could not kill you in reality?
> Colonel G. H. F. L. M. Rock: I believe nothing of the sort.]

Harry then shoots the colonel and leaves the building. That afternoon the colonel's body is found and deemed a case of suicide. However, the gun is found eight paces away from the body. And the building superintendent thinks that he might have seen someone leaving the colonel's apartment.

Schneider's short story seems to have been more or less forgotten by contemporary readers, but it deserves special attention in this study, as it exemplifies my contention that suicides in GDR fiction are not primarily realistic reflections of real suicides in GDR society, and that GDR fiction is more complicated than many readers of GDR literature (or GDR cultural authorities) have assumed. Further, the story, on a meta-level, theorizes the problem of suicide in GDR literature, insisting that the fictional suicide functions not as a representation of sociological phenomena but rather as a complex literary trope. Along those lines, the story theorizes the complex interrelationship between fiction and reality, namely that fiction can affect reality at least as much as the other way around. The imaginary friend kills the colonel, just as fiction heightens communist paranoia, affects Party rhetoric, and unravels literary heritage. The imagination is powerful, indeed. While the colonel is aging and quite possibly has some mental health issues, the end of the story suggests that something else is at work in the narrative. Was Harry a real person all along? Or did the colonel imagine everything, kill himself, and somehow drop the gun in a way that left it eight paces away? Neither of these possibilities suit a careful reading of the text. Assuming that the narrator, who recounts the story from a third-person, presumably extradiegetic narrative situation, is not an unreliable narrator, then Harry must both be imaginary and kill the colonel. The colonel's death could be considered a case of worker's suicide—if one were to categorize soldiers as workers—as his combat experience, one could postulate, may contribute to his mental health issues. However, the colonel is no Bienkopp. Schneider's "Imagination" represents something other than a worker's suicide. It queries the reality of the imaginary. And it liberates suicide as a literary device and foreshadows the development of fictional suicides in the 1970s.

In short, suicides in GDR fiction before the Honecker era were relatively sparse. There were explicit antifascist suicides, but those aided rather than subverted the Party rhetoric, and most of them were written before the GDR was even founded. The category of the workers' suicide in the GDR is nebulous. *Ole Bienkopp* is perhaps the only clear example of it. Johnson's works, while about the GDR, were never published in the GDR. While Müller's *Der Lohndrücker* subverts the figure of the worker-hero in a way that perhaps paved the way for *Ole Bienkopp*, it does not contain a suicide. And although two of Christa Wolf's works from the 1960s led critics to consider whether their protagonists were suicidal, they cannot be said to contain suicides per se. I count the death of the colonel in Rolf Schneider's "Imagination" as a suicide, an important one in terms of the literary potential of fictional suicide. While there were only relatively sparse manifestations of suicide in GDR literature of the 1950s and 1960s, there was no shortage of such fictional suicides in GDR literature of the 1970s.

2: Suicide and the Fluidity of Literary Heritage: Ulrich Plenzdorf's *Die neuen Leiden des jungen W.*

THE PUBLICATION OF Ulrich Plenzdorf's *Die neuen Leiden des jungen W.* caused a commotion. As scholar Dieter Sevin declared: "Neben Christa Wolfs erstem erfolgreichen Werk *Der geteilte Himmel* wurde kaum ein anderes literarisches Werk bei seiner Veröffentlichung in der DDR mit so viel Furore rezipiert wie Ulrich Plenzdorfs *Die neuen Leiden des jungen W.*"[1] (Apart from Christa Wolf's first successful novel *Der geteilte Himmel*, hardly any other literary work in the GDR was received with such furor as Ulrich Plenzdorfs *Die neuen Leiden des jungen W.*). Gundula M. Sharman even went so far as to compare the impact of the publication of Plenzdorf's novel with that of Goethe's *Die Leiden des jungen Werther*.[2] Indeed, while many young adult readers, in East Germany and West Germany alike, awarded the book cult status, GDR apparatchiks lambasted it. And West German critics were divided. The range of opinion on the subject of the novel may be demonstrated by juxtaposing several different responses to it: that of East German lawyer and mystery writer Friedrich Karl Kaul's letter to the editor of *Sinn und Form* (where Plenzdorf's novel was originally published), Wilhelm Girnus, on June 12, 1972; that of writer Stephan Hermlin's response to Kaul in *Sinn und Form* in 1973;[3] that of an East German secondary school student referred to as Monika Sch.; and those of two different West German critics.

Kaul makes his opinion clear:

> Mich ekelt geradezu . . . die . . . Inbezugsetzung eines verwahrlosten . . . Jugendlichen mit der Goetheschen Romanfigur an; von dem Fäkalien-Vokabular, in dem des langen und breiten über die innige Funktionsverbindung von Niere und Darm der Plenzdorfschen Figur abgehandelt wird, ganz zu schweigen.[4]
>
> [It makes me sick . . . the comparison . . . of the slovenly . . . youth with the character from Goethe's novel; not to mention the fecal vocabulary with which the functional connection between the kidneys and the intestines of Plenzdorf's character is described at length.]

Kaul does not like the juxtaposition of Goethe with youth culture and with scatological images. This is indicative of the extent to which Goethe was revered in GDR cultural politics, in part as a result of the writings of Georg Lukács. (It is ironic, furthermore, that Kaul uses an abjective metaphor of vomiting in order to describe his disgust with the abjection in Plenzdorf's novel.) Kaul goes on to declare that Edgar Wibeau is not representative of the youth in the GDR, indicating perhaps how distant GDR cultural authorities had become both from GDR youth culture and from the works of literature that they, the authorities, so fiercely defended. Indeed, part of the reason why Plenzdorf's novel caused such a lively response, both among supporters and detractors, is that it offers a reading of Goethe's novel that is active, contemporary, and relevant.

Hermlin's response to Kaul makes several interrelated points. He defends *Die neuen Leiden* as "ein authentisches Stück neuer Kunst" (an authentic piece of new art) and notes that cultural authorities always criticize truly innovative art (and not just in the GDR). He further notes that the dichotomy of healthy versus sick literature, which Kaul used to lambast Plenzdorf's text—a dichotomy that Kaul borrowed from Lukács—is problematic, as each person views himself as healthy. Hermlin also declares that Kaul, whom Hermlin knew personally, was, in fact, profoundly out of touch with young people in the GDR.

One of the most telling pronouncements on the novel, however, is a statement by Monika Sch. During an interview by the periodical *Neue Deutsche Literatur* with Monika, two university students, and a construction apprentice, she declares:

> Zum erstenmal haben die unter die Tischdecke geguckt! Sonst sieht alles immer von oben so schön glatt aus und so schön weiß! . . . Edgar will eben nicht immer alles nach Plan machen. Bei uns ist alles zu sehr im voraus organisiert, die Ausbildung, der ganze Lebensweg. . . . Immer den geraden Weg so langgehn, der so schön vorgeschrieben ist und glatt, das hat ihm nicht gefallen, deshalb ist er in diese Laube gegangen nach Berlin.[5]
>
> [For the first time, they looked under the tablecloth! Otherwise, everything always looks so nice and smooth from above! . . . Edgar just doesn't want to do everything according to plan. Everything here is organized too much ahead of time: the education, the whole path of life. . . . Always going in the same direction, just like they tell us to, he didn't like that. That's why he went to the garden shed in Berlin.]

Monika Sch. sees in *Die neuen Leiden* a dialectic that functions against the lip service of "dialectics" among GDR cultural authorities. She describes

Plenzdorf's novel as looking under the proverbial tablecloth. For Monika Sch., underneath the tablecloth things never go according to plan, a matter that apparatchiks were not willing to concede. Although she likely means a tablecloth of GDR youth culture, an idea that is not inaccurate, her statement also applies to the tablecloth of GDR literary heritage. Building upon Hermlin and Monika Sch., I read Plenzdorf's novel as an indication that readings of canonical texts change over time with the changing perspective of the reader, a fact that proved problematic for the sclerotic literary heritage of the GDR. That is, literary heritage cannot be controlled any more than youth culture can.

In the Federal Republic, the journalistic criticism tended to argue either that Plenzdorf had created a new style of writing, a new relationship to language (Fritz J. Raddatz), or that the novel was of questionable literary value, but that it was still important because it articulated a new type of subversion (Marcel Reich-Ranicki). At the risk of constructing a straw-man argument, it should be noted that Reich-Ranicki's position here is at least as wrongheaded as that of Kaul. In my estimation, it is precisely the rich literariness of Plenzdorf's novel that makes it so subversive, a point that both Raddatz and Hermlin seem to support.

But why was the novel received in such varied and vociferous ways? On the surface, the novel seems only moderately subversive and even quite silly. Some plot summary is necessary here before moving beyond the surface to answer that question. Plenzdorf's *Die neuen Leiden des jungen W.* narrates the events leading up to the death of Edgar Wibeau, who runs away from home, finds refuge in a garden shed, creates abstract paintings, and works with a construction brigade. Edgar finds a copy of Goethe's *Die Leiden des jungen Werther* in the garden shed, uses the title page and the introduction pages as toilet paper, and later reads the volume without knowing the title or author or anything about the reception of the work, as he shit on those pages that would have provided him with some context. Amused by Goethe's language, he reads excerpts from Werther's letters aloud and records them onto cassette tapes, which he then sends to his friend Willi. Edgar strikes up a friendship with a preschool teacher named Charlie and desires an amorous relationship with her, but she is engaged to Dieter, who has recently returned from military service and is beginning to study German literature at the university. Edgar develops an electric paint sprayer to help his work brigade and is electrocuted while testing his invention, fully aware that the voltage is much too high. The novel has several narrators: the posthumous voice of Edgar, the tapes of Edgar quoting Werther's letters, obituaries from newspapers, Willi, Edgar's parents, Edgar's colleagues, and Charlie.

Returning to the question of why the novel made such big waves, a couple of reasons have emerged in the secondary literature. Peter J. Brenner posited that the impact of Plenzdorf's novel can be traced back to two factors: its exposure of the tension between the individual and society in the GDR, especially the role of the youth individual in GDR society, and its use of a classic text as a tool for dealing with contemporary problems.[6] Of course, there is also a third issue: suicide. The first point is important but also rather obvious. Further, that first point has been addressed by scholars such as Michael Douglas Schleihauf Zimmermann and Siegfried Mews. However, transtextuality is an important mechanism in the novel, one that fortifies and enriches the youthful individualism in the novel. The transtextuality in Plenzdorf's novel, combined with the suicide, is what makes the work such a watershed event in GDR literary history.

In May 1971, Erich Honecker came to power in the GDR, replacing Walter Ulbricht as the First Secretary of the Socialist Unity Party (SED) and promising a new approach to cultural politics, partly because Honecker was twenty years younger than Ulbricht. In 1965, at the infamous Eleventh Plenum, Ulbricht had declared that rock-and-roll music is the "Monotonie des Je-Je-Je"[7] (monotony of yeah, yeah, yeah) and his Central Committee of the SED banned eleven new GDR films, virtually the year's entire film production. In most cases those films were banned simply because they were vaguely deemed to be frivolous. In December 1971, in an apparent effort to enliven GDR cultural production in the aftermath of Ulbricht's heavy-handed censorship, Honecker, the former leader of the Free German Youth (FDJ), declared that there were to be no taboos in German literature as long of the writer was a socialist.

> Wenn man von der festen Position des Sozialismus ausgeht, kann es meines Erachtens auf dem Gebiet von Kunst und Literatur keine Tabus geben. Das betrifft sowohl die Fragen der inhaltlichen Gestaltung als auch des Stils—kurz gesagt: die Fragen dessen, was man die künstlerische Meisterschaft nennt.[8]
>
> [If one starts firmly from the standpoint of socialism, there can, in my opinion, be no taboos in the field of art and literature. That applies to content as well as style—in short: those questions of what one regards as artistic mastery.]

This declaration only thinly concealed who (the Party) would judge which authors were beginning "firmly from the standpoint of socialism." As is often pointed out in scholarship on *Die neuen Leiden*, the novel is in part a response to Honecker's declaration. Suicide was no doubt a problematic topic in the GDR, one that Plenzdorf also addresses in the film he made with Heiner Carow, *Die Legende von Paul und Paula* (The Legend of Paul and Paula).[9] With *Die neuen Leiden*, Plenzdorf was also flirting with the taboo of reading canonical texts in a humorous, though ultimately entirely serious, manner, in a way that engages the context of East Germany in the early 1970s, reading Goethe's novel as a living text rather than as a museum piece.

That is, Edgar's reading of Goethe is a subversive case of Gérard Genette's concept of proximation. In fact, Genette also notes this matter. He uses Plenzdorf's novel in his taxonomy of hypertextuality, *Palimpsests: Literature in the Second Degree*, which is in turn part of his five-part taxonomy of transtextuality. Genette defines proximation as follows: ". . . the habitual movement of diegetic transposition is a movement of proximation: the hypertext transposes the diegesis of its hypotext to bring it up to date and closer to its audience (in temporal, geographic, or social terms)."[10] In other words, proximation is a type of serious transformation that involves transposing a story from its original setting into a more contemporary one. Genette points out correctly that such "diegetic transpositions" occur more or less throughout literary history, giving examples such as Joachim Heinrich von Campe's *The German Robinson* (1779) and Thomas Mann's *Doktor Faustus* (1947). As will become evident, Goethe's *Die Leiden des jungen Werther* also entails its own series of proximations, including that of Klopstock, for example. Plenzdorf's novel, then, in proximating Goethe's novel to the context of the early 1970s GDR, brought both the proximation of Goethe's *Werther*—a work lauded as part of the GDR literary heritage, thanks in part to Lukács's positive reception of it—and the suicide depicted in it into the rhetorically charged discourse of GDR literary heritage.

Proximation allows literary reception to be fluid and to cross borders. In its toying with literary heritage, proximation invites the destabilization of that heritage. The proximation involved in Plenzdorf's novel, furthermore, instigated the type of semiotic change that Soviet semiotician and cultural critic Yuri Lotman calls explosion,[11] that is, a sudden, sharp semiotic change resulting from the collision of two semiotic systems. Such an explosion occurs, in part, through Edgar's reading of Werther, but it also occurs, literally, at the moment when Edgar's electrical paint sprayer explodes, killing him. Metaphors of currents (both aqueous and electric) in the text provide a conceptualization of transtextuality and the way in which Plenzdorf's novel subverts GDR literary heritage. That is, literary reception is fluid, and Plenzdorf's novel, as well as that of Goethe, depicts such fluidity through the flow of metaphorical currents. Indeed, the fact that Edgar cannot control the flow of paint with his contrived machine represents the fact that the cultural authorities in the GDR could not control literary reception with their contrived literary heritage. Further, just as the electrical current from Edgar's power source is too high in voltage for his electrical paint sprayer, so too is the literary value of Goethe's epistolary novel too rich and varied for the GDR's narrow official view of Goethe. The proximation of *Werther* with GDR youth culture zaps GDR literary heritage just as the excess voltage zaps Edgar and his electric paint sprayer. As such, Plenzdorf's novel is all about currents—aqueous, electric, and literary—and the borders they cross.

Edgar's Currents

Edgar Wibeau's autopsy report states that his death was a "Stromsache"[12] (matter of electricity) This is true on several levels. One type of current that kills Edgar is electrical: Edgar electrocutes himself. The obituary in the *Berliner Zeitung* from December 26—which the reader encounters on the very first page of the novel—declares that Edgar is "mit elektrischem Strom umgegangen" (7; someone who dealt with electrical current). And this current is powerful. The machine's engine runs on 380 volts. Rather than safely avoiding the outdated machine with its high voltage, Edgar thinks as follows: "Das heißt, ich mußte die zweihundertzwanzig in der Laube erst hochtransformieren" (142–43; That means that I first had to transform the 220V in the garden shed to the higher voltage). He is well aware of the danger of high voltage and of the transformation of the voltage, a factor that, combined with the novel's allusions to *Werther*, leads readers to consider Edgar's death a suicide. After describing how he transformed the voltage with ersatz tools, Edgar describes how dangerous the machine is as he tries to turn it on by pushing the button that he adapted from the doorbell on the garden shed: "Auf die Art mußte die Spannung natürlich ungeheuer hochgehen, und wenn einer die Hand daran hat, kommt er nicht wieder los. Das war's. Machts gut, Leute!" (145; In this way, the voltage must have increased tremendously, and if you have your hand on that, it won't come off again. That's all she wrote. Take care, people!)

Edgar also works with hydraulic current. One of the obituaries cited at the beginning of the novel is signed "VEB (K) Hydraulik Mittenberg" (8). ("VEB" stands for Volkseigener Betrieb [publicly owned operation]. The "K" stands for "kreisgeleitet" [managed by the district]. "Hydraulik" means hydraulics, the focus of the operation. "Mittenberg" is the name of the district.) Edgar's brigade is trying to design a paint sprayer without an excessive cloud of mist. Edgar's colleague Addi tries to design such a machine with air pressure, a design that fails. Edgar, in the meantime, tries to salvage a hydraulic paint sprayer he finds under the brigade's trailer, a design that he defends before he even tries it (without asking why the earlier design had been stored away in the first place), and a design that likewise fails. As it turns out, Edgar's insistence on using hydraulics turns out to be not an allegiance to hydraulics as such but rather an annoyance at the hydraulic machine being in his way, as well as a curiosity about it. "Es lag da unter unserem Salonwagen rum. Ich war schon mindestens dreimal darüber gestolpert und hatte es auch schon beschnarcht. Aber ich hätte mir doch lieber sonstwas abgebissen, als einen danach zu fragen, was das für ein Apparat war und so" (97; it was just lying around underneath our trailer. I tripped over it at least three times. I had also examined it curiously, but I would rather have bit the bullet than to have asked somebody what the thing was for.) But Edgar soon discovers what kind of machine it is. It sprays paint without creating a cloud of mist, but the pressure is too great and a hose bursts, creating a mess. The air-compression painting machine creates a cloud of mist, and the pressure involved in the hydraulic machine is too great for the hoses to contain. Paint, like economies and literary reception, cannot easily be controlled.

When Honecker came to power in the GDR, changes were made not only in cultural policy but also in economic and technological policy.[13] Technology had long been an important part of Eastern Bloc policy. The latter part of the Ulbricht years saw the technological and economic push known as the Neues Ökonomisches System der Planung und Leitung (NÖS or NÖSPL, sometimes referred to in English as the New Economic System), which lasted from 1963 to 1970 and was intended both to offer incentive for technological advancement and to jumpstart the economy. It was also a reaction both to economic crisis and events and discourse in the Soviet Union.[14] The program (NÖSPL) involved optimistic economic planning and an interdependency between technology and political rhetoric.[15] With the switch from Ulbricht to Honecker came, as Benjamin Robinson fondly points out, a switch from the political and economic planning of NÖSPL to cybernetics,[16] and, as Raymond G. Stokes demonstrates at length, a switch from investment in high technology to an investment in consumer goods production, a switch that left the field of electronics in a rather backward condition.[17] This technological and economic regime change helped to set the stage for Plenzdorf's *Die neuen Leiden*, with its technological metaphors.

As historian Dolores L. Augustine observes, technology played a large role in the East German literary imagination, starting at the latest in the 1960s. Augustine points out how writers such as Christa Wolf and Volker Braun were critical of the notion that technology would assist in the march toward socialist utopia, but she goes on to read Plenzdorf's *Die neuen Leiden* as being affirmative of such technophilia. Although technology plays a large role in the novel, and Augustine's monograph is otherwise admirably well thought-out and well written, seeing the novel as affirming utopian technophilia is simply a dubious reading of the novel. On a basic plot level, it is technology that kills Edgar Wibeau. Moreover, the garden shed in which Edgar finds refuge is being demolished in the name of technological advancement. Edgar uses a tape-recorder to play music and to send quotations from Goethe's *Die Leiden des jungen Werther* to his friend Willi, and he likes cinema, but this is no gesture toward advancing East German technological prowess. He likes technology the same way he likes blue jeans and slang and J. D. Salinger and Louis Armstrong.

He likes technology because it is fun, because it ties into his youth culture. Edgar's abstract paintings, moreover, are critical of scientists. "Wir malten durchweg abstrakt. Eins hieß Physik. Und: Chemie. Oder: Hirn eines Mathematikers" (20; We always painted abstractly. One was called Physics. And: Chemistry. Or: Brain of a Mathematician). That is, Edgar does not take the GDR reverence for science and math seriously. He satirizes that reverence with silly paintings. Edgar's mother wants him to find an "ordentlichen Beruf" (20; proper career). But he wants to be a painter, and he mocks the practical careers with his paintings. Edgar works as a painter with a construction brigade, but he works in construction not because he is interested in a technophilic, communist utopia but rather because he needs money and has no practical skills. As the posthumous Edgar puts it:

> Klar wollte ich Geld verdienen! Wenn einer keine Tonbänder mehr kaufen kann, muß er Geld verdienen. Und wo geht er in diesem Fall hin? Zum Bau. Motto: Wer nichts will und wer nichts kann, geht zum Bau oder zur Bahn. Bahn war mir zu gefährlich. Da hätten sie garantiert nach Ausweis und Aufenthaltgenehmigung gefragt und dem Käse. Also Bau. Auf dem Bau nehmen sie jeden. Das wußte ich.[18]
>
> [Of course I wanted to earn money! When one can no longer afford to buy cassette tapes, one has to earn money. And where will one go in such a case? To the construction site. Motto: Whoever doesn't want to do anything and can't do anything goes either to construction or to the railway. The railway was too dangerous for me. They surely would have asked for my ID and residence permit and so on. So, I went into construction. At the construction site, they'll take anybody. I knew that.]

Edgar's relationship to technology, construction, and engineering is playful, youthful, but not affirmative in a teleological sense of promising utopia. Plenzdorf's *Die neuen Leiden* simply does not "depict engineering as a higher calling," as Augustine maintains.[19]

If technology in the novel is not a hymn to the great prowess of East German engineering, what role does technology play in the novel, besides Edgar's youthful enjoyment of it? Technology, especially electric current, in the novel represents both the means by which Edgar kills himself and another metaphor of flowing current as the fluidity of literary reception. It transforms Goethe's *Die Leiden des jungen Werther* by allowing it to collide with the context of GDR youth culture. When Edgar's electric paint sprayer malfunctions, killing him, it also kills the sclerotic literary heritage of the GDR. Yuri Lotman divides semiospheric changes—the semiosphere always changing—into gradual changes and explosions, the latter being a sharp and unexpected shift.[20] The appearance of Plenzdorf's *Die neuen Leiden* represents an explosion in the literary heritage of the GDR. It sharply changed the reception of Goethe's *Die Leiden des jungen Werther* and, more generally, Goethe, in the GDR and fundamentally disrupted the official literary history of the GDR, with its dichotomous, Lukácsian paradigm of classicism, realism, and rationalism (and above all Goethe) versus romanticism, modernism, and irrationalism. Although Lotman's diachronically informed theory of semiotics is both groundbreaking and useful, it is not difficult—even without Lotman—to see the appearance of Plenzdorf's novel, with its literal, diegetic explosion, as an explosion in a metaphorical sense. Indeed, Peter J. Brenner writes that the Plenzdorf Debate "sprengte"[21] (exploded) the restrictive literary critical framework.

Before the appearance of Plenzdorf's novel, the reception of *Die Leiden des jungen Werther* in the GDR was set, in large part, by Lukács's chapter on that novel in *Goethe und seine Zeit* (Goethe and His Age)—which, published in 1947, slightly predates the GDR)[22]—in which he downplays the influence of Sturm und Drang (Storm and Stress) on romanticism and counterintuitively emphasizes the relationship between Sturm und Drang and the Enlightenment.[23] That is, he defends Sturm und Drang while criticizing romanticism, although the latter is typically viewed as an heir to the former. He portrays *Werther* as a work of realism, which allows him to see it as a forerunner of nineteenth-century realism. He appreciates the fact that Goethe based the work loosely around real events, and he praises Werther's admiration of Homer, Klopstock, Goldsmith, and Lessing. Lukács, furthermore, sees the novel as one of social rebellion against both feudalism and the emerging bourgeoisie. The fact that he sees Werther primarily as a figure who engages in social protest is also part of the reason why *Die neuen Leiden* seemed so subversive to critics such as Kaul. If Werther protests the social conditions of his age, and Edgar Wibeau is a Werther-figure, then Edgar must be protesting the social conditions of the GDR. Such a reading is misguided, however, as the novels of both Goethe and Plenzdorf are more complex than that. Edgar states, for example, that he has no problems with communism in and of itself, and Werther has issues beyond those involved in his social environment. Indeed, Lukács the philosopher uses almost no textual evidence to support his claims. Nonetheless, Lukács's take on *Werther* provided a common measuring stick for later GDR scholarship on *Werther*.

Peter Müller's 1965 dissertation on *Werther*, published as a monograph in East Berlin in 1969, performs a close reading and favors the novel as a prized piece of literary heritage for the GDR.[24] Müller, in part, sees Werther as rebelling against feudal aristocracy but as a willing participant in the emerging bourgeoisie, thereby also a torchbearer of literary heritage. There was some backlash against Müller's book, claiming that while he remained true to the text, he did not remain true to Marxism-Leninism (although both Marx and Lenin were enthusiastic readers of bourgeois literature).[25] Critics such as Hans-Georg Werner, for example, wanted to return to Lukács's view.[26] All in all, however, the reception of *Werther* in the GDR until the early 1970s was overwhelmingly positive. Indeed, criticizing Goethe would have been a dangerous move politically for any critic.

Edgar, however, reads Goethe's novel somewhat differently, not only from Lukács and Werner but also from Müller. But he also performs rather unorthodox readings of other novels (as does Werther). In that sense, he understands Werther better than those trained Goethe scholars do. He declares that Salinger's *Catcher in the Rye* (1951) and Defoe's *Robinson Crusoe* (1719) are his two favorite books. In addition to reading, he listens to the songs of Louis Armstrong and Ella Fitzgerald, and he watches the film *To Sir, with Love* (1967), starring Sidney Poitier. What function do these texts play in the novel? Kirsten Scherler notes that Edgar's two favorite books, *Catcher in the Rye* and *Robinson Crusoe*, both portray a main character who is isolated: Crusoe literally stranded on an island and Holden Caulfield socially isolated.[27] Edgar's affinity for jazz and the blues creates an incongruous juxtaposition with the established cultural norms of the GDR. Priscilla Layne argues that Edgar associates with figures of black culture as a means of establishing rebellion.[28] There is, however, another function that such texts, especially *Catcher in the Rye* and *Robinson Crusoe*, play in the novel: they also contain readers, namely readers who (like Werther) set the stage for Edgar's reading practices. Holden Caulfield mishears the song "Comin' Through the Rye" by Robert Burns. This mishearing allows Holden to construe the song as an anthem for angst-ridden youth. Robinson Crusoe has only the Bible to read, symbolizing the Protestant doctrine of *sola scriptura*. There is surely a connection between these figures' isolation and their reading practices. They are reading alone with no context, dialogue, or access to secondary literature. Edgar likewise reads without any context, especially regarding Goethe's *Werther*. He does not know anything about the GDR reception of that work. In fact, he defecates on the cover, title page, and afterword of the book, those parts which would have provided some context for the novel. He finds the novel in the bathroom in the garden shed, as he realizes that there is no toilet paper there. "Ich hatte das aus dieser alten Schwarte oder Heft. Reclamheft. Ich kann nicht mal sagen, wie es hieß. Das olle Titelblatt ging flöten auf dem ollen Klo von Willis Laube"[29] (I got it out of this old doorstop, a Reclam volume. I can't even say what the name of the book was. The dang title page went down the dang drain of the toilet in Willi's garden shed). He later describes what he does with this "Reclamheft" in greater detail:

> Und kein Klopapier, Leute. Ich fummelte wie ein Irrer in dem ganzen Klo rum. Und dabei kriegte ich dann dieses berühmtes Buch oder Heft in die Klauen. Um irgendwas zu erkennen, war es zu dunkel. Ich opferte also zunächst die Deckel, dann die Titelseite und dann die letzten Seiten, wo erfahrungsgemäß das Nachwort steht, das sowieso kein Aas liest. Bei Licht stellte ich fest, dass ich tatsächlich völlig exakt gearbeitet hatte. (35)
>
> [And there was no toilet paper, people. I fumbled around like a crazy person all over the bathroom. And in the process, I managed to get this book in my hands. It was too dark to see what it was. I sacrificed the cover, then the title page, and then the last pages, where the afterword usually is, that stuff that nobody reads anyway. When it was daylight again, I discovered that my work had been exact.]

That is, Edgar uses exactly the cover, the title page, and the afterword as toilet paper, then flushing them down the toilet. He then has only the text to read with no title, author name, or commentary. He does not know when the text was written or what the cultural authorities in the GDR had written about it. He then reads the text in the context of his life as a teenager in East Germany in the early 1970s. But Edgar is not the only character in literary history to read a text without context or commentary.

Werther's Currents

Goethe's *Die Leiden des jungen Werther* was always already, in part, an exploration of proximation (although other critics do not employ that particular Genettean term) and the fluidity of literary reception.[30] Werther reads Homer, Ossian, Lessing, the Bible, and Klopstock, among other texts, and his readings highlight fluidity, including, among other things, the fluidity of literary reception. In addition to transforming the role of *Werther* in GDR literary heritage—or rather as a way of transforming it—Edgar also reads as Werther does: as an interpreter who proximates literary texts with his contemporary context and, in the process, often highlights fluidity. Secondary literature on *Werther* that focuses on Werther's readings tends to accuse Werther of misreading or reading selectively. (I agree that Werther has a habit of misreading. However, I contend that Werther's misreading—and Edgar's misreadings—are productive.) Bruce Duncan maintains: "The reader of Goethe's novel becomes—or should become—aware that Werther experiences these works inappropriately."[31] Arnd Bohm even goes so far as to assert that "Werther betrays his obligations as a Christian reader . . ." by missing the role of divinity in Klopstock's ode.[32] Similar claims have been made about

Edgar Wibeau's reading of *Werther* and other texts. Both Werther and Edgar, furthermore, focus on metaphors of fluidity. Before returning to Edgar's readings, then, it is in order to examine Werther's readings.

Werther reads Homer enthusiastically—mentioning the poet seven times—and, as Tobol and Washington indicate, he reads selectively. He admires Homer as an ancient poet concerned with nature and mythology. His reading of the poet's works, however, reveals much more about Werther than it does about Homer. Tobol and Washington are particularly concerned with Werther's assertion, in his May 13 letter to Wilhelm, that Homer's works provide him with a much-needed lullaby (*Wiegengesang*).[33] The poet's works, they note, are full of gruesome battles and dangerous adventures, scenes not typically thought to be conducive to lullabies. In his June 21 letter Werther tells Wilhelm that he sees himself in Penelope's suitors in Homer's *Odyssey*, as he waits with Lotte while Albert is away. The suitors are described in Homer's work, however, as being greedy, impatient, and arrogant. Werther's unconventional reading of Homer is also reflected in (and perhaps caused by) his reading of the Westein edition, which contains no commentary.[34] Just as Edgar reads a copy of *Werther* that now has no afterword or title page, Werther begins on August 28 to read the Westein edition of Homer, a gift from Albert, rather than his five-volume Ernesti edition with commentary, a matter that allows Werther to read Homer without the literary historical baggage attached to the poet. On October 12, however, after Lotte and Albert have wed, Werther puts aside Homer and begins to read Ossian.

In the letter from that same day, Werther tells Wilhelm, in the letter dated October 12, that he is now reading Ossian rather than Homer (he says "Ossian hat in meinem Herzen den Homer verdrängt" (Ossian has ousted Homer from my heart), a change in reading that reflects Werther's change in affect. Indeed, as Goethe remarked to Henry Crabb Robinson in 1829, Werther reads Homer "while he retained his senses" and reads Ossian "when he was going mad."[35] As Swales, Duncan, Bahr, and Koelb all have indicated, Werther's reading of Ossian is complex, if also misguided. Indeed, twelve pages of *Werther* are dedicated to narrating Goethe's reading of Ossian. Ehrhard Bahr has demonstrated that Werther reads Ossian (with Lotte) to index the parallels between women in Ossian's text—first Colma, then Daura—who are torn between rivals and the situation involving Lotte, Werther, and Albert. Werther also focuses in his reading on duels between rival men over women, a theme that parallels the tension between Werther and Albert over Lotte.[36] Werther, furthermore, reads his own translation of Ossian, a matter that amplifies the interpretive nature of his reading of the text.[37] Werther thus reads Ossian selectively, and, as Bahr maintains, Werther's Ossianism is quite different from that construed by James Macpherson under the pseudonym of Ossian.[38] But Homer and Ossian are certainly not the only authors that Werther reads.

Werther also reads Lessing's *Emilia Galotti*, a play in which a father kills his daughter in order to protect her honor. The play is open on Werther's lectern as he shoots himself in the head. The same play, it should be noted, was open in Karl Wilhelm Jerusalem's room when he killed himself in November 1772; Goethe based *Werther*, in part, on Jerusalem's suicide, and Werther's reading of *Emilia Galotti* was surely influenced by reports that Jerusalem had read it before killing himself.[39] Duncan demonstrates that Werther's reading of Lessing's play, like Werther's other readings, allows him an ironic association with Emilia Galotti. That is, Werther sees parallels between Emilia Galotti's situation and his own, when in fact such parallels are difficult to discern. Odoardo kills his daughter Emilia in order to save her honor and restore order. Werther kills himself, a suicide that is difficult to perceive as restoring order. Werther's readings of Homer, Ossian, and Lessing indicate instability in literary reception. He proximates the works to his contemporary situation, thereby working against the grain of established literary history. Other readings by Werther go beyond such ironic interpretations to focus on metaphors of fluidity and currents within those works, further indicating that literary heritage is fluid.

Metaphors of fluidity abound in *Werther*. When Werther and Lotte read Ossian, for example, tears flow from their eyes, and Werther describes Ossian's text, in his letter dated October 12, using the words "in dampfenden Nebeln" (in the vaporous mists) and "Waldstrom" (roar of a forest torrent), that is, a waterfall gushing from a cliff in the woods. But two other works that Werther reads provide myriad metaphors of fluidity: the Bible and Klopstock. Werther's allusions to the Bible relate, for the most part, to flowing water and to drinking. Werther compares young women fetching water from a well to young women in the Bible doing the same.[40] Clayton Koelb indicates that this is surely an allusion to the story of Rachel and Jacob from the Hebrew Bible.[41] Werther's allusion to that story highlights his desire to court, as Jacob and Rachel meet and court at the well. In addition, the allusion to the well directly precedes a passage in which he mentions his reading, subtly implying that his readings are also fluid. At the end of his letter dated May 12, he writes: "wie um die Brunnen und Quellen wohltätige Geister schweben. O der muß nie nach einer schweren Sommertagswanderung sich an des Brunnens Kühle gelabt haben, der das nicht mitempfinden kann" (I sense the benevolent spirits that watch over springs and wells. Oh, anyone who cannot share this feeling must never have refreshed himself at a cool spring after a hard walk on a summer's day).

Then at the beginning of his letter dated May 13, he writes:

> Du fragst, ob du mir meine Bücher schicken sollst?—Lieber, ich bitte dich um Gottes willen, laß mir sie vom Halse! Ich will nicht

> mehr geleitet, ermuntert, angefeuert sein, braust dieses Herz doch genug aus sich selbst; ich brauche Wiegengesang, und den habe ich in seiner Fülle gefunden in meinem Homer.
>
> [You ask if you should send me my books?—My dear fellow, I implore you, for God's sake keep the things from me! I do not want to be led on, stimulated, inspired any more, for this heart of mine is turbulent enough of its own accord; what I need is soothing lullabies, and I have found them in abundance in my Homer.]

That is, literary meaning, necessarily mediated by interpretation, like spiritual nourishment, can be represented as a fluid substance taking the shape of the container in which it is contained. Further, Werther is reluctant to read beyond Homer, an ironic statement, given the extent to which he is stimulated by other texts later in the novel. Werther's other allusions to the Gospels of the New Testament, like his allusions to the Hebrew Bible, deal mostly with drinking fluids. In an allusion to John 18:11 in his letter dated November 15, Werther, foreshadowing his own death, compares himself to Christ who was ordained "seinen Becher auszutrinken" (to drink the cup of bitterness). In addition, he is subtly implying that biblical meaning is fluid, as his renditions of biblical passages are willful. Werther's incorporation of metaphors of fluidity is even more evident in his reading of another author.

Werther and Lotte both read Klopstock with great enthusiasm. This becomes evident in Werther's letter to Wilhelm written on June 16, in which he describes a rain and lightning storm that befalls Wetzlar during an evening ball. At the height of the storm, Lotte touches Werther's hand and says "Klopstock!" Werther recalls to Wilhelm how he (Werther) immediately understood the allusion. "Ich erinnerte mich sogleich der herrlichen Ode, die ihr in Gedanken lag, und versank in dem Strome von Empfindungen, den sie in dieser Losung über mich ausgoss"[42] (At once I remembered the glorious ode she had in mind, and was lost in the sensations that flooded me on hearing the name). The ode to which Lotte refers is Friedrich Gottlieb Klopstock's "Frühlingsfeier" (1771), which celebrates the divine interconnectivity of everything through images of a storm with rain, thunder, lightning, heavy winds, flooding, and finally even a worm is interconnected with the storm and the divine. Lotte mentions the ode in connection with the storm, leading Werther to associate the ode with the interconnectivity he feels with Lotte. He then bends down, kisses her hand, and cries.

Again, Werther appropriates the poem about fluid currents for his contemporary situation (in Genette's terms, Werther proximates Klopstock's poem). Klopstock's work is about the pervasiveness and sublime nature of the divine, the divine interconnectedness of everything.

Lotte alludes to Klopstock's consideration of the divine as portrayed by the thunderstorm, Klopstock's ode also using imagery of a thunderstorm. Werther, however, associates the ode with his affection for Lotte, proposing a reading of the poem that is quite different from the established one. Just as the poem uses metaphors of water and fluidity ("Ozean der Welten," "Tropfen am Eimer," "Strom des Lichts," "zusammenströmten," "ich weine," "diese Thräne," "Ergeuß," "schwül," "durchströmen," "dampft," "Regen"; ocean of worlds, drop of a bucket, stream of light, flow together, I cry, these tears, gush, moist, flow through, steam, rain), so too does Werther's description of his interaction with Lotte at the moment when Lotte mentions Klopstock. In his letter dated July 16, Werther describes sinking into a current of emotions that Lotte pours over him. "Wenn sie gar im Gespräch ihre Hand auf die meinige legt und im Interesse der Unterredung näher zu mir rückt, daß der himmlische Atem ihres Mundes meine Lippen erreichen kann:—ich glaube zu versinken, wie vom Wetter gerührt." (If she places her hand on mine when we are talking and, excited by the conversation, moves closer, so that her divine breath brushes my lips—I feel as if I shall sink into the ground, as if I had been struck by lightning.)[43]

The currents in the Klopstock ode also describe the way that Werther allows texts to flow, to change meaning based on his contemporary situation. As will become evident, metaphors of currents, reading without literary historiographical baggage, and Werther's reception of Klopstock play a large role in Plenzdorf's *Die neuen Leiden des jungen W.*

Klopstock's Currents

Secondary literature on Plenzdorf's novel that addresses intertextuality tends to focus either on Goethe's *Werther*, clearly the most important hypotext for Plenzdorf's work, or on Salinger's *Catcher in the Rye*, which is also an important hypotext. However, *Werther* and *Catcher in the Rye* are not the only hypotexts in Plenzdorf's novel. One text that Werther and Lotte discuss in *Werther* is also an important—and entirely overlooked—hypotext in Plenzdorf's work: Klopstock's poem "Frühlingsfeier." Neither Klopstock nor his famous ode is mentioned by name in Plenzdorf's novel, but its presence, as will become evident, is unmistakable. But what was the role of Klopstock in the GDR?

Klopstock, the theologically minded father of *Sturm und Drang*, was received positively in the GDR. Three of Klopstock's poems are included in the 183 works that comprise the *Deutsches Lesebuch: Luther bis Liebknecht* (German Reader: Luther to Liebknecht), edited by Stephan Hermlin and published in 1976 by the Leipzig-based publisher Reclam (the same press that published the edition of *Werther* that Edgar reads). Compared with the eight poems by Goethe, the three poems by Andreas

Gryphius, and the two poems by the first Minister of Culture of the GDR, Johannes R. Becher, Klopstock is represented strongly. And one of those three poems by Klopstock included in the volume is "Frühlingsfeier." Klopstock had heavily influenced early GDR poets such as Johannes Bobrowski, Erich Arendt, Georg Maurer, and Karl Mickel.[44] And evidence of his influence can be seen in Volker Braun as well.[45] In 1971, one year before Plenzdorf's *Die neuen Leiden* appeared in the East German literary journal *Sinn und Form*, a one-volume edition of Klopstock's works with an introduction by Karl-Heinz Hahn was published.[46] And in 1974, Klopstock's 250th birthday was celebrated in the GDR, complete with a Klopstock conference in Halle.[47] Indeed, Klopstock, with his anti-feudalism and anti-absolutism, was salvaged for the GDR, despite his deep religious faith. In short, Klopstock was put to work for political purposes as part of the GDR's literary heritage.[48]

Flowing water is present in Plenzdorf's novel in ways that are remarkably similar to the water in Klopstock's ode. Klopstock is not explicitly mentioned in *Die neuen Leiden des jungen W.*, but then neither is Goethe. In any case, water is abundant in *Die neuen Leiden*, especially when Edgar touches and kisses Charlie, just as water is especially abundant in Goethe's *Die Leiden des jungen Werther* at the ball when Lotte touches Werther's hand and Werther kisses Lotte's hand. The scene between Edgar and Charlie occurs when, despite the fact that it is raining, Charlie wants to go boating with Dieter, her fiancé, who has recently returned from the army and is now studying *Germanistik*. Dieter maintains that it makes no sense to go boating in a rainstorm and continues typing up a *Germanistik* seminar paper. Charlie then angrily leaves and goes boating with Edgar. As they are in the boat being soaked by rain, Charlie puts her arm around Edgar and leans her head on his shoulder. Edgar in the meantime drives the boat in sharp turns so that centrifugal force causes Charlie to be pressed firmly against him. Then, as if not enough fluids are being tossed around, Charlie has to urinate, or as the posthumous Edgar puts it: "Sie mußte mal. Das verstand ich. Wenn es regnet, geht einem das immer so" (133; She had to go. I understood that. When it rains, you always have to go). Finally, Charlie asks Edgar: "Willst du einen Kuß von mir?" (133; Do you want a kiss from me?). Just as the kiss in Goethe's *Die Leiden des jungen Werther* comes during a rain storm and just after tears begin pouring from Werther's eyes, the kiss in Plenzdorf's *Die neuen Leiden* comes during a rain storm and just after Charlie urinates. In both cases, transtexuality is at work.

Key to understanding how the appearance of Plenzdorf's *Die neuen Leiden des jungen W.* creates an explosion in Lotman's sense is Genette's notion of proximation. Elements of the narrative are plucked out of eighteenth-century Germany and placed into the setting of East Germany in the early 1970s. As such, two very different cultures collide. Moreover, such proximation forces the reader to rethink both Werther and East German culture. The effects of this proximation are radical. The transposition implies that there are arbitrary laws in the GDR that do not support workers. It implies that there are outsiders in the GDR. It also highlights the likelihood that young people in the GDR did not read canonical texts in the ways that the regime had intended, or that young people did not even recognize such texts. It also reveals that Werther, far from being rational, is himself also a problematic figure, just as much of a misunderstood, miscreant, rebellious youth as Edgar is. These implications, furthermore, demonstrate the arbitrariness of literary heritage.

As Edgar pushes the button on his electric spray gun and electrical current passes through his body, much changes; he becomes a GDR Werther, a painter who misreads (that is, productively proximates) literary texts, deals in currents (whether aqueous or electric), and subversively kills himself. The moment when he posthumously describes the current passing through his body is also the moment when he mentions that he almost understands Werther's suicide.

> "Das letzte, was ich merkte, war, daß es hell wurde und daß ich mit der Hand nicht mehr von dem Knopf loskam. Mehr merkte ich nicht. Es kann nur so gewesen sein, daß die ganze Hydraulik sich nicht bewegte. Auf die Art mußte die Spannung natürlich ungeheuer hochgehen, und wenn einer dann die Hand daran hat, kommt er nicht wieder los. Das war's. Macht's gut, Leute! . . .[49] Schätzungsweise war es am besten so. Ich hätte diesen Reinfall sowieso nicht überlebt. Ich war jedenfalls fast so weit, daß ich Old Werther verstand, wenn er nicht mehr weiterkonnte."[50]

> [The last thing I noticed was that it got bright and that I couldn't take my hand off of the button. I didn't notice anything else. It could be that the whole hydraulic didn't move. In this way, the voltage must have increased tremendously, and if you have your hand on that, it won't come off again. That's all she wrote. Take care, people! . . . It was probably for the best that way. I wouldn't have survived this letdown anyway. In any case, I was just about to the point where I understood Old Werther, when he just couldn't carry on anymore.]

This is the point at which the allusions to Werther cease to be silly and instead become quite serious. When Edgar stops poking fun at Werther and himself dies, the transtextuality of *Werther* collides more forcefully with the culture of the GDR. And that transtextuality also includes the works of those writers to which Werther alludes: Homer and Ossian, for example, and, in this case, especially Klopstock. Klopstock's ode is about the interconnectedness of nature and the divine. Werther reads Lotte's naïve allusion to it as pointing toward the interconnectedness between him and Lotte. And interconnectedness in the sense of transtextuality is already at work in *Werther*. Edgar, furthermore, realizes, although in a superficial way, that texts are interconnected: "Sowieso sind meiner Meinung nach in jedem Buch fast *alle* Bücher" (32, italics in original; In my opinion, almost *all* books are in every book anyway.) Klopstock's fluid current, which flows through *Werther* and into *Die neuen Leiden*, is modernized into an electrical current, being transformed and transforming all along the way. Edgar's declaration, "Das heißt, ich mußte die zweihundertzwanzig in der Laube erst hochtransformieren"[51] (That is, I first had to transform the 220V in the shed to the higher voltage), might even be read as a description of the process by which the electrical current is transformed by the Klopstock current, and that current is explosive.

Explosive Border Crossings

Fluid currents can flow across borders in ways that rigid items cannot. With its proximation and fluid use of intertexts, Plenzdorf's novel is also in large part about the ramifications of currents crossings borders. But the border crossings in the novel are not limited to the intertextual. There are three others: abjection/dejection, epistolarity, and haunting, all of which, in the context of Plenzdorf's novel, are related to proximation. Edgar is a deject. That is, following Julia Kristeva's theory of abjection and the deject, he urinates, defecates, and flees spatially.[52] Kristeva posits that representations of corporeal elements, such as feces or vomit, leaving the body indicate a symbolic act of disturbance. However, for Kristeva, it is not so much the presence of biological waste and its lack of hygiene that is disruptive. Rather, it is the fact that it crosses a border; it flows out in ways that are not always controllable. Or rather, such disruption causes abjection. That is, abjection symbolizes disturbance. As Kristeva notes: "It is thus not lack of cleanliness or health that causes abjection but what disturbs identity, system, order. What does not respect borders, positions, rules."[53] She goes on to write that the person who experiences abjection, the deject, also does not respect borders but is in a constant state of flight. Edgar fits this description. He urinates and defecates, namely at the same time:

> An sich wollte ich mich bloß verflüssigen, aber wie immer breitete sich das Gerücht davon in meinen gesamten Därmen aus. Das war ein echtes Leiden von mir. Zeitlebens konnte ich die beiden Geschichten nicht auseinander halten. Wenn ich mich verflüssigen mußte, mußte ich auch immer ein Ei legen, da half nichts.[54]
>
> [I really just wanted to pee, but like always the rumor got around in my whole innards. That was a real problem of mine. My whole life I

could never keep those two stories apart. Whenever I had to pee, I also had to take a dump. I just couldn't help it.]

The abject is at work here in that Edgar urinates and defecates. Kristeva's theory of abjection might otherwise be rejected as silliness—given that all animals including human beings excrete biological waste regularly—but in the case of *Die neuen Leiden* it describes the symbolism of Edgar's excretion so accurately. Further, Edgar's waste continues to flow like literary disturbances: two kinds of abject matter, urine and feces, flow together in the water, further disrupting order. Most telling, however, is Edgar's use of the word "Geschichten" to describe the two types of abject matter. Again, two types of currents, as it were, connect, symbolizing proximation. And if urine were not already "Strom" enough for such an interpretation, Edgar reports, "Ich hätte einen Trocknen machen können in jeden See"[55] (I could have done a number two in every lake), mixing again solid excrement with fluid.

Furthermore, the first time that Edgar defecates and urinates together ("die beiden Geschichten nicht auseinander halten") in the novel is also the first time that he comes in contact with Goethe's *Werther*. In addition to not being able to keep his urine and feces separate, Edgar cannot keep *Werther* separate from other stories, including his own. Part of the reason for this is that he uses the title page of the book and any pages that would give him a context for Goethe's epistolary novel as toilet paper. As he literally shits on the context of Goethe, he opens the text of *Werther* to new interpretations, allowing him to interpret from his perspective as a teenager in the early 1970s in the GDR. Had Edgar read the afterword to *Werther*—instead of wiping his ass with it—he might not have taken the text seriously.

Edgar's electronic epistolarity, that is, his act of recording his readings of *Werther* onto cassette tapes and mailing them to his friend Willi, also represents a disruptive border crossing. They also represent changes made in the text through proximation. Just as Edgar's painting becomes electrical, electrifying Werther's hobby, Edgar's letter writing, Werther's other activity, also becomes electrical. Edgar's modernizing of epistolarity parallels the modernizing of his reading of the text. This is fitting, as Edgar's "letters" are Werther's letters. They are not just Werther's letters, however, they are Edgar's recordings of Werther's letters. They change as Edgar records them. They are also different in that Willi receives them and listens to them, as opposed to Wilhelm receiving them and reading them. With the different medium, the different addressee, and the different historical context, the letters have now changed quite a bit. That is, not only does Edgar read Werther's letters differently, Willi perceives them differently still, not only because they are in a different medium, but also because he listens to the recordings without knowing even the narrative context of *Werther*.

Edgar also crosses "über den Jordan"[56] (over the Jordan), as he says, that is, into death. Even in death he seems like something of a vagabond. Edgar speaks from the dead—both via the recorded tapes and through his posthumous narration—a different type of fluid border crossing altogether. Edgar hints that haunting is something that occurs in the minds of the living (which is not to say that it does not exist), and, again, he notes the border between the living and the dead in the metaphor of the River Jordan: "Ansonsten ist Bedauern jenseits des Jordan nicht üblich. Wir alle hier wissen, was uns blüht. Daß wir aufhören zu existieren, wenn ihr aufhört, an uns zu denken" (16–17; Otherwise, regret is not something that happens much over the Jordan. Here, we all know what becomes of us. That we cease to exist when you cease to think about us.)[57] That is, the presence of the dead in the minds of the living affects the thoughts of the living. Lotman also suggests that the crossing of the border between life and death, in either direction, comes with great semiotic ramifications.[58] One reason for this is the radical proximation that occurs with that border crossing. That is, through haunting, the thoughts of the living come into contact with the presence of the dead, who are otherwise not present. As such, haunting is also a metaphor for transtextuality.

These border crossings—abjection, epistolarity, and haunting—as well as the proximation of Goethe's *Werther* with the GDR of the early 1970s, culminating in the malfunction of Edgar's electric paint sprayer, create the kind of semiotic change that Lotman calls explosion. Lotman writes: "The moment of explosion is the moment of unpredictability."[59] That is, such semiotic change cannot easily be controlled. He goes on to explain that explosion is a juxtaposition of signs or sign systems that leads to new possibilities. Plenzdorf's *Die neuen Leiden* represents a turning point in GDR cultural politics and literary production in that it creates the possibility of rereading GDR literary heritage against the context of everyday life in the GDR. The explosion caused by the proximation in Plenzdorf's novel led not only to changes in cultural politics and literary production, but, related to those changes, it also led to literary historiographical changes. That is, the works of writers such as Goethe and Klopstock were viewed differently. In particular, the largely homogenous uncritical affirmation of Goethe was finally questioned. After the appearance of Plenzdorf's novel, Goethe's status in the GDR was never fully restored, a matter that will become evident again in the chapter on Wolf's *Kein Ort. Nirgends.* As such, Plenzdorf's *Die neuen Leiden* disrupted the official literary heritage of the GDR. In the realm of cultural politics, Kurt Hager, chief ideologist of the SED, attempted to lead a movement to restrict literary production to the limitations in place before Honecker's "No Taboos" speech of December 1971. In May 1973, Honecker spoke again before the Central Committee of the SED, trying to retighten GDR cultural restrictions. This effort, however, was in vain. At the 7th

Writers' Congress in November 1973, a relatively open assembly involving many writers, the easing of restrictions regarding literary production was confirmed. Although tensions flared again, most notably during the Biermann Affair of November 1976, the notion of an immovable literary heritage for the GDR had already begun to unravel.

Literary Responses to Plenzdorf

In the realm of literary production, there were initial reactions to Plenzdorf's novel that attempted to provide a different view of the teenage outsider in the GDR. Peter Brenner lists three such novels: Wolfgang Joho's *Der Sohn: Nachrichten aus der Bender Welt* (The Son: Reports from Bender's World, 1974), Rolf Schneider's *Die Reise nach Jarosław* (The Journey to *Jarosław*, 1974), and Volker Braun's *Unvollendete Geschichte* (Unfinished Story, 1975).[60] Those novels, while clearly responses to Plenzdorf's *Die neuen Leiden*, seem, in part, to try to reconcile the will of youth culture with the project of socialism. In Joho's novel, the son protests against his actor-father's lack of creativity, but then the generational conflicts are solved through communication and self-criticism, largely in the context of a courtroom trial with a warm and rational judge. In Schneider's novel, the protagonist Gittie is not accepted into the "Erweiterte Oberschule" (EOS), roughly the East German equivalent of the West German Gymnasium, that is, a college preparatory school, so she runs away to Poland. *Die Reise nach Jarosław* is an explicit response to Plenzdorf's *Die neuen Leiden*, as Gittie meets a young man at the Friedrichstraße train station who has long hair, wears blue jeans, and is named Ed. However, the problematic of the teenage outsider is, to some extent, belittled and rendered comical in Schneider's novel. Braun's novel, through one character's reading of Plenzdorf's novel, is also an explicit response and hints that *Die neuen Leiden* poses appropriate questions about the tension between the individual and society in the GDR but does not fully answer them. That is, it does not probe to the core of the matter. Another novel that is a direct response to Plenzdorf and that Brenner does not mention is Günter Görlich's *Eine Anzeige in der Zeitung* (A Notification in the Newspaper, 1978), which tells the story of an unorthodox teacher, Manfred Just, who commits suicide. It is narrated by a colleague of Just's. Görlich's novel responds to that of Plenzdorf, as both involve schools and teenagers. However, the person who commits suicide in Görlich's novel is a teacher and not a student. As such, it is not so much about youth culture. However, it is, among other things, about the relationship between transtextuality and suicide. *Eine Anzeige in der Zeitung* also contains, above all, a discourse on Russian futurist poet Vladimir Mayakowsky's poetry on suicide (Mayakovsky, 1893–1930, also killed himself). Furthermore, Görlich's novel, which has been read as a pedagogical novel that is relatively affirmative of the GDR (although I see the novel as being richer than such readings imply), contains several other elements that point to Plenzdorf's novel, including newspaper statements, the metaphor of death as a border crossing, and the fact that his suicide is not a protest against communism. Although, as Brenner correctly notes, these novels appeared in the wake of Plenzdorf's novel, engaged its problematic of individual versus society, and would be unthinkable without it, there are other works that responded to *Die neuen Leiden* in other ways. The most important of these are works that deeply engage the literary heritage of the GDR. The first of these that will be examined here is Werner Heiduczek's often-overlooked novel *Tod am Meer* the focus of the next chapter.

3: Remembering to Death: Werner Heiduczek's *Tod am Meer*

On June 9, 1978, the Soviet ambassador to the GDR, Pjotr Andrejevich Abrassimov, and his Bulgarian counterpart showed up at the home of none other than Erich Honecker to protest the appearance of Werner Heiduczek's novel *Tod am Meer* in December of 1977.[1] Although censorship was rampant in the GDR, appeals for censorship made directly in the residence of the First Secretary of the SED were rare. What is it about this novel that Abrassimov found so subversive? In his official statement, Abrassimov cites the portrayal of Soviet soldiers as "ungehobelte Grobiane, als brutale Leute und Ignoranten"[2] (crude brutes, as brutal people and ignoramuses). He goes on to cite passages in which Soviet soldiers rape German women and otherwise insult the German people. And he reports an absence of the atrocities committed by German Fascists in the Soviet Union during the Second World War. Indeed, as Carsten Wurm indicates, the novel was barely approved by the censors, and was likely approved as a result of the censors being hesitant to cause another stir in the immediate wake of the Biermann affair, the massive response to which had created a real political crisis.[3] As Michael Hametner states, the novel was, for many readers "ein Kultbuch—für die Zensur in der DDR ein Ärgernis"[4] (a cult book—a nuisance for the GDR censors). Abrassimov's visit to the Honecker residence had consequences. The novel was banned and not rereleased until 1987 in the wake of Mikhail Gorbachev's *glasnost* and *perestroika*. From Abrassimov's appeal to Honecker in 1978 until the collapse of the GDR, Heiduczek published only children's literature.[5]

While Abrassimov's observations of the novel's offensiveness are accurate, *Tod am Meer* is also subversive in its rewriting of Thomas Mann's *Tod in Venedig* (Death in Venice), Mann being an otherwise accepted writer in the Lukácsian realist paradigm that was favored by GDR cultural authorities. Much is subversive in the novel's relationship to Mann's novella. One could point to the fact that the novel's main character, Jablonski, kills himself rather than having to return to the so-called workers' and peasants' paradise on German soil. In addition, the novel is subversive in its constant hinting that the Stalinist system is itself self-destructive. These three points: the rewriting of Mann; Jablonski's self-destruction; and the representation of the Stalinist system as self-destructive are, furthermore, interconnected. A narratological matter allows each of these three points to come to the fore: vocalization, that is, the textual transformation from a non-autodiegetic narrator to an autodiegetic one. Genette explains that ". . . vocalization . . . substitutes an I . . . (that is, a person, a narrating character) for the nonperson of a narrator who had previously been external to the story, impersonal and transparent. . . . a shift from the third to the first person."[6] In other words, vocalization is the narrative shift that allows the protagonist to tell his own story. Whereas Mann's *Tod in Venedig* is narrated by a third-person narrator, *Tod am Meer* is narrated largely by the novel's main character and Aschenbach figure, Jablonski. This distinction is crucial, as it allows the reader to see Jablonski's life through his own commentary, revealing his past, his suicidal character, and his analysis of the self-destructive nature of Stalinism. All this is only possible through the text's reworking of Mann's famous novella.

Heiduczek's *Tod am Meer* needs to be viewed through three different lenses, each view arriving more or less at the same conclusion. The first of these lenses involves a conscious reading of the relationship between Mann's *Der Tod in Venedig* and Heiduczek's *Tod am Meer*. The second involves reading *Tod am Meer* as detective fiction, an approach that allows for an examination of Jablonski's eyewitness account of his own life and his detective-like search through his past for the moment at which his life went awry. The third juxtaposes Jablonski's autobiographical work with his biographical work on Stalin and compares Jablonski to Stalin, as both Jablonski and Stalin were, in their own ways, self-destructive and both officially died of cerebral hemorrhaging. These three approaches combined reveal just why Heiduczek's novel was so subversive: its shift in narrative situation both undermines Mann's venerable position in the official literary heritage of the GDR and highlights the self-destructive elements at work in the Eastern European socialist experiment.

The reader of Heiduczek's *Tod am Meer* is informed—in both the first and last sentences of the novel—that Jablonski is dead. On the surface, Jablonski's death is ambiguous. A physician declares the official cause of death to be a hemorrhage of the brain. However, the text later makes it fairly clear that his death is a case of suicide or at least that he was self-destructive and wanted to die, given his seemingly hopeless state of existence and his allusions to Werther (Goethe's fictional character who shoots himself in the head), Vladimir Mayakovsky (the Russian futurist poet and painter who shot himself to death in 1930), and Arthur Schopenhauer (the nineteenth-century philosopher who wished to decriminalize, if not encourage, suicide), not to mention the novel's titular allusion to Thomas Mann's *Der Tod in Venedig* (in which the main character self-destructively remains in cholera-infested Venice knowing that it will likely lead to his death). This chapter reads Jablonski's death as a suicide and asks what it represents.

Jablonski narrates his own downfall. In his lengthy, yet fragmentary letter written to his former hospital roommate, Jablonski, who is recovering from illness (among other things) in a hospital on the Black Sea in Bulgaria, writes of his life at the end of the war and throughout the 1950s. He describes how a sergeant major sadistically abused both his soldiers and civilians and how his (Jablonski's) friend Wanda later killed that officer and was hanged for murder. He laments how he joined the SPD only in order to receive 100 Marks and how, only a couple of weeks after he joined the Party, it merged with the KPD to form the SED. He writes about his experience in a postwar teacher-training curriculum, his experience as a school director, and his experiences with three different women: a woman he loved, a prostitute he knew before the end of the war, and a potential lover who attempted suicide. He regrets how he was coerced by a young professor to confront a respected Kantian philosophy professor with questions about Stalin that led to the philosophy professor's dismissal. He describes his experience with the workers' uprising of June 17, 1953, and how a young Stalinist professor attempted to quell the protesters and was killed by a protester's rock. Jablonski's anecdotes are telling, but they do not fit together into a coherent whole. They are fragmentary and do not lead to a climax. Jablonski's narration only makes sense with the intervention of the fictional editor and Jablonski's three acquaintances. The fact that there is no clear central message in Jablonski's letter leads perhaps to the main point of the novel: Jablonski feels a need to communicate, but for a variety of reasons he cannot. He is a professional writer who can no longer write; he experiences writer's block. The main doctor in the hospital forbids him from writing. Perhaps worst of all, he cannot seem to find the heart of the matter. He cannot find the language to express what it is that bothers him so. Jablonski's inability to write parallels Werther's inability to paint and, more so, Aschenbach's inability to write. Indeed, *Tod am Meer* fits into the category of anti-Bildungsroman, of which *Die Leiden des jungen Werther* and *Der Tod in Venedig* are prime examples. Jablonski's narration illustrates the self-destructive nature of himself and of the society in which he lives.

Little has been written about *Tod am Meer*. A handful of reviews were written shortly after the novel's appearance, the most worthy of mention being those by Werner Liersch[7] and Hans Jürgen Geerdts,[8] as those critics approach the novel as a work of literature. Achim Trebeß includes two pages on the novel in his 2001 essay on the motif of death in GDR literature.[9] Trebeß accurately notes the text's non-linear narration and compares the structure of the novel to that of a fairy tale, a comparison that is not readily evident. Udo Grashoff briefly mentions the novel in his monograph on the history of suicide in the GDR, noting its dark tone.[10] These works serve their purposes and will be discussed further later in this chapter. Of these critics, only Werner Liersch has mentioned Heiduczek's allusion to Mann's *Der Tod in Venedig*, and he does so only to assert that Heiduczek's novel is different from Mann's novella, damning the former and praising the latter. Nor has anyone dared to read Jablonski's death explicitly as a case of suicide, even though suicide is suggested in the novel by the fictional editor of Jablonski's diary. However, Trebeß does call Jablonski's death "ein Krankheitstod, der auf Konflikte des Individuums mit sich und mit der Gesellschaft hinweist"[11] (a death due to illness that points to conflicts within the individual and with society), a description that is also not inaccurate. Grashoff discusses the novel in the context of suicide, mentioning the suicide of a minor character whom Jablonski calls "der traurige Habicht" (the sad hawk) but failing to read Jablonski's death as a suicide. The present chapter combines Liersch's observation that the novel alludes to Mann's novella with Trebeß's observation that the narrative situation of Heiduczek's novel is peculiar. A juxtaposition of the narrative situations of Mann's novella and Heiduczek's novel reveals much about Jablonski's narration and his self-destruction. As none of the critics quite see Jablonski's death as a case of suicide, however, this point deserves to be clarified first.

Jablonski is self-destructive and kills himself. There is no doubt that Jablonski is, for the bulk of his life, suicidal. Even as a young *Flakhelfer* (anti-aircraft artillery assistant) in the Second World War, Jablonski considered suicide and mulled over which method would be best.

> Ich spielte mit dem Gedanken, mir das Leben zu nehmen. Aber ich wußte nicht, wie ich es anstellen sollte. Mich aufzuhängen schien mir schrecklich, und mich vom Dachgarten des Admiralspalastes auf das Steinpflaster zu stürzen, dazu hatte ich zuviel Angst. Ich stellte mir vor, wie ich da aufknallen würde, und die bloße Vorstellung nahm mir jeglichen Mut. Der beste Tod schien mir der Tod durch eine Kugel. Aber ich hatte keine Pistole. Ich hätte sie dem Oberleutnant stehlen müssen, doch ich fand keine Gelegenheit dazu.[12]
>
> [I toyed with the thought of taking my own life. But I didn't know how I should do it. Hanging myself seemed too horrendous, and I was too afraid to fling myself from the rooftop garden of the admiral's palace onto the pavement. I imagined the thwack that I would make there, and just the thought of it robbed me of all courage. The best death seemed to me to be with a bullet. But I didn't have a pistol. I'd have to steal one from the lieutenant, but I never found the opportunity to do that.]

Jablonski did not kill himself as a young man because he did not have a gun (unlike Werther, Mayakovsky, and Kleist) and because he did not like the other methods, a matter that he expresses in a darkly humorous manner. Whether he would have shot himself had he had the means, the reader cannot know. What is clear, however, is that he considered the possibility of suicide in detail. To be sure, this is not the last time that Jablonski considers suicide. After the war, while thinking about his friend Ellen, who rescued him when he was ill at war's end, who was later dismissed from a teacher-training program after the administration found out that she had worked as a prostitute for Nazi officers during the war, Jablonski went into a state of depression that he describes as follows: "Ich befand mich in einer Stimme, in der man Schlaftabletten nimmt oder den Gashahn aufdreht" (93; I found myself in a mood in which you take sleeping pills or turn the gas on). Jablonski finds himself in a self-destructive state of this sort often throughout his life. After his death, fictional commentators on Jablonski also suggest that he was suicidal. His colleague M.—a playwright—confirms this, as he states: "Er war niemals frei von Depression und Zweifel" (307; He was never free of depression and doubt). Anissa states that Jablonski suffered from his art and fell ill due to his own doubt about himself. When Jablonski repeatedly visits the theater to see his estranged wife, an actress who has left him, perform, he is repeatedly beaten by the henchmen of the theater director, who is Jablonski's wife's boyfriend. Thinking back on the situation, Jablonski writes, "Sollen sie mich totschlagen, dachte ich. Manchmal wünschte ich es geradezu" (179; Let them beat me to death, I thought. Sometimes I wished they would). Later, in the clinic in Burgas in Bulgaria, Jablonski stands on the third floor balcony, looks down, and, having apparently overcome his fear of death by jumping off of a building, confesses "ich möchte mich hinabstürzen" (85; I would like to fling myself off here). Again, he is denied the chance to follow through with the act, as he is interrupted by the nurse Weska. At another point he considers leaping off a cliff. He also ponders jumping out of a window. It is no secret that he ponders death in Burgas. He contemplates: "Vielleicht ist Burgas meine letzte Station. Fast wünsche ich es" (86; Maybe Burgas is my last station. I almost wish it is). As his doctor warns him of the seriousness of his condition, Jablonski sums up his suicidal position as follows: "Ich fürchte nicht den Tod, den Dr. Assa mir androht, ich fürchte das Leben, wie ich es bisher gelebt hatte" (180; I'm not a afraid of the death that Dr. Assa threatens me with. I'm afraid of life the way I've lived it to this point). He later formulates this in a more urgent manner: "Ich möchte sterben und muß leben. Und weiß nicht, wie. Und weiß nicht, wie. . . ." (295; I would like to die and must live. And don't know how. And don't know how. . . .)

The fact that Jablonski wanted to die, one might argue, is no proof that he in fact killed himself. Although the official cause of Jablonski's death is given as cerebral hemorrhaging, there is ample textual evidence that suggests that his death is a case of suicide. In the first two pages of the novel, the fictional editor repeatedly suggests this. For instance, he says, "Mir will jedoch scheinen, Jablonski ist nicht an den Folgen eines Gefäßrisses gestorben, sondern an dem Versuch, sein leben zu korrigieren" (5; But it seems to me that Jablonski didn't die as a result of his aneurysm, but rather from his attempt to correct his life). In other words, he examines his life to such an extent that he perishes. Although Jablonski is ill, the fictional editor suggests that he might have lived longer had he returned to Leipzig, as demanded by Dr. Assa: "Ich glaube, er blieb in Burgas, obwohl er wußte, daß Hitze und Feuchtigkeit hier ihm den Tod bringen konnten" (6; I believe he stayed in Burgas, even though he knew that the heat and the humidity could bring about his death here), a statement that alludes to the case of Gustav von Aschenbach, who remained in Venice rather than returning to Munich, knowing that it likely meant his death. The fictional editor goes on to elaborate on his position that Jablonski remained in Burgas despite knowing that he might die there: "Und je länger ich über Jablonski und sein Ende nachdenke, um so stärker drängt sich mir der Verdacht auf, daß er Angst hatte, in sein gewohntes Leben zurückzukehren" (6; And the more I think about Jablonski and his death, the more I suspect that he feared returning to the life that he was used to). As we will see, there are several reasons why Jablonski's life is not pleasant. The fictional editor also suspects that Jablonski was suicidal: "Vielleicht suchte er den Tod" (6; Maybe he was searching for death). Citing Kant, as Jablonski does in his manuscript, the fictional editor posits that Jablonski sought death, "um sich aus der 'selbstverschuldeten Unmündigkeit' zu befreien" (6; In order to liberate himself from his "self-imposed immaturity"), an allusion to Immanuel Kant's call for enlightenment. To this end, as the fictional editor writes, Jablonski did not passively wait for death, but rather, in the course of three months, actively wrote himself to death (6; sich . . . geradezu in den Tod schrieb).

This statement is more than mere speculation. Dr. Assa sees that writing is destructive for Jablonski and forbids him to write at all. Still, Jablonski continues to write. Jablonski himself even writes of the self-destructive force in writing: "Immer wenn ich schreibe, fühle ich mich gehetzt, trinke, rauche und habe Kreislaufstörungen" (285; Every time I write, I feel agitated, drink, smoke, and have circulation problems). In spite of—perhaps because of—this knowledge, Jablonski writes more and more. He is fully committed to writing his manuscript to the end, both to the end of the manuscript and to his own end. In a passage somewhat reminiscent of Hamlet's famous "to be or not to be" soliloquy, Jablonski writes: "Ich weiß nicht, was auf mich wartet. Das Leben oder der Tod."[13] (185; I don't know what awaits me. Life or death.) Knowing that Anissa will arrive in a week to take him back to Leipzig, he adds, as a subtle indication that he will choose to die: "Aber ich habe keine andere Wahl. Sieben Tage. Anissa soll kommen. Sie soll kommen. Bis dahin werde ich das Letzte aufgeschrieben haben." (273; But I have no other choice. Seven days. Anissa is supposed to come. She's supposed to come. By then, I'll have written the last of it.) That is, Jablonski decides to write himself to death before Anissa arrives in Bulgaria to take him back to his accustomed life in Leipzig. At the end of his manuscript there is the following sentence, written in all capital letters: "DER TOD IST EXAKT" (304; DEATH IS EXACT). Below that is the name "Rainer Maria Rilke," hinting that the sentence may be a quotation from Rilke.[14] It is unclear whether the sentence is Jablonski's ending to his manuscript or whether the fictional editor later added it to the manuscript. The sentence attributed to Rilke, in any case, implies that Jablonski's death is no accident. But the allusion to Rilke is not, as we have already seen, the novel's only allusion to writing of the early twentieth century.

Jablonski and Aschenbach

The work of Thomas Mann was received favorably in the GDR, a matter that may seem baffling given Mann's early defense of German imperialism, his positive reception of Nietzsche and Schopenhauer, and his writings' emphasis on decadence, illness, and self-destruction. Indeed, Bertolt Brecht held Mann's bourgeois aesthetics in contempt, writing, for example, that he could not understand why the German people "nicht nur die untaten des hitlerregimes, sondern auch die romane des herrn mann geduldet hat"[15] (not only tolerated the atrocities of the Hitler regime but also tolerated mr. mann's novels). Brecht's aesthetics and his opinions of Thomas Mann, however, were markedly different from those of Georg Lukács, who viewed the German bourgeoisie as an important part of the trajectory from humanism to socialism. Lukács, furthermore, believed that Mann represented all that was best in the German bourgeoisie. And Lukács's views of Mann took precedence in the writer's reception in the GDR. Alfred Kurella, an important cultural functionary in the SED, similarly revered Mann, writing, for example, that "ich persönlich habe Thomas Mann erlebt als den Höhepunkt der letzten großen Welle der realistischen deutschen Prosa des 19. Jahrhunderts"[16] (I personally experienced Thomas Mann as the high point of the great wave of German realist prose of the nineteenth century). Although there were some scattered attacks on Mann in later GDR literary criticism, the positive evaluation of Mann set up by Lukács and Kurella remained largely intact throughout the course of the GDR.

Among Mann's works, *Der Tod in Venedig* was particularly valued in the GDR, and Lukács was key in shaping the work's reception there. Between 1944 and 1955 Lukács wrote five essays praising the novella. In the first of these he sees the novella's main character as representing the lack of any future for the German bourgeoisie.[17] That is, Lukács sees

Aschenbach largely as a personification of bourgeois Prussia, ill and dying. In the second and third essays, he perceives social criticism embedded in the novella and praises Aschenbach's composure and self-criticism.[18] In the last two of the essays, Lukács claims that Aschenbach's self-critical and artistic tendencies foreshadow those of the German bourgeoisie during and after the First World War.[19] In all of these essays, Lukács sees Aschenbach as representing the dying bourgeoisie, both its positive aspects and its lack of a future. Lukács's essays on Mann's novella were not the only criticism that shaped its reception in the GDR, but they were by far the most influential. So how does Heiduczek's *Tod am Meer* subvert the GDR reception of *Der Tod in Venedig*?

The relationship between the two works must be examined. Following Gérard Genette's typology of transtextuality, there is, first of all, a paratextual relationship between *Der Tod in Venedig* and *Tod am Meer*. That is, there is an allusion to the former in the latter, but not in the body of the text itself. In this case, the allusion to *Der Tod in Venedig* is in the title *Tod am Meer*. The word "Tod" is included in both titles, and—excluding the definite article in the former—both titles consist of three words, and in each case the last of the three words is a place. In addition, the titular prepositional phrase "am Meer" also describes the location of Aschenbach's death in *Der Tod in Venedig*, that is, on the Lido in Venice, next to the Adriatic Sea. The titular paratextuality invites readers to compare *Tod am Meer* with *Tod in Venedig*. The two literary works are also similar enough that one may consider their textual relationship to be one of hypertextuality, that is, *Tod am Meer* is a reworking of *Der Tod in Venedig*. Both works involve an older German writer experiencing writers' block who dies near a sea in southern Europe. In both cases, the protagonists' deaths can be read as illness-related suicides. And both deaths can be read metonymically as the downfall of something greater than the protagonist himself.

Although there is an element of proximation in *Tod am Meer*—Mann's narrative is moved to the mid-twentieth century and to Bulgaria—there is also another important hypertextual shift at work here: vocalization, Genette's term for that narrative transformation that allows a character to tell his own story. The downfall of Aschenbach is recounted by a heterodiegetic narrator (that is, one who is not also a character in the narrative), whose focalization (that is, what the narrator sees, perceives, knows) shifts from external to internal over the course of the narrative (that is, at the beginning of the narrative, the narrator perceives and knows more or less the same things that Aschenbach perceives and knows, but later in the narrative, the narrator perceives and knows less, or perhaps different things, than Aschenbach). In other words, the narrator, who is not Aschenbach, sees the story largely from Aschenbach's perspective at the beginning of the narration, but becomes less and less able to see Aschenbach's perspective as the narration progresses, an unorthodox, dynamic narrative situation explained by narratologist Dorrit Cohn.[20] Jablonski, on the other hand, tells of his own downfall with an autobiographical narrative that comprises the bulk of the novel. This difference is key. The seemingly objective, heterodiegetic narration in *Der Tod in Venedig* allows for the Lukácsian reading of the novella, which posits that Aschenbach, although previously admirable, has taken a wrong turn. Were the narrator not heterodiegetic, it might be difficult for a reader to see that point. Jablonski also thinks that his life has gone awry, but—telling his own story—he cannot simply distance himself from his own life. His attempt to do so proves self-destructive. Before further examining how his narration and his attempt to purge the unsavory events of his earlier life from his being function, it is necessary to examine the spatial semantics of his downfall.

Central to both texts is the crossing of semiotic borders. Although little has been written about *Tod am Meer*, an incredible amount of scholarship has been produced on *Der Tod in Venedig*. Matias Martinez uses literary scholar and semiotician Yuri Lotman's spatial semiotics and his theory that narrative consists largely of semiotic border crossings to describe the transition involved in Aschenbach's trip from Munich to Venice.[21] Martinez outlines three semantic binaries. The first describes psychological and physical changes in Aschenbach. The second describes the semantic opposition between Munich (clean, attractive, bourgeois) and Venice (dirty, ugly, degenerate). The third highlights the divide between the familiar and the foreign. As Martinez's essay demonstrates, Lotman's spatial semiotics apply well to *Der Tod in Venedig*. Indeed, an enormous amount of semiotic transition occurs as Aschenbach's travels from Munich to Venice. Read together, the essays by Cohn and Martinez show that as the landscape changes, Aschenbach changes, and the narrator's perception of Aschenbach also changes.

What Cohn and Martinez establish narratologically—roughly stated, that Aschenbach undergoes great change as he travels from North to South—had already been posited in other terms by earlier critics.[22] Some of the more sociologically and politically motivated of these earlier critics argue that the change, or rather downfall, of Aschenbach represents the downfall of bourgeois society. Inge Diersen, for example—a critic from the GDR—makes this explicit: "Und doch signalisiert Aschenbachs Untergang Bedrohtheit und Brüchigkeit einer gesellschaftlichen Ordnung"[23] (But Aschenbach's downfall symbolizes the endangerment and fragility of a societal order). The endangered societal order that Diersen describes is the pre–First World War, bourgeois, capitalist German society, experiencing early symptoms of what would become a long descent into fascism, a typical GDR view of that society. Regardless of whether Diersen's estimation of Imperial Germany as a precursor of fascism is accurate, she is correct in saying that Aschenbach undergoes a change on his journey from Munich to Venice, a change with major ramifications.

Martinez shows, however, that while opposing meanings can certainly be linked to opposing ends of a geographical binary in the novella, there is also a system of multiple, imcompatible meanings that exist simultaneously within the figure of Aschenbach.[24] Martinez illustrates this point with the example that the story of Aschenbach is at once both realistic, with a historical background and real geographical locations, as well as mythical, with its numerous transcendental figures. There are both outer and inner elements, a matter that leads back to Cohn's insight that at some point in the novella the narrator ceases to understand the inner Aschenbach and is only capable of describing him from the outside, although he is clearly undergoing inner change. The matter, however, is even more complicated. The paradox of Aschenbach not only has to do with the simultaneous existence of the realistic (outer) meanings and the mystical (inner) meanings, but also that Aschenbach's transformation is not entirely one from rationalism, composure, and health in Munich to irrationality, self-destruction, and illness in Venice (and all the other characteristics and associations that he embodies in each of the two cities), but rather that all these things are, to some extent, always at work in Aschenbach. While the associations linked with Munich are frequently read to be positive and those with Venice negative, both sets of characteristics contain a wealth of associative meanings. In other words, the change that occurs in Aschenbach represents change in the inner workings of a system, whether psychological or societal. At the societal level, this is largely in tune with Diersen's reading: proto-fascist elements in German society at the beginning of the twentieth century, however slight they were then, eventually got the upper hand in a way that led the system to self-destruct.

Heiduczek's *Tod am Meer* enacts a reworking of Mann's *Der Tod in Venedig* to describe a similar self-destructiveness at work in the German Democratic Republic. Before examining the inner changes in Jablonski himself, it is necessary to outline some of the politico-societal events he describes. Although a succession of historical events are recounted in *Tod am Meer*, two postwar events in particular seem to stand out starkly in Jablonski's mind. The first event is the absorption of the SPD by the KPD and the nominal creation of the SED. Jablonski joins the SPD in order to receive the hundred-mark signing bonus that the Party is offering. Shortly thereafter, the SPD is dissolved into the KPD, and the KPD becomes the SED, leaving Jablonski stuck in the SED. He repeatedly exclaims how bitter he is about the matter. The other event that seems to plague Jablonski's memory is the failed workers' revolution of June 17, 1953, which was violently suppressed by the Soviets. Related to both of these events, voices were silenced and history was simplified. Seeing

Tod am Meer as a reworking of *Der Tod in Venedig* for the GDR suggests correctly that *Tod am Meer* represents a case of proximation, that form of textual transformation that brings a story into contact with a contemporary situation. That is, if *Der Tod in Venedig* represents the self-destructive downfall of the German bourgeoisie, then *Tod am Meer*, being a reworking of *Der Tod in Venedig* set in the East Bloc, represents the self-destruction involved in Eastern European communism. But that is not the whole picture. Unlike Aschenbach, Jablonski narrates his own story—that is, a major element of Heiduczek's reworking of Mann's novella is vocalization—a matter with ramifications that deserve examination.

Jablonski as Detective

One way of examining Jablonski's narrative situation is to read the novel as detective fiction. Such a reading sees Jablonski as an eyewitness to his own story. That is, through vocalization, he is like a detective who is trying to find out what went wrong in his life. And in the process of investigating his own life, Jablonski excavates much about German history. Detective fiction looks backward to past events, often by way of flashbacks and eyewitness testimony, in order to establish previously unknown (or rather un-narrated) details, most often in the form of the question: Who murdered the victim? Or as connoisseurs of the genre say: whodunnit? Marxist philosopher and literary critic Ernst Bloch offered a more eloquent definition of detective fiction, listing three main criteria for the genre: "die Spannung des *Ratens*" (the suspense of *guessing*); "das *Entlarvende, Aufdeckende*" (that which *unmasks and uncovers*); and "das *Unerzählte . . . , Vorgeschichtehafte . . .*" (the *un-narrated . . .* , that which happened before the narrative begins).[25] For Bloch, the third criterion is the most important and arises through the first two. Before any narration begins, a criminal act (*Untat*), usually murder, is committed. The narration, then, looks primarily backward in time in order to reconstruct and thus explain the act.[26] Bloch further notes that the narration of detective stories often begins with the discovery of a corpse.

All of these criteria apply to *Tod am Meer*. The first sentence of the novel complies with Bloch's formula perfectly: "Jablonski ist tot" (5; Jablonski is dead). The rest of the novel seeks to investigate this mysterious death. Not only does the narration take an analeptic turn to a time before Jablonski's death; it goes as far back as his childhood in the 1930s, implying that the explanation of Jablonski's death lies that far back in the past. Jablonski sets up both the timeframe and the gravity of his story with the following sentence: "Als in Hindenburg die Synagoge brannte, war ich ein Kind"[27] (When the synagogue in Hindenburg burned, I was a child). Jablonski's narration then proceeds through the war, capitulation, and well into the GDR years. All the while he asks at what point things began to go wrong: “Ich suche den Punkt, von dem aus mein Leben anfing, falsch zu laufen” (21; I’m searching for the point at which my life started to go down the wrong path). The fictional editor also queries where Jablonski’s life took a wrong turn. A careful consideration of Jablonski’s and the fictional editor’s questions reveals the relevance of detective fiction as a paradigm for a reading of *Tod am Meer*. Before delving further into such a reading, however, it is necessary to look at another definition of detective fiction, one that considers the character of the detective, in order to establish more firmly the importance of vocalization for *Tod am Meer*.

Given the lack of a detective in the sense of a police officer or a professional private investigator in *Tod am Meer*, one may be tempted to ask whether the work might belong simply to crime fiction rather than the more specific genre of detective fiction. British writer and renowned theorist of detective fiction and crime fiction Julian Symons distinguishes the two on eight grounds that mostly boil down to detective fiction having a detective who looks backward in time to investigate the crime in the spirit of a puzzle.[28] Symons’s criteria not only support the claim *Tod am Meer* can, indeed, be read as a work of detective fiction; they also help to describe the work’s narrative situation and the ramifications thereof. The first criterion, like Bloch’s third criterion, is the assertion that analeptic reconstruction is necessary. The second criterion states that in detective fiction there must be a character who questions and investigates. Further, Symons states that the detective need not be a professional and that the detective is often the main character. In this case, Jablonski fits the bill. The third criterion states that the method of murder is of great importance and is often strange. Although, as I argue, Jablonski’s death is a matter of self-destruction, the method is both strange and of great importance to the story. The fourth criterion states that detective fiction offers many clues, which are often explained by the detective figure. This is certainly the case with *Tod am Meer*. Jablonski excavates Central European history, finding and explaining clues all along the way. The fifth criterion states that the detective figure is the main character and that all other characters are minor. Such is without doubt the case in *Tod am Meer* (and in Mann’s novella, Aschenbach is also the only main character, although he is no detective). The sixth criterion states that the bulk of the narration takes place before the murderous deed occurs. That is, the investigation leads to a telling of what happened in the past, through flashbacks, witness testimony, or clues that point to the past. Much of *Tod am Meer* takes place long before Jablonski’s death. The eighth criterion states that solving a puzzle or a mystery is of great importance. As quoted above, Jablonski explicitly cites his search for a point at which his life began to spiral downward as the driving force behind his narration. Of Symons’s criteria, only the seventh criterion is somewhat problematic for *Tod am*

Meer. However, it is also problematic in itself. It states that detective fiction must have a conservative social stance. Symons, however, does not offer a definition of conservative, nor does he assert whether it is the detective, the narrator, or the author who ought to be conservative. In any case, *Tod am Meer* fulfills at least seven of Symons's eight criteria of detective fiction as opposed to crime fiction and may legitimately be read as detective fiction.

The elements that make *Tod am Meer* not seem like detective fiction are, in large part, the elements that make *Tod am Meer* different from *Der Tod in Venedig*. The most important of these is that Jablonski is detecting his own case. He narrates his own demise. There are no suspects he can ask whether they have alibis. There is no one the police can arrest. The detection lacks the scientific rigor of Auguste Dupin or Sherlock Holmes, nor are there any forensic laboratories. This is all because the scene of the events is Jablonski's memory. Nonetheless, there is a question that leads to detection, and there is, in accordance with Symons's second criterion, a character who detects, although the victim and the detective are the same character.

Again, the mystery that Jablonski seeks to solve is how his life turns out to be so miserable. How does he go about this detective work? In searching for that point in his life, he is both detective and one of several witnesses—the main witness, in fact. He perceives his own story. To use Genette's terms, which are adopted by Martinez and Scheffel in the German context, he is an autodiegetic narrator (that is, he tells his own story), at least in his manuscript, which makes up the bulk of the novel. He recounts the events of his own life.

Jablonski never does find a singular point at which his life goes awry. Instead, nearly every event in his life is such a point. He introduces several episodes by stating that his negative life turn may have begun with the episode that he is about to narrate. He recounts numerous failed, amorous relationships, deaths, and political and personal fiascos. The National Socialists hang Jablonski's girlfriend Wanda (52). Paul, a fellow soldier, murders his friend Wysgol in the war. He unsuccessfully attempts to navigate his way westward after the war. He joins the SED more or less against his will. The communists dismiss his friend Ellen from the teacher-training program. Jablonski manipulates the girl known as the "traurige Habicht" (sad hawk) into a suicide attempt and greatly regrets it. He ruins his relationship with Hermine—director of the teacher-training program, an older woman with whom he has an amorous relationship—by sleeping with her daughter. At the instigation of the Stalinist pseudo-intellectual Imme (Immanuel Feister), he brings about the downfall of a Kantian philosophy professor by baiting him into criticizing Stalin during a lecture for which Imme had artificially filled the lecture hall with Party members, an episode that he later greatly regrets. For a moment, he places the blame of his miserable life on Imme. He states three times, "Imme ist schuld" (185; It's Imme's fault). He points out, "Ohne ihn wäre mein Leben anders verlaufen" (192; Without him, my life would have taken a different course). But as soon as he blames Imme, he acknowledges that the matter is more complicated: "Ich habe ihn gefürchtet, und ich habe ihn geliebt" (192; I was afraid of him, and I loved him). He later goes so far as to claim that Imme's death is his (Jablonski's) downfall. Jablonski sums up the failure of his life with the pithy sentence, "Mein ganzes Leben ging schief" (22; My whole life went awry). The major event that destroys Jablonski, however, is the act of detection itself.

Before examining how Jablonski detects himself to death, it is worth examining Jablonski's spaces of detection—not the spaces that he detects, but rather the spaces from which he investigates: the sea and his hospital bed—as they emphasize the narrative shift toward vocalization. Both spaces highlight Jablonski's self-destructiveness and the way that he perceives it. The space of the sea, already mentioned in the novel's title, again juxtaposes the novel with *Der Tod in Venedig*. Both Aschenbach and Jablonski die next to the sea, but whereas Aschenbach's story is narrated by an outside narrator—what Dorrit Cohn, following Franz Stanzel, calls a second author[29]—from an unknown location, Jablonski's story is narrated by Jablonski himself, by the sea. In describing the role of the sea in *Der Tod in Venedig*, Matias Martinez writes:

> In der Novelle steht das Meer in bedeutungstragender Opposition zum Festland. Aschenbach kommt aus dem kontinentalen München. Seine Reise ans Meer scheint nur ein geographischer Ortswechsel zu sein. Im Laufe der Erzählung werden jedoch Hinweise eingestreut, die das Meer über seine denotative Bedeutung hinaus mit konnotativen Zusatzbedeutungen aufladen.[30]
>
> [In the novella, the sea stands in meaningful opposition to the land. Aschenbach is from the continental city of Munich. His journey to the sea seems at first to be only a geographical change of place. But in the course of the narrative, clues are interspersed that charge the sea with connotative meaning on top of its denotative meaning.]

In the case of Jablonski, the Black Sea is not only a semiotic opposition to his home on solid ground in Leipzig; it also represents the absence of solid ground on which to erect his search for cause and effect. In other words, it represents forgetting and oblivion (in the sense of the ancient Greek mythology of Lethe). If the sea is a symbol of fluid forgetfulness, then it makes sense that Jablonski narrates his life story by the sea. Jablonski's memory, which provides the basis of his narration, indulges in analepsis and prolepsis: he does not craft a solid, chronologically continuous narration, but rather his memory drifts without an apparent destination. Although Leipzig also has a waterfront in the form of the river Elster, there are significant differences between Leipzig's river and Burgas's sea. The river flows linearly toward a destination, whereas the sea ebbs and flows and contains waves. Except for Burgas, the towns Jablonski has lived in have all been located on rivers. As he puts it, "Mein Leben ist dadurch gekennzeichnet, daß ich es an stinkenden Flüssen zubringen muß: Schwarze Elster, Beuthener Wasser, Mulde" (293; My life is marked by the fact that I must live it on stinking rivers: the Black Elster, Bytomka, and Mulde Rivers). On these rivers, history has been narrated as a linear, teleological narrative, whether by National Socialism or by Stalinism. On the wavy, tidal Black Sea, Jablonski's memory drifts along as it wishes. If, however, Jablonski's memory is liberated at sea, that is no luxury for him. He knows Burgas is on the sea and will be a place where he can remember freely, writing: "O Burgas, das mich hergeholt hat, damit Totes in mir wach wird" (52; O Burgas, that brought me here, so that dead things will awaken in me). He knows that remembering in Burgas will stir up things that are perhaps better left alone. He also implies that he understands how destructive such remembering in Burgas might be, acknowledging that it might lead to his death. He is, furthermore, well aware of the myth of Lethe but he also recognizes that memory can be self-destructive: "Lethe trinken, ins Nirwana eingehen. Der Mythos kennt schöne Namen. Aber so oder so, ich bin verdammt, mich zu erinnern." (259; Drinking Lethe, entering into nirvana. The myth knows beautiful names. But either way, I'm damned to remember.) Jablonski feels forced to try to remember in Burgas on the Black Sea, knowing that it will be his demise.

There is, however, another site of narration where Jablonski's self-destruction manifests itself: his hospital bed. For although the hospital lies next to the Black Sea, Jablonski narrates more specifically from the restricted space of his hospital bed. Monika Ankele describes the hospital bed—in the context of women's psychiatric institutions around 1900—as a restricted space in which the patient further restricts herself.[31] That is, the restricted space of the bed—a space to which psychiatrists at the time thought it healthy to confine women with psychiatric disorders—instigates in the patient a drive to flee further within herself, creating "einen Raum im Raum"[32] (a space within a space). Ankele's examples of this include patients such as Helen Prager, who hid objects as well as animals under her bed sheets; the painter Bertha Gertrud Fleck, who kept her eyes shut even while not sleeping, so as to be able to see things that were not there in or around her bed; several patients who hid under their bed sheets as a measure similar to closing their eyes but with the added protection against being seen by others; and Auguste Opel, who even ate under her bed sheets.[33] Although Jablonski is neither a woman, nor lives around 1900, nor literally keeps his eyes closed or hides under his bed sheets, he does flee within himself. In his hospital bed he remembers his life to the point of self-destruction. He is ill, so he remembers, and the more he remembers, the more ill he becomes.

As Jablonski replays his life looking for the moment in which it went awry, he explores instances of unpredictability in GDR history. In explaining his notion of explosion (the catalyst of unpredictability), Yuri Lotman mentions detective fiction as a potential site for unpredictability. He creates a dichotomy between detective fiction that offers a single offender and tends toward predictability and detective fiction that exposes unpredictability. Lotman offers Edgar Allan Poe as a representative author of the latter kind of detective fiction: "The artistic strength of the works of E. A. Poe consists precisely in the fact that he lays before the reader riddles which cannot be solved. . . . E. A. Poe opens before the reader a way without end, a window onto unpredictability."[34] This is precisely the kind of detective fiction that *Tod am Meer* is. It offers a "window onto unpredictability." It questions GDR history, and instead of offering a "sly or simple 'explanation,'"[35] it exposes a riddle "which cannot be solved." In doing so, it forces both Jablonski and the reader to consider unpredictable possibilities. Such consideration of unpredictability works against the Eastern European communist reverence for linear, logical history. Jablonski surely understands this, as he was a historian.

Jablonski and Stalin

Although the underlying cause of Jablonski's death is his obsessive remembering, a symptom of the illness that he thrusts upon himself is cerebral hemorrhaging: an important symbol for the novel. It is an abjective act—in Kristeva's sense—that enacts the self-destruction involved in Jablonski's act of detecting his past. It also indexes the life and death of a figure Jablonski knew well, one who officially died of cerebral hemorrhaging: Joseph Stalin. The relationship between cerebral hemorrhaging, abjection, and Stalinism must be examined. First, however, it is in order to note the relationship between the causes of Jablonski's and Aschenbach's deaths.

In *Tod in Venedig*, Aschenbach remains in Venice knowing that he will likely die of cholera, a waterborne bacterial infection of the small intestine. The main symptoms of the disease are extreme, chronic diarrhea and vomiting, both of which lead to fatal dehydration. In other words, the system that is the human body rids itself of fluids in an attempt to flush out the bacteria, but this leads to death. This purging of fluids can be seen as abjection. The narrator of Aschenbach's story gives the reader no details of Aschenbach's abjective symptoms, in part because Aschenbach does not tell his own story.[36] At this point in the narrative, as Cohn indicates, the third-person narrator does not understand Aschenbach's experiences.

Jablonski, however, tells his own story and describes his abjective symptoms. Long before he writes himself to death, when he is a soldier in the Second World War—an episode that is without doubt related to his misery and later suicide—he contracts a waterborne bacterial illness, likely dysentery or typhoid fever. His symptoms include fever, diarrhea, and extreme vomiting. Here in the midst of the Second World War is where Jablonski's abjection begins. It continues later in the form of his writing, by means of which he purges the painful details of his life story.

Not only does Jablonski's abjection parallel that of Aschenbach, but Jablonski's cerebral hemorrhaging points toward another narrative, one all too familiar to Jablonski: Joseph Stalin died on March 5, 1953, of cerebral hemorrhaging. At least, this is the official cause of Stalin's death, which would have been familiar to both Jablonski and Heiduczek. A recently emerged earlier draft of the medical report on Stalin's death, which was locked away for decades, describes the vomiting of blood, pointing toward stomach hemorrhaging.[37] In any case, the brutal, paranoid dictator died of abjective symptoms very similar to those that accompanied Jablonski's death. Again, Jablonski was trained in the history and philosophy of Stalin. First, Imme has Jablonski set up the downfall of Kantian philosophy professor by tricking him into criticizing Stalin in front of a phony audience. Then, after Jablonski completes his studies at the university, Imme sends him to the regional Party school to be trained as a Stalin biographer. Not only does Jablonski mention Stalin often in his manuscript, but he explicitly mentions Stalin's death.

> Im Frühsommer dreiundfünfzig drohte in unserem Land die Emotion die Vernunft zu erdrücken. Stalin war gestorben. Die Pläne, Deutschland zu neutralisieren, waren gescheitert. Nato und Warschauer Vertrag. Rüstung. Rüstung. Rüstung. Es drohte ein neuer Krieg. (260)
>
> [In early summer of fifty-three, emotion was threatening to suppress reason in our country. Stalin had died. The plans to neutralize Germany had failed. NATO and Warsaw Pact. Armament. Armament. Armament. A new war was imminent.]

Here Jablonski mentions Stalin's death in the context of the insecurity of Cold War Germany. This association, taken at face value, seems to imply that Jablonski thinks everything was better when Stalin was alive. However, the case is more complicated than this. Although trained as a Stalin biographer, Jablonski is no great defender of Stalin. But it must also be stated that he does not denounce Stalin as harshly as one might hope. For example, when, even before his training as a Stalin biographer, he learns that Stalin let his own son die in a Nazi prisoner-of-war camp rather than exchanging imprisoned German officers for him, Jablonski notes how cruel the act is, but then admires Stalin's persistence.

> Sein Vater hätte ihn gegen hohe deutsche Offiziere austauschen können. Aber er hat den Sohn hingeopfert. Es schien mir eine schreckliche Tat, zugleich bewunderte ich die Unbedingtheit gegen sich selbst. Mir kam das Geschehen vor wie in einer griechischen Tragödie. Ich verstieg mich so weit, Stalin mit Ödipus zu vergleichen. (205)
>
> [His father could have traded high German officers for him. But he sacrificed him instead. It seemed to me to be a horrendous deed, but, at the same time, I admired his unconditionality against himself. To me, it looked like something that happens in a Greek tragedy. I even went as far as comparing Stalin to Oedipus.]

Jablonski appears almost to admire Stalin or at least his persistence. Further, not only might Stalin's sense of persistence be compared to that of Oedipus (traditional readings of Sophocles's *Oedipus Rex* see persistence as a tragic flaw in Oedipus, leading to his downfall), but also to that of Aschenbach and Jablonski.[38] Aschenbach's favorite word is, in fact, "Durchhalten"[39] (perserverance).

Neither Aschenbach nor Oedipus, however, is a cruel dictator who murdered millions of people. Jablonski's ambiguous attitude toward Stalin and the SED must be further examined. Jablonski is no apparatchik. Once he even exclaims, "Ich scheiß auf die Partei" (233; I shit on the Party). Still, he is a member of the Party, even if he joined it on a fluke. He makes sarcastic statements about others who romanticize Stalin: "Hermine sprach von Stalin wie Goethes Lotte von Klopstock, gleichsam verzaubert" (214; Hermine spoke of Stalin like Goethe's Lotte speaks of Klopstock, equally spellbound). However, he learns to be a Stalin biographer, well knowing that he is going to be a cog in the Party propaganda machine. And even though he sometimes curses the Party, there are moments when he feels great allegiance to it, even if he now thinks back on it ironically:

> Lach mich aus, lach mich aus, eines Nachts wurde ich wach, sprang aus dem Bett und hielt eine große Rede. Es war ein Ruf an alle. Ich konnte nicht anders. Saulus war Paulus geworden. Es hätte nicht viel gefehlt, und ich hätte neben Marx und Lenin und Stalin den lieben Gott beschworen. (235)
>
> [Laugh at me. Laugh at me. One night I woke up, jumped out of bed, and held a great speech. It was a call to everyone. I couldn't help it. Saul had become Paul. It wouldn't have taken much, and

> I would have evoked God almighty in addition to Marx and Lenin and Stalin.]

This passage shows how mixed up Jablonski is at times. A Catholic, Jablonski not only swings back and forth between hating the Party and willingly participating in it; he also ironically mixes two belief systems that are normally thought to be starkly opposed to one another. Even as he curses Stalinism, it is internalized in him. In another passage Jablonski curses Stalin, among other things, not because the dictator murdered millions of human beings, but rather because he associates Stalin with his unhappy relationship with Hermine:

> Ich war plötzlich wütend auf Mauritius [a member of the SPD who fled to the West in protest against the unification of the SPD and the KPD] und den traurigen Habicht. Ein Unstern leuchtete über mir, seit ich so leichtfertig in die SPD eingetreten war. Die hundert Mark brachten mir miserable Zinsen. Von der SPD war ich zur SED gekommen, von der SED zu Immanuel Kant, von Immanuel Kant zu Imme, von Imme zu Stalin, von Stalin zu Hermine. Ihretwegen saß ich nun mit durchnässten Hosen und einem geschenkten Pullover, dessen Ärmel mir zu kurz waren, in einem Zimmer der Landesleitung und mußte mich von Imme anschreien lassen. (232–33)

> [I was suddenly angry at Mauritius and the Sad Hawk. A black cloud hung over my head ever since I had so frivolously joined the SPD. The hundred Mark brought me miserable interest. From the SPD, I had come to the SED, from the SED to Immanuel Kant, from Immanuel Kant to Imme, from Imme to Stalin, from Stalin to Hermine. And because of Hermine I now sat there with soaked pants and a hand-me-down pullover with sleeves that were too short for me in a room at the Party headquarters getting yelled at by Imme.]

This passage combined with the previous one shows how Stalinism and Jablonski's life are intertwined. He finds his way to Stalinism much as a protagonist in a *Schelmenroman* moves through life. He meanders here and there, and Stalinism becomes part of his life, whether he likes it or not. In this passage he condemns Stalin, but mostly for the reason that he is not satisfied with his life, which is intertwined with Stalin. To emphasize the constant juxtaposition of Jablonski and Stalin, it is furthermore worth mentioning that during the war Jablonski was called "heiliger Josef" (44; Saint Joseph), though the text leaves open whether his first name is really Josef.

Jablonski's inability to separate himself from Stalinism and other things that he does not like leads back to the abject. Jablonski, the detective, looks for the point at which his life turned sour. He wants to rid himself of whatever it is that led to his misery. He cannot find that point, or rather his whole life is that point. He tries to expel elements from his life until he is no more. Abjection is the violent attempt to separate oneself from something that exists within oneself. Or as Kristeva writes in explaining the term: "L'abjection is something that disgusts you, for example, you see something rotting and you want to vomit—it is an extremely strong feeling that is at once somatic and symbolic, which is above all a revolt against an eternal menace from which one wants to distance oneself, but of which one has the impression that it may menace us from the inside."[40] Jablonski's vomiting and later bleeding in the head—in line with Kristeva's notion of abjection—both occur at times when he attempts to distance himself from things that are so deeply woven into the fabric of his life that he cannot expulse them without harming himself. They also symbolize his project of self-destructively remembering his life in order to purge it of unsavory elements. As he writes early in his manuscript: "Mein ganzes Leben ging schief" (22; My whole life went awry). He thus wants to distance himself from everything that he is. He revolts against menaces that are inside him. His entire inner being menaces him, and his revolt against these menaces brings him to the point of self-annihilation.

Jablonski, however, is not the only character in the novel who suffers symptoms of abjection. In fact, many characters in the novel do. The "dicke Zigeunerin" (fat gypsy) in the hospital vomits into the sink and clogs the drain. Paul, the soldier who kills Wysgol, hits his head on the corner of a table and bleeds heavily. The "traurige Habicht" slashes her wrists open and nearly bleeds to death. Anissa nearly bleeds to death as the result of a botched abortion. Vunja—a patient in the hospital in Burgas—has the same illness as Jablonski and has had an aneurysm. Dr. Assa warns both her and Jablonski of the "Wildheit der Liebe . . . Der physiologische Vorgang könne einen neuen Gefäßriß provozieren"[41] (Wildness of love . . . The physiological act could instigate a new aneurysm). Tscherwuchin—a melancholy teacher from Siberia serving as a cultural officer in the Soviet Occupation Zone—appears one night at Jablonski's room with an unexplained bloody forehead (243). In the middle of Jablonski's description of how demonstrators stormed the building of the Ministerium für Staatssicherheit (Ministry for State Security, Stasi headquarters) on June 17, 1953, he describes how he saw a man with a bloody face. All of this abjection seems—at least in Jablonski's mind—to be interwoven with Stalinism, which, as will become evident, can also be seen as abjective and self-destructive.

Two other characters, in particular, lead lives interwoven with the history of Stalinism and are associated with abjection. Imme receives a bleeding head wound during the uprising of June 17, 1953. Imme, the character who convinced Jablonski to train in matters pertaining to Stalin, defends

Stalin and Stalinism to the death. That is, he defends Stalin and Stalinism until he, Imme, dies, roughly three-and-a-half months after Stalin. Imme says over and over again, "Die Macht geben wir nicht aus der Hand" (253; We won't let go of the power). The power, however, does not leak out of his hands, but rather out of his head. As protesters assemble on the market square on June 17, 1953, Imme runs to the square, climbs up a wooden pole, and tries to yell over the protesters' loudspeakers. He demands that they turn off the speakers and return to work. Jablonski thinks Imme is crazy, and the words Jablonski uses to describe this thought are telling. "Ich dachte: Dem springt der Kopf auseinander" (268; I thought his head would bust open). And that is exactly what happens. A protester throws a rock at Imme, hitting him precisely in the head. When he instinctively holds his injured head, he falls from the mast. He lies on the ground, blood flowing from his head, rainwater flowing into his mouth. The border between subject and object is fluid. And he dies.

Another character who deals with abjection and is self-destructive in a way similar to Jablonski is Schippenschiß (Willi Hutkessel), about whom Jablonski is writing a film script. Schippenschiß earns his nickname, from which he cannot possibly escape, through an act of abjection.

> Während seiner Zeit als Heizer auf einer Lok fragte ihn jemand: "Was machst du denn, wenn's dich ankommt? Du kannst doch nicht den Hintern in den Wind hängen?" Hutkessel antwortete treuherzig: "Ich scheiß auf die Schippe, und rein ins Feuerloch." Alle, die dabeistanden, wollten sich einpissen vor Lachen. Seit jenem Tag hieß Willi Hutkessel "Schippenschiß." Es kränkte ihn so, daß er bei der Reichsbahn kündigte. Aber die Flucht half ihm nicht. Er hätte nach Kanada auswandern können, nach Australien, auf eine gottverlassene Insel, der Name wäre ihm vorausgeeilt. (274)
>
> [During his time as a stoker on a steam locomotive, someone asked him: "What do you do when you have to go? You can't just hang your behind out in the wind?" Hutkessel answered sincerely: I shit onto the shovel, and it goes straight into the fire." Everyone who was standing there just about pissed his pants laughing. From that day on, Willi Hutkessel was known as "Schippenschiß." He was so bothered by it that he quit his job with the railway. But that didn't help him. He could have moved to Canada, to Australia, to a God-forsaken island; the name would have hurried ahead.]

His nickname is perhaps the only thing that remains constant in his life. Besides working as a locomotive stoker, he works as a construction equipment operator and as an aluminum fabricator. He goes on to win a national literature prize and become director of the Kulturpalast, a job from which he is later fired along with being dismissed from the Party.

Schippenschiß's roller coaster career and his rise and fall in the Party represent a political ambiguity similar to that of his abjective act. When he shovels his shit onto the fire that powers the State locomotive, is he symbolically shitting on the State, or is he adding organic fuel to the fire? This is the political ambiguity faced by both Jablonski and Schippenschiß.

Jablonski and Schippenschiß are, indeed, quite similar, so much so that Jablonski writes: "Schippenschiß war Jablonski und Jablonski war Schippenschiß" (275; Schippenschiß was Jablonski and Jablonski was Schippenschiß). They are the same age and even share the same birthday. They have had similar careers or at least similar career ups and downs. Just as Schippenschiß moves from being a simple worker to a major figure in GDR cultural policymaking and then gets kicked out of the Party, Jablonski, as a result of the Bitterfelder Weg movement,[42] begins his writing career while working with a locomotive carbide oven and undergoes a series of ups and downs in his relationship to the Party. Indeed, Jablonski and Schippenschiß are not only similar to each other, but they also both represent the paranoia and self-destructiveness of the Stalinist system that were omnipresent in the GDR at the time.

Much of Jablonski's film script deals with such characteristics of the Stalinist system. Jablonski writes that his film is meant to shock. The reader does not have the opportunity to view the fictional film. But shock is exactly what Heiduczek's novel does. The East German writer Dieter Noll was, as Udo Grashoff put it, "schwer schockiert" (severely shocked) by the book.[43] Furthermore, Hans Koch, a cultural functionary in the SED, was appalled by the "selbstzerstörische Züge" (self-destructive strains) in the novel.[44] Koch was correct that at its core the novel is about self-destruction. Jablonski's self-destructive abjection represents the self-destructive elements of Stalinism, that is, show trials, purges, murder, and, specific to the context of the GDR, population hemorrhaging. Not only are characters in the novel, such as Schippenschiß, dismissed from the Party on mysterious grounds, but others leave their jobs or even leave the GDR. In describing a Bitterfeld-related work program to Jablonski for the sake of his film, Schippenschiß explains the hemorrhage of the GDR work force (and indeed of the citizenry at large).

> Wir haben gelebt wie in einem Kloster. Nein, schlimmer. Planerfüllung hundertzwanzig Prozent, nicht saufen, nicht huren, keine Bummelschicht, Dichterlesung, Beethoven und Neues Deutschland. Nach einem Monat liefen die ersten davon. Ich weiß nicht mehr, wie viele durchhielten. Keine fünfzig Prozent. Und von denen, die durchhielten, blieben die meisten nur wegen der Prämie.[45]

> [We lived as though we were in a monastery. No, it was worse. A hundred-and-twenty percent production quota. No drinking. No

> whoring. No fiddling around. Poetry reading, Beethoven, reading the Party newspaper. After a month, the first ones ran away. I forgot how many stuck it out. Less than fifty percent. And of those who made it through, most of them stayed only because of the premium.]

In this case, the treatment of the workers is counterproductive. They are pushed so hard to work harder that they actually produce less, and perhaps even leave the country.[46] Jablonski himself states three times that he traveled to Bulgaria in order to flee the GDR. He tells Imme that five engineers defected to the West in the previous month, and Imme replies that more will leave in the future. Jablonski goes on to explain that Imme, in his paranoia, wants more to leave: "Imme war für klare Verhältnisse. Am liebsten hätte er die Hälfte aller Betriebsleiter aus dem Werk gejagt. Für ihn waren sie Saboteure und Agenten." (255; Imme was for transparent conditions. He would have preferred to have chased half the managers out of the factory. For him, they were saboteurs and spies.) Imme's paranoid desire is representative of the abjective at work in the Stalinist system. As Jablonski describes the uncomfortable position of Eschenreuter, Jablonski's successor as director of the school in Kreppin, who is torn between Imme and Lüderitz (a local pastor, who is as dogmatic in his Christianity as Imme is in his Stalinism), Jablonski wonders why Eschenreuter does not flee: "Ein Anderer wäre vielleicht nach dem Westen geflohen" (259; Anybody else might have fled to the West). Indeed, in the Stalinist GDR, in which, as Imme states, "Wer nicht mit uns ist, ist gegen uns" (250; Whoever's not with us is against us), many did flee to the West.

Nikolai Bukharin, during his show trial in 1937, is reported to have declared: "I won't shoot myself because then people will say that I killed myself so as to harm the party. But if I die, as it were, from an illness, then what will you lose by it?" Slavoj Žižek describes this scene in his essay "When the Party Commits Suicide,"[47] which is in part a review of *The Road to Terror: Stalin and the Self-Destruction of the Bolsheviks* by Getty and Naumov.[48] One chapter of Getty's and Naumov's volume particularly strikes Žižek's attention: "The Storm of 1937: The Party Commits Suicide," which describes the purges and executions of 1937 and 1938, including the execution of Bukharin. Žižek is struck by the fact that Bukharin, a dedicated Stalinist, was willing to publicly confess to political sins that he did not commit if the Party needed him to. Bukharin understood that elements of the Party must be ritually abjected. But he wrote a private letter to Stalin asking him to tell him secretly that he had not really committed sins against Stalin. Bukharin was such a dedicated Stalinist that he was willing to die for the Party, but he could not bear the thought that Stalin might really think him guilty. Žižek declares: "Once we enter the Stalinist universe of the ridiculous sublime, the ultimate form of sacrifice is no longer the tragic fate of the fighter dedicated to the Cause, but a much more radical self-sacrifice." The Party's need to purge such key elements, that is, to execute such a loyal member, is abjective and self-destructive. Werner Heiduczek was also well aware of such self-destruction, describing it with the sentence, "Im Namen des Sozialismus töteten Sozialisten Sozialisten" (In the name of socialism, socialists killed socialists).[49] The blood that hemorrhages within Jablonski's head represents such paranoid political abjection. Jablonski, narrating his own experience of Stalinism, destroys himself trying to abject the elements of Stalinism from his life.

Jablonski is self-destructive in a similar way to Aschenbach. *Tod am Meer* uses transtextual momentum from *Der Tod in Venedig*, which was relatively well received in the GDR, to criticize, among other things, the self-destruction of Stalinism. Jablonski tries to separate himself from everything about his life that he does not like. He searches for moments in his biography from which he can distance himself and finds that his entire life is a sequence of failures. This will to separation from the displeasurable—what else is abjection?—functions like Imme's exclamation "Wer nicht mit uns ist, ist gegen uns," which turns into the self-destructive paranoid belief that everyone is against us, to the point that there is no more us. Or in Jablonski's case, he investigates his own problematic life, removing elements of it until there is no more Jablonski.

4: Suicide and the Reevaluation of Classicism: Christa Wolf's *Kein Ort. Nirgends*

CHRISTA WOLF'S *KEIN ORT. NIRGENDS* (1979) was influenced by the November 1976 expatriation of singer-songwriter Wolf Biermann.[1] Whereas Heiduczek's *Tod am Meer* was written before the Biermann affair took place (and published two months after the affair), Wolf's novel was written after the affair, an event that had a profound effect on Wolf. She had signed a petition against the decision to expatriate Biermann and consequently faced restrictions and later dismissal from her leadership position in the *Schriftstellerverband* (Writers Union).[2] Wolf purportedly felt as though she had her back against the wall, a statement she made during an interview with Frauke Meyer-Gosau for the West German periodical *alternative* in the winter of 1982, implying that Wolf felt that her political and literary possibilities had become limited in the GDR.[3] But neither Biermann nor Wolf wanted out of the country, at least not permanently. In November 1976, Biermann gave a concert in Cologne and wanted to return to the GDR, but he was forced to remain outside the country. Like Biermann, Wolf had some freedom to travel, visiting Greece in 1980, for example, but she always willingly returned to the GDR. For Wolf, being in the GDR and being a writer were intertwined. She made a pact with Franz Fühmann that if one of them became incapable of writing, that person would leave the GDR.[4] She continued to write and remained in the country. As David Bathrick describes, writers such as Wolf understood that leaving the GDR would only strengthen the rhetorical binaries of the Cold War, in particular the literary historiographical binary of ill, irrational, capitalist literature versus healthy, rational, communist literature. If her literary works are any indicator, Wolf wanted to reevaluate the literary heritage of the GDR, rather than merely run from it. Indeed, *Kein Ort. Nirgends*, written after the Biermann affair, is the first major instance in Wolf's oeuvre of such reevaluation. Others were to follow. The impact of the Biermann affair on *Kein Ort. Nirgends* has long been acknowledged. Ann Stamp Miller, for example, writes:

> After Biermann's expatriation, the writers had to find other ways of expressing their voices, either by coding their literature or writing as voices from a more distant past. For instance, Christa Wolf turned

> to the Romantic Period and Greek literature . . . In so doing, their works provided a platform whereby they could vent their frustration and voice their subtle call for political reform with less fear of censorship because of questionable interpretation.[5]

Wolf did turn to the romantic period and to Greek literature, and in doing so certainly made the censors' task more difficult. However, her turn to the romantics and the Greeks, I argue, was much more than a mere sleight of hand to trick the censors. Rather, her transtextuality represented a bold subversion of GDR literary heritage.

Kein Ort. Nirgends employs the theme of suicide not as a means of escape, not as a way out, but rather as a method of subversion, as a means of questioning the limits and boundaries of the GDR literary heritage, and as a way of exploring unpredictability in GDR literary heritage. This chapter examines the suicidal thoughts of semi-fictional characters Kleist and Günderrode, particularly their dreams in the work, in which they imagine scenes that correspond to each other's actual writings. Using the taboo theme of suicide, *Kein Ort. Nirgends* probes the official literary heritage of the GDR beneath the surface into romanticism but also into ancient Greek literature, the ways in which German Romanticism received ancient Greek literature differently from the way that German classicism viewed it, and the ramifications of such a difference for the GDR context.

Ute Brandes points in this direction in her astute essay on quotation in *Kein Ort. Nirgends*, as she writes, ". . . the structure of citation underlying the text functions to connect the spirit of the early romantic epoch with the *Zeitgeist* in the GDR."[6] Indeed, Wolf quotes Kleist's and Günderrode's letters and literary works in a manner that has relevance for the GDR. Although the story is set in 1804, the narrator reveals that it is a fiction that has contemporary relevance: "Daß sie sich getroffen hätten: erwünschte Legende"[7] (The claim that they met: a legend that suits us). Even before that passage, the narrator notes that the figures on which the story is based are centuries dead, implying that the narrator is speaking around the time that the book was written, and that we, the narrator's contemporaries, are "immer noch gierig auf der Aschegeschmack der Worte" (5; still greedy for the ashen taste of words, 3). The narrator also indicates that the message that may be gleaned from those words is no exact historical message, but rather is an "Echo, ungeheuer, vielfach gebrochen" (6; echo, monstrous, bouncing off innumerable barriers, 3–4). While Brandes locates unmarked quotations in Wolf's work, demonstrating the fruitful manipulation of Kleist's and Günderrode's writings at the sentence level, this chapter shows how Wolf adopts their disruption—particularly through the trope of suicide—of the literary heritage constructed by German classicism, utilizing it to disrupt the literary heritage of the GDR.

The type of rewriting as disruption used by Kleist, Günderrode, and Wolf is what Genette calls transvaluation, a value shift away from the hypotext, an emphasis on, or rearrangement of, some part of the narrative that instigates a wholly different interpretation of the story. In Genette's words, transvaluation is "any operation of an axiological nature bearing on the value that is implicitly or explicitly assigned to an action or group of actions: namely, the sequence of actions, attitudes, and feelings that constitutes a 'character.'"[8] Further, Genette goes on to posit that Kleist's *Penthesilea* is the most radical example of transvaluation that he knows: "I do not wish to leave the subject of transvaluation without mentioning its most dramatic and yet most enigmatic manifestation: Kleist's *Penthesilea* (1808)."[9] This chapter shows how Wolf uses the transvaluative weight of Kleist's *Penthesilea* and Günderrode's poetry to force a transvaluation of GDR literary heritage.

Günderrode Dreams of Kleist's Penthesilea

Kleist was not part of the literary heritage of the GDR, in part because of the positive reception of Kleist by the National Socialists, and in part because Georg Lukács saw Kleist as a conservative and an irrationalist.[10] Kleist, however, was not altogether frowned upon in the GDR. Anna Seghers, who deeply influenced Christa Wolf, defended Kleist as one of the great German writers, one whose shock value was necessary in times of crisis.[11] While Kleist was only sparsely received in the GDR in the 1950s and 1960s, engagement with Kleist in the GDR became more frequent among both scholars of literature and writers in the 1970s and 1980s.[12] In this period, writers such as Günter Kunert, Heiner Müller, Christa Wolf, Jürgen Rennert, Erich Arendt, Rainer Kirsch, Klaus Schlesinger, Rudo Melchert, and Roland Müller dealt explicitly with Kleist in literary works.[13] Kleist was a problem for the maintenance of the official literary heritage of the GDR.[14] The authorities in the GDR could afford neither to ignore Kleist completely nor to accept him wholeheartedly into the GDR literary heritage. Although he was never officially condoned during the entire forty-year existence of the GDR, he became an ambiguous and much discussed figure in the 1970s and was a large part of the crisis of the GDR literary heritage in the wake of Honecker's "No Taboos" speech of 1971.[15] As Günter Kunert pointed out, the *Lexikon deutschsprachiger Schriftsteller*, which was published in the GDR in 1972, characterized Kleist's works as "eigentümliche Vermischung von . . . Gesundheit und Krankhaftigkeit"[16] (peculiar mix of health and morbidity). Kunert, in citing this passage, identified this peculiarity of Kleist in the GDR. Kunert, indeed, had much to say about Kleist and his reception in the GDR.

In 1976, three years before the publication of Wolf's *Kein Ort. Nirgends*, Kunert composed and aired a radio play based on Kleist's suicide entitled *Ein anderer K.*,[17] in which the voices of Kleist's acquaintances contemplate why Kleist killed himself.[18] The character Grollhammer poses the question as follows: "Mir ist der Tod meines Freundes ein Rätsel. Er mag exzentrisch gewesen sein, doch einen anderen Menschen ins Herz und sich selber in den Kopf—da müssen doch tiefere Gründe vorliegen, greifbare, ersichtliche!" (The death of my friend is a mystery to me. He might have been eccentric, but to shoot another person in the heart and then to shoot himself in the head—there must be deeper reasons that are tangible and evident!)[19] Other characters in the radio play then attempt to answer this question of why Kleist killed himself. The Prussian official Gruner mentions rumors that the act might be a signal to the Prussian state that it has strayed from its political goals. Grollhammer later implies that Kleist might have been schizophrenic. The widower Vogel tells Grollhammer that there is no concrete reason, but rather that Kleist was "eben ein Dichter"[20] (a poet, after all). Other figures defend similar positions. In the end, however, Kunert gives the semi-fictional Kleist (who at this point in the radio play is dead) the final word.[21] And it is the semi-fictional Kleist's final monologue, with its description of the possibilities for perception, that leads to Kleist's transvaluation that is so important for my reading of *Kein Ort. Nirgends.* It is important enough to quote in full:

> Die wahre Erkenntnis erscheint nicht in der Sprache alltäglicher Unterhaltung, nicht in der Sprache des Militärs oder der Büchsenmacher, auch nicht in der Kanzleisprache, sie erscheint nur in Bildern und Gleichnissen, denn das Paradies hat sich hinter uns geschlossen und ist verriegelt. Wir müssen die Reise um die Welt machen und sehen, ob es vielleicht von hinten irgendwo offen ist. Denn die Welt ist ringförmig, und es gibt einen Punkt, wo sie wieder ineinandergreift. Erst wenn dieser Punkt erreicht ist, erst wenn alles Getrennte erneut sich zusammenfügt, kann Leben so werden dass es nicht länger notwendig ist, es noch darzustellen. Weil dann seine reale und seine wirkliche Erscheinungsweise eins geworden sind. Zu diesem Punkte also müßte sich die Menschheit aufmachen, falls sie überhaupt eine werden will.[22]
>
> [True perception does not appear in the language of everyday conversation, nor does it appear in the language of the military or of the gunsmith, and also not in bureaucratic language. It only appears in images and allegories, for paradise closed the door behind us and sealed it shut. We have to travel around the world and see if maybe there is a back door open somewhere. The world is ring-shaped, and there is a seam at which it interlocks again. It is only at this point, only when everything that has been divided connects again, that life becomes such that it is no longer necessary to represent it, because

> then its material and virtual modes of appearance become one. At that point, humanity would have to open itself up, if it ever wants to become humane.]

This passage contains stark allusions and unmarked quotations from the historical Kleist's essay "Über das Marionettentheater," in which Kleist, referring to the biblical story of Adam and Eve, according to which they eat from the forbidden fruit of the tree of knowledge (Baum der Erkenntnis), comments: "Doch das Paradies ist verriegelt und der Cherub hinter uns; wir müssen die Reise um die Welt machen, und sehen, ob es vielleicht von hinten irgendwo offen ist" (But Paradise is locked and bolted, and the cherubim stands behind us. We have to go on and make the journey round the world to see if it is perhaps open somewhere at the back).[23] The semi-fictional Kleist, in this passage, begins by locating the appearance of *Erkenntnis* (that is, perception, recognition), stating that *Erkenntnis* is not located in any of a variety of language registers that reflect surface reality in a one-to-one manner, but rather that real *Erkenntnis* is to be found in images and comparisons.[24] Kleist's notion of *Erkenntnis* peers beyond surface realism. For the semi-fictional Kleist here, paradise has closed behind us and is sealed, an appropriate image for a space that exists and at the same time does not exist. In order to enter the paradisiacal (no)space, according to this semi-fictional Kleist, one needs images and comparisons. This is work that Wolf's text does. Christa Wolf's *Kein Ort. Nirgends* picks up where Kunert's *Ein anderer K.* leaves off and utilizes the trope of suicide, among others, to reevaluate literary history. By probing deeply into the literary heritage of the GDR—through German Romanticism and into Romanticism's reception of ancient Greek literature—*Kein Ort. Nirgends* reaches beyond the common Party understanding of the literary heritage of the GDR, thereby disrupting it.

Through Kleist, Wolf is able to examine contrasting valuations of Greek literature. Kleist's Penthesilea, like Günderrode, kills herself with a dagger to the heart. This, in addition to his biographical, bullet-induced suicide, is where Kleist plays a role. One of the keys to understanding the double suicides in Christa Wolf's *Kein Ort. Nirgends* is Kleist's play *Penthesilea*.[25] The eponymous Amazon queen in that play kills herself—even after her sister Prothoe takes away her dagger and her arrows—with a poisonous, ideational dagger that she forms from her own emotions.

> Denn jetzt steig' ich in meinen Busen nieder
> Gleich einem Schacht, und grabe, kalt wie Erz,
> Mir ein vernichtendes Gefühl hervor.
> Dies Erz, dies läutr' ich in der Glut des Jammers,
> Hart mir zu Stahl; tränk es mit Gift sodann,
> Heißätzendem, der Reue, durch und durch;

Trag es der Hoffnung ew'gem Amboß zu,
Und schärf' und spitz es mir zu einem Dolch;
Und diesem Dolch jetzt reich' ich meine Brust:
So! So! So! So! Und wieder—Nun ist's gut.
(Sie fällt und stirbt.)

[For now I shall descend into my breast,
And dig a shaft, and quarry out the cold
Ore of a feeling that annihilates.
This ore I purify in fire of grief
To hardest steel; in poison then, of bitter,
Burning remorse, I soak it, through and through;
Now carry it toward Hope's eternal anvil,
And grind and sharpen it into a dagger;
And to this dagger now I yield my breast:
So! So! So! So! Again!—Now it is done.
(*She falls and dies.*)][26]

Penthesilea, the breastless archer-queen of the Amazons, has fallen in love with the Greek warrior Achilles, and he has likewise fallen in love with her. After arguing about which kingdom they will live in, he challenges her to another battle in order to settle the matter. He goes to the battlefield alone, without armor, with only a spear. She, in a mad rage of love, shoots an arrow through his neck and, along with her dogs, bites his flesh to pieces. Upon coming back to her senses, she is told that she has killed him, and worse, mangled his beautiful body. This is when she forms her ideational steel dagger, soaks it in ideational poison, and stabs herself five times until she drops dead.

The figure of Penthesilea and Kleist's play *Penthesilea* are well known to Christa Wolf—she wrote an essay about the Kleist play,[27] and the figure of Penthesilea appears in her book *Kassandra*.[28] However, Penthesilea and her suicide in the Kleist play also have much to do with Wolf's *Kein Ort. Nirgends*. The clues are subtle, but once spotted, they are telling. As Günderrode sees a deer being shot in the neck with an arrow, she fantasizes about dying the deer's death. This scene is pronouncedly similar to Achilles's death in Kleist's Penthesilea. The two passages are juxtaposed below, beginning with Wolf's text.

Der Druck auf der Brust, seit dem Morgen schon, seit dem Traum, der jetzt wieder auftaucht. In einer Gruppe von Personen ging sie in einem kargen, sanften Gelände, fremd und zugleich vertraut, in ihrem weißen fließenden Kleid, zwischen Savigny und der Bettine. Savigny hob plötzlich einen Bogen an die Wange, spannte ihn, zielte mit stumpfem Bolzen. Da sah sie: am Waldrand das Reh. Der Schreckenslaut, den sie sich ausstoßen hörte, kam wie immer zu spät, der Bolzen holte ihn ein. Das Reh, am Hals getroffen, stürzte. Die Bettine an ihrer Seite, die sie nicht aus den Augen ließ, nahm als erste das Unheil wahr. Lina! Rief sie klagend. Die Wunde war an ihrem Hals, sie mußte nicht nachfühlen. Der Bettine weißes Tuch färbte sich rot, daß die Günderrode staunen mußte, wie kräftig im Traum Farben sind. Es käme ihr so natürlich vor, zu verblüten.

[The pressure on her chest which she has felt ever since morning, ever since the dream which now is surfacing again. She was walking with a group of people in an infertile, gentle tract of country, at the same time alien and familiar, in her flowing white dress, between Savigny and Bettine. Suddenly Savigny raised a bow to his chest, drew the string, aimed the blunt arrow. Then at the edge of the woods she saw the doe. As always, the sound of horror she heard herself utter came too late, the arrow overtook it. The doe, struck in the throat, sank to the ground. At her side Bettine (she never took her eyes off her) was the first to notice the calamity. Lina! She cried, a lament. The wound was in her throat, she did not have to feel for it to know it was there. Bettine's white handkerchief turned red, so that Günderrode felt astonished at how bright colors are in dreams. Bleeding to death would have seemed to her so natural.][29]

And here is Kleist's text:

Inzwischen schritt die Königin heran,
Die Doggen hinter ihr, Gebirg' und Wald
Hochher, gleich einem Jäger, überschauend;
Und da er eben, die Gezweige öffnend,
Zu ihren Füßen niedersinken will:
Ha! Sein Geweih verrät den Hirsch, ruft sie,
Und spannt mit Kraft der Rasenden, sogleich
Den Bogen an, daß sich die Enden küssen,
Und hebt den Bogen auf, und zielt und schießt,
Und jagt den Pfeil ihm durch den Hals; er stürzt!
Ein Siegsgeschrei schallt roh im Volk empor.
Jetzt gleichwohl lebt der Ärmste noch der Menschen,
Den Pfeil, den weit vorragenden, im Nacken,
Hebt er sich röchelnd auf, und überschlägt sich

[And all the while the Queen was drawing near,
Her pack of dogs apace behind her, scanning
The woods and towering mountains, like a hunter;
And just as he begins to part the boughs
In order to sink down before her feet:
Aha! The antlers give away the stag,
She cries, and, with the strength of madness, draws

> The bow until the two ends kiss,
> And raises up the bow and aims and shoots,
> And drives an arrow through his throat; he falls][30]

The similarities here are remarkable. Achilles is referred to as a deer in the Kleist play, and it is a deer that is killed in the passage from the Wolf piece. Both are hunted. Both Achilles and the deer are killed with a bow and arrow, and in both cases the arrow hits the neck. The verbs "aufheben," "spannen," and "zielen" are used in both passages to describe the movements of the archer, and the verb "stürzen" is used in both passages to describe the reaction of the creature shot in the neck. Furthermore, both scenes take place at the edge of the forest, the noun "Wald" being used in both.

Günderrode's dream of dying the deer's death that is similar to that of Kleist's Achilles shines much light on *Kein Ort. Nirgends* in at least three ways. First, it reinforces Günderrode's wish to die. She fantasizes that she is the deer that is being impaled with the arrow. On the one hand, she thinks how natural such a death would be. "Es käme ihr so natürlich vor, zu verblüten." Indeed, the death of the deer occurs in nature in the sense that they are at the edge of the forest. The deer runs wild, rather than being domesticated—encaged in a way that would be symbolic of the bourgeois life represented by the figures inside the salon—and then systematically slaughtered. On the other hand, that death is unnatural in that the deer is intentionally killed by Savigny. Reading the passage from Kleist's *Penthesilea*, furthermore, one might ask to what extent Achilles's death may be considered suicide. He perhaps did not expect that Penthesilea would kill him, but he did—himself vulnerably unarmed—approach an armed warrior in battle. Günderrode wishes to die the deer's—or maybe Achilles's—death.

Second, it points to gender disidentification. The historical Günderrode wanted to be a man. Indeed, her unhappiness as a woman is the main reason she gives for wanting to die. In a diary entry dated August 29, 1801, an entry that Wolf quotes at the beginning of her essay "Der Schatten eines Traumes: Karoline Günderrode—Ein Entwurf" (1978), Günderrode, after belaboring her wish to die, writes: "Warum ward ich kein Mann! Ich habe keinen Sinn für weibliche Tugende, für Weiberglückseligkeit." (Why was I not born a man! I'm not interested in female virtues or womanly felicitousness.)[31] The historical Kleist also experienced gender disidentification.[32] Focusing on gender in Wolf's *Kein Ort. Nirgends* is nothing new.[33] But doing so in the context of Günderrode's dream is. It further indicates the parallel between the dream and Kleist's *Penthesilea*. There is, on one level, already a reversal of gender roles in Kleist's play.[34] Achilles submits, while Penthesilea is a warrior. And it is Achilles who is penetrated.

Third, it allows *Kein Ort. Nirgends* to be read not only in terms of Günderrode's dream but also in terms of Kleist's play *Penthesilea.* Penthesilea kills the person she loves. She kills herself with a dagger. And that dagger is an idea. This same progression holds true in the case of Wolf's fictional Kleist and Günderrode. It is not revealed in the text whether one of them kills the other first and then kills himself—as in the historical case of Kleist and Henriette Vogel—or whether they somehow kill each other at the same time, or whether they each kill themselves at the same time. But they do agree to die together. Much, however, is made of Günderrode's dagger in the novel. She wears it around her neck and touches the place on her chest where she knows the insertion of the dagger would kill her. Later, she drops it, and Kleist hands it back to her. Everyone at the salon sees the dagger and is perplexed that she has such a weapon. Kleist, however, is amazed.[35] Such representation of Günderrode's dagger fortifies the notion of Kleist's *Penthesilea* as a hypotext in Wolf's *Kein Ort. Nirgends.* It is Kleist who understands Günderrode's attraction to the dagger. Kleist and Günderrode, furthermore, both understand that the dagger has ideational value.

With the example of *Penthesilea,* three elements of Kleist's oeuvre that are important for Christa Wolf, especially for *Kein Ort. Nirgends,* become evident: the relationship between self-destruction and love, character transformation, and transtextuality, especially transvaluation. In her essay on Kleist's *Penthesilea*—Kleist's work that perhaps mostly starkly concerns love and self-destruction—Christa Wolf writes: "Kleists Helden, flatternden Gewissens zwischen unsichere Gebote gestellt, die einander ausschließen, aber unbedingten Gehorsam beanspruchen, zerfleischen sich selbst. Kein schöner Anblick. Die Moderne beginnt." (Kleist's protagonists, torn with a flittering conscious between competing and mutually exclusive imperatives that each demand absolute allegiance, mutilate themselves. That is not a pretty sight. Modernity begins.)[36] This statement also describes several protagonists in Wolf's oeuvre, above all Kleist and Günderrode in *Kein Ort. Nirgends.* Themes of self-destruction, destroying objects of love, and self-destruction via love are common in Kleist's oeuvre. In "Die Verlobung in St. Domingo," a Swiss colonizer on the island of Santo Domingo[37] falls in love with a woman of African descent, thinks she has betrayed him—it later becomes clear that she intended to help him avoid harm—and kills her. In "Der Findling," a man adopts a child, loves him as his own, and later kills him, as the adopted son had been responsible for the death of the father's wife and has legally evicted the father from his own home. Before the father is hanged for murder, he refuses to take sacraments, as he wishes to further avenge the adopted son in hell. In "Der Zweikampf," Jakob Rotbart dies after apparently winning a duel, as a minor cut to his wrist becomes fatally infected, and his opponent Herr Friedrich loses the duel, being injured severely, but is nursed back to health. Both these men were fighting for the love of Littegard, with whom Rotbart thinks he has had sexual intercourse, and whose chastity Friedrich dares not question. In "Michael Kohlhaas," the eponymous main character, in defending his property and his horse, carries out a number of increasingly violent acts of revenge until he is sentenced to capital punishment. In "Das Erdbeben in Chili," Jeronimo and Josephe are initially punished for loving each other. He is in prison, she in a convent. They escape death by grace (that is, an earthquake) and meet again in a loving embrace, only to be put to death later on different terms.

Second, inner transformation in characters is a hallmark of both Kleist's and Wolf's narratives, although the transformations occur in markedly different ways in the two respective writers' works. Kleist's works represent an extreme in that there are sharp turns in Kleist's plots, and with these plot turns come inner transformation in the characters. There are natural disasters, legal declarations, fights, and deaths, for example. Indeed, Eberhard Lämmert cites Kleist as the foremost German example of what he calls the "Geschehenserzählung,"[38] that is, a narration in which the outward plot is emphasized more than other elements of the narrative such as societal development or inner, affective or psychological, development. In Lämmert's spectrum of emphasis on outer plot versus emphasis on inner development, Kleist is placed far at the outer plot end, and Christa Wolf would be far at the inner development end, as Rita Seidel overcomes her love for Manfred and affirms her allegiance to the communist project, as Christa T. comes to herself, as the narrator in *Was bleibt* ponders finding her own language, as the semi-fictional Kleist and Günderrode confirm their status as outsiders, and as Kassandra reflects upon her development as a prophet, for example. However, as Lämmert himself insists, this polarization is a spectrum—not a concrete dichotomy—designed to give insight into the broad nature of narrative. The implication is that all narratives have some amount of development on each side of the spectrum, although the emphasis may be much higher on one side or the other. Kleist and Wolf, then, represent dialectical opposites of each other, not just dialectical in the sense that they are opposites, but dialectical in the sense that they are two sides of the same coin. On the inner development side of the spectrum, there is a high ratio of inner development to outer plot development, but, nonetheless, inner development happens along with outer plot development within the coordinates of time and space. Rita Seidel's inner development is a response to Manfred's crossing of the border into West Berlin and time she spends with her fellow workers in locomotive production. Likewise, sharp outer plot turns have inner ramifications for the characters within the narrative. After Michael Kohlhaas participates in much action and is sentenced to death, he is changed. After Penthesilea kills Achilles, she has undergone such inner change that she is capable of crafting a blade made from her inner affect and kills herself with it. *Penthesilea*, indeed, is an example of a work that particularly disturbs Lämmert's spectrum of outer plot development versus inner development. Martin Greenberg writes of the action-filled third scene, in which Penthesilea gallops quickly to intercept Achilles: "This isn't so much action as feeling, the love and violence, tenderness and aggression, submissiveness and domineeringness which are tragically confused inside the breast of the Amazonian queen."[39] In this case, the narration (narrated here in Aetolian's speech as he discusses the action with Dolopian and Myrmidon) of action portrays intense emotion. For Penthesilea, indeed, action and emotion are not polar opposites, just as she does not perceive love and violence to be polar opposites. The interaction between outward action and inner change, furthermore, is connected to and represented largely by the self-destruction indicated in the previous paragraph. And this holds true, in large part, for Kleist and Günderrode in *Kein Ort. Nirgends* just as it does for Penthesilea and Achilles in Kleist's *Penthesilea*.

Third, most of Kleist's works contain heavy transtextual elements.[40] As Genette indicates, *Penthesilea* is one of the most prominent examples of transvaluation not just in Kleist's oeuvre but in the entirety of Western literature.[41] In Kleist's version of the play the violence of battle and the violence of love come to the fore, and Penthesilea is at least an equal agent to Achilles. Indeed, in the Kleist version, Penthesilea kills Achilles, whereas other versions of the story have Achilles killing Penthesilea. Kleist's *Amphitryon*, furthermore, also has a strong transtextual element, and is also an example of transvaluation, inasmuch as the character of Amphitryon in the Kleist play is not a cuckolded fool to be lampooned as in other versions of the story but rather a serious general experiencing a metaphysical crisis. In Kleist's narrative fiction, he often begins with a historical or mythological story, which he then valuates. Indeed, transvaluation is at work in much of Kleist's writings. Christa Wolf, in *Kein Ort. Nirgends*, adopts Kleist's technique of transvaluation, a technique that is also at work in the writings of Karoline von Günderrode.

Kleist Dreams of Günderrode's Adonis

Karoline von Günderrode, at the fringes of German Romanticism, remained, like Kleist, outside the official literary heritage of the GDR.[42] She also became part of the crisis surrounding the official literary heritage of the GDR in the 1970s and 1980s, albeit it on a smaller scale.[43] Anna Seghers, however, defended Günderrode along with Kleist as early as 1937, challenging Lukács's narrow view of them, which became and remained the official view of romanticism in the GDR until the 1970s.[44] Whereas a multitude of GDR writers and scholars engaged with Kleist in the 1970s and 1980s, Christa Wolf worked alone to pique interest in Günderrode. Wolf was first introduced to Günderrode through Seghers. She confessed this in a letter to Seghers: "Du warst die erste, durch die ich ihren Namen [Günderrode] überhaupt gehört habe"[45] (You were the first person I ever heard the name Günderrode from). Indeed, Wolf recognizes Seghers as directly influencing *Kein Ort. Nirgends*. In an earlier letter to Seghers, Wolf writes:

> Ich habe den Sommer über an einer Erzählung geschrieben, die ist noch nicht fertig, ich weiß noch nichtmal, ob ich sie wirklich schaffe. Aber Du bist mit Schuld an dem Thema: Ich versuche, eine Begegnung zwischen Kleist und der Karoline von Günderrode zu schildern, die vielleicht einmal stattgefunden hat (wahrscheinlich nicht), aber ich glaube, das habe ich Dir im Frühjahr schon erzählt
>
> [I spent all summer writing a story. It's not finished yet. I don't even know if I'll ever finish it. But I got involved in the theme because of you. I'm trying to depict a meeting between Kleist and Karoline von Günderrode that may have happened once (but probably didn't). But I guess I already told you about it in the spring.][46]

In addition to including a semi-fictional Günderrode in *Kein Ort. Nirgends*, Wolf edited a volume of Günderrode's poetry, prose, and correspondence and wrote a lengthy essay on Günderrode, which she included in the volume.[47] She also corresponded about Günderrode with others, writing to Brigitte Reimann, for example: "Kennst Du die Günderrode? Mit ihr beschäftige ich mich ein bisschen, dabei mit dem Umkreis der Romantik-Weiber. Gar nicht uninteressant, kann ich Dir sagen." (Do you know Günderrode? I've been occupied with her a bit, and also with the circle of female romantics. It's pretty interesting I can tell you.)[48] And in May 1970 on trip to West Germany, she visited Günderrode's grave in Winkel am Rhein,[49] from where she wrote to Anna Seghers: "Wir sind nun in Winkel am Rhein, wo die Günderrode sich erdolcht hat, die Stelle am Fluß findet man natürlich nicht, aber den Stein auf dem Friedhof." (Now we're in Winkel am Rhein, where Günderrode stabbed herself to death with her dagger. Of course, nobody knows where the exact spot is on the river where she did it, but the gravestone is here.)[50] Given Wolf's enthusiasm about Günderrode and the edited volume of Günderrode's work, many in the GDR were likely introduced to Günderrode through Wolf. There is, however, no large amount of literary reworkings of Günderrode in the GDR.[51] Nonetheless, the inclusion of Günderrode in *Kein Ort. Nirgends* further fortifies the work's transvaluation of Greek literature.

It is, in part, Günderrode's technique of transvaluation that makes her works so pathological[52] for Lukács and, at the same time, so vital for Anna Seghers and Christa Wolf. There is, on the surface, a lack of the life-affirmation that one might expect to be part of Lukács's realism. Günderrode was both ill and suicidal, and some of this may be seen in her texts. But Lukács also appreciated works by Thomas Mann that include ill, dying, and even suicidal protagonists, as well as Goethe's *Die Leiden des jungen Werther*, in which the protagonist both defends and commits suicide. The works of Günderrode do not fit into Lukács's notion of realism for two other reasons. First, they emphasize the transformation inherent in death. Second, they receive Greek mythology in ways that counter the reception of Greek mythology in German classicism. These two points are, furthermore, related. An overview of transtextuality in the works of Günderrode may begin to clarify these points.

Like those of Kleist, Günderrode's works tend to have strong relationships with other texts. The short poem "Ariadne auf Naxos" engages with a number of figures from Greek mythology. Her ballad "Don Juan" transforms Mozart's eponymous opera. Her brief dialogue "Des Wanderers Niederfahrt" is a romanticization of Goethe's poem "Wanderers Nachtlied." Her poem "Brutus II" addresses the murder of Julius Caesar made (in)famous in Shakespeare's play *Julius Caesar* from the guilt-laden perspective of Brutus. Her poems "Buonaparte in Egypten" and "Mahomets Traum in der Wüste" allude, respectively, to the historical figures Napoleon Bonaparte and Mohammed. Her one-act play, or "dramolet" as she calls it, "Immortalita" has figures from Greek mythology participate in dialogue with the feminine personification of immortality. She also wrote poems about Melete and Adonis, which will later be helpful in revealing the connection between death and transformation for Günderrode.

Günderrode's dialogue "Die Manen," furthermore, reads as a theory of the relationships among texts. In the dialogue, a student tells a teacher about how, upon visiting the catacombs of Gustav Adolph, he came to the realization that stories only exist insofar as they are received and that stories change over time. Walter Benjamin makes this point in part in his essay on the storyteller, and Christa Wolf addresses the matter in the opening pages of several of her books as well as in several essays. "Die Manen," like Benjamin's essay on the storyteller, connects such transformations in stories to death. Rather than annihilating something, death represents merely a shift in energy. The teacher figure in the dialogue states: "Der Tod ist ein chemischer Prozeß, eine Scheidung der Kräfte, aber kein Vernichter, er zerreißt das Band zwischen mir und ähnlichen Seelen nicht."[53] (Death is a chemical process, a separation of forces, but not an annihilator. It doesn't destroy the bond between me and kindred souls.) Death thus changes matters, but it does not stop the matter from being relevant to the present and future. He goes on to ask the student figure, "Eine Verbindung mit Verstorbenen kann also statt haben, in so fern sie nicht aufgehört haben, mit uns zu harmonisieren?" (128; So a connection with the deceased can take place in so far as they haven't stopped harmonizing with us?). He then answers his own question with the statement, "Es kommt nur darauf an, diese Verbindung gewahr zu werden" (129; It's just a matter of becoming aware of this connection). This dialogue, which Christa Wolf cites in her essay on Günderrode, highlights much about transtextuality in Wolf's works. Günderrode's discourse on death and transformation, furthermore, emerges in Christa Wolf's *Kein Ort. Nirgends.* While "Die Manen" utilizes Nordic history, many of Günderrode's works transvaluate Greek mythology.

Greek mythology plays a particularly large role in Günderrode's readings, as the previous overview of transtextuality in her works indicates. Friedrich Creuzer often sent her his translations of Greek texts[54] and was teaching her about Greek history.[55] In Creuzer's letter to her dated March 21, 1805, for example, he mentions her affinity for Pythagoras of Samos.[56] Günderrode also worked on Creuzer's four-volume *Mythologie und Symbolik der alten Völker, besonders der Griechen*, published 1810–12.[57] Günderrode's *Studienbuch* indicates that she carefully studied the journal *Athenäum*, edited by August Wilhelm Schlegel and Karl Wilhelm Friedrich Schlegel, which contained translations of Greek elegies and essays on Greek literature.[58] Her knowledge of Greek mythology and Greek history is also apparent in her literary writings. Although it was common for writers in Günderrode's day to engage with the myths of Ancient Greece, Günderrode's engagement with them was starkly different from German classicist writers, Goethe being the most obvious example. Whereas the German classicist writers perceived Greek literature as rational and heroic, Günderrode perceived it as morbid and irrational, characteristics that drew her to it. Günderrode's intervention in the reception of Greek literature combined with her interest in the transformative aspects of death were subversive in the context of the GDR. Günderrode's Adonis poems, along with Christa Wolf's subtle allusion to them in *Kein Ort. Nirgends*, provide an example of this.

While Günderrode's dream of dying the deer's death in *Kein Ort. Nirgends* alludes to Kleist's play *Penthesilea*, Kleist, in *Kein Ort. Nirgends*, has a dream, which he conveys to his fiancée Wilhelmine, that alludes to two poems in Günderrode's *Melete*, namely "Adonis Tod" and "Adonis Todtenfeyer." In this dream, which the narrator indicates is the first and only dream that this semi-fictional Kleist mentions (36), and which has haunted Kleist since he left the military (37), Kleist chases a wild boar, "ein zottiges Tier, einen Eber wohl, ein wildes, schönes, rasendes Geschöpf" (37; a shaggy beast, it seemed to be a boar, a wild, beautiful, raging creature, 28), trying to put reins on it and mount it. He is, however, never able to catch up with it completely. Finally, he grabs a musket and shoots the beast dead (37). After he conveys the dream to

Wilhelmine, she cries and declares that the relationship between her and Kleist is going nowhere (38). On the surface, this dream indicates perhaps that Kleist attempted to maintain standing in the Prussian military (or in Prussian society) and was unable to do so. Juxtaposed with two poems by Günderrode, however, the dream points to something much richer.

The first two poems in Günderrode's collection *Melete*, after the quatrain "An Melete" and the sonnet "Zueignung," deal explicitly with the ancient Greek myth of Adonis, the god of rebirth and vegetation and the lover of both Aphrodite and Persephone; he was pierced in the heart by a wild boar's tusks and died in Aphrodite's arms.[59] In some versions of the myth, Ares, disguised as a wild boar, murders Adonis out of vengeance because he, too, loves Aphrodite. The first of these two poems, "Adonis Tod," consists of two sonnets and describes the death of Adonis ("den Jäger traf des Thieres wilde Wuth": the hunter was met with the wild anger of the beast) and the sorrow of Aphrodite ("Die Göttin sinkt in namenlosem Leide": The goddess sinks in unnamed sorrow). As Edith Hamilton writes of Aphrodite and her sorrow at Adonis's death, ". . . the Goddess of Love, who pierces with her shafts the hearts of gods and men alike, was fated herself to suffer that same piercing pain."[60] Aphrodite, however, realizes the transformation occurring at the moment of death, as the blood of Adonis makes a rose grow, and her sorrows turn to song

The second poem, "Adonis Todtenfeyer," is a meditation on the transformative nature of death. The line "Wandeln ist unsterblich Sterben" (transformation is dying immortally) epitomizes such sentiment. A transformation occurs when something of the dead lives on. Günderrode even suggests that the divine is present in such transformations:

> Leben wiederkehrt zum Leben.
> Also ist der Gott erstanden
> Aus des dumpfen Grabes Banden.
>
> [Life returns to life
> Thus God is arisen
> From the dull bonds of the grave.]

Life does not simply persist beyond death: it is transformed at the moment of death. This thought parallels that of Yuri Lotman (as part of his theory of spatial semantics) that the crossing of the border between life and death—in either direction—is often a border crossing of great semantic importance.[61] But what does this have to do with *Kein Ort. Nirgends*?

Günderrode's Adonis poems juxtaposed with the reception of Adonis in German classicism indicate Günderrode's radical reinterpretation of Greek mythology. Whereas Günderrode's portrayal of Adonis deals with death and transformation, the German classicist portrayals of Adonis deal primarily with beauty. The following passage from Goethe's *Briefe aus der*

Schweiz, in which he compares Ferdinand to Adonis, is indicative of the German classicist imagining of Adonis.

> Ich veranlaßte Ferdinanden, zu baden im See; wie herrlich ist mein junger Freund gebildet! Welch ein Ebenmaß aller Teile! Welch eine Fülle der Form, welch ein Glanz der Jugend, welch ein Gewinn für mich, meine Einbildungskraft mit diesem vollkommenen Muster der menschlichen Natur bereichert zu haben! Nun bevölkere ich Wälder, Wiesen und Höhen mit so schönen Gestalten; ihn seh ich als Adonis dem Eber folgen, ihn als Narziß sich in der Quelle bespiegeln!
>
> [I induced Ferdinand to bathe in the lake. What a glorious shape my friend has! How duly proportioned his limbs are! What fulness of form! What splendour of youth! What a gain to have enriched my imagination with this perfect model of manhood! Now I can people the woods, the meadow, and the hills with similar fine forms. I can see him as Adonis chasing the boar, or as Narcissus contemplating himself in the mirror of the spring.][62]

Here there is no mention of Adonis's gruesome death. There is also no mention of his being mourned by a goddess or his transformation. Goethe—in congruity with Winckelmann's ideas about young Greek boys in general—imagines Adonis to be beautiful, youthful, and athletic.

Another example of the reception of the Adonis myth in German classicism is located in Schiller's sonnet "Nänie" (1800).

> Auch das Schöne muss sterben! Das Menschen und Götter bezwinget
> Nicht die eherne Brust rührt es dem stygischen Zeus.
> Einmal nur erweichte die Liebe den Schattenbeherrscher
> Und an der Schwelle noch, streng, rief er zurück sein Geschenk.
> Nicht stillt Aphrodite dem schönen Knaben die Wunde,
> Die in den zierlichen Leib grausam der Eber geritzt.
> Nicht errettet den göttlichen Held die unsterbliche Mutter,
> Wann er am skäischen Tor fallend sein Schicksal erfüllt.
> Aber sie steigt aus dem Meer mit allen Töchtern des Nereus,
> Und die Klage hebt an um den verherrlichten Sohn.
> Siehe! Da weinen die Götter, es weinen die Göttinnen alle,
> Dass das Schöne vergeht, dass das Vollkommene stirbt.
> Auch ein Klagelied zu sein im Mund der Geliebten ist herrlich;
> Denn das Gemeine geht klanglos zum Orkus hinab.
>
> [Beauty itself must die! Though it subjugate men and immortals,
> Yet it can never appeal unto the Stygian god.
> Love but once in his life could move the ruler of Hades,
> Who on the threshold then sternly regretted his vow.
> Not Aphrodite herself could heal the wounds of Adonis,

> Torn in his delicate skin by the redoubtable boar.
> Nor was the hero saved at Troy by his mother immortal
> When at the gate he died, falling as destiny bade.
> But from the deep she rose with all the daughters of Nereus,
> Wailing long and loud for her illustrious son.
> Gods and goddesses all lament in unanimous anguish
> That the beautiful dies, fades the ideal away.
> Even a dirge of lament we prize from the lips of our dear ones,
> For the dishonoured and mean creep into Orcus unsung.][63]

Here too, Adonis is twice (lines 1 and 12) described as being beautiful. And with Adonis, beauty, the reader is informed, must perish. The description of the death of Adonis here implies a transformation at the moment of death, but it is a lamented passing of the beautiful, which is quite different from the positive unlocking of the divine through death described in Günderrode's Adonis poems. Whereas death represents the end of Adonis and his beauty for Schiller, it represents a transformation for Günderrode.

In Günderrode's Adonis poems, Adonis undergoes a transformation. Both Kleist and Günderrode receive Greek literature radically differently from the Weimar classicists, such as Wieland, Goethe, and Schiller, all influenced by Winckelmann. Whereas the Weimar classicists view the ancient Greeks as being both beautiful and rational, Kleist and Günderrode focus on the irrational, the paradoxical, the violent, and the mortal in Greek literature. They both also focus on bodies in Greek literature that can be maimed, wounded, and destroyed. But there is always a transformation involved in these deaths. Günderrode in particular was interested in death and its transformative value in Greek literature. In fact, as Markus Hille and Steven D. Martinson indicate, it was Günderrode's interest in death and transformation—in addition to Friedrich Creuzer's influence on her—that first led her to study Greek mythology.[64] So many of her works—and in particular the Adonis poems—support the notion of death that she establishes in the fragment "Die Manen":

> Er [death (der Tod)] ist ein chemischer Prozeß, eine Scheidung der Kräfte, aber kein Vernichter, er zerreißt das Band zwischen mir und ähnlichen Seelen nicht, das Fortschreiten des Einen und das Zurückbleiben des Andern aber kann wohl diese Gemeinschaft aufheben, wie ein Mensch, der in allem Vortrefflichen fortgeschritten ist. (128)

> [Death is a chemical process, a separation of forces, but not an annihilator. It doesn't destroy the bond between me and kindred souls. But the advancement of the one or the lag of the other can annul this companionship, like a person who is advanced in everything admirable.]

Christa Wolf, too, is interested in death and transformation, and this is particularly evident in *Kein Ort. Nirgends.* The fictional Günderrode in the novel dreams of being killed by an arrow like a deer and like Achilles, and the fictional Kleist dreams of killing a wild boar similar to the one that kills Adonis in Greek myth and in Günderrode's Adonis poems. Both of these scenes imply a will for transformation through death via literary history. Kleist and Günderrode, in Wolf's novel, reevaluate Weimar classicism, locating transformative death, rather than rationality and life-affirmation, in Greek literature. Kleist tells Günderrode: "Der Geheime Rat [that is, Goethe], denk ich, hat keinen dringlichen Hang zur Tragödie, und ich glaube zu wissen, wieso" (107; The Privy Councilor of Weimar, I think, has no particular penchant for tragedy, and I believe I know why, 83). Günderrode asks him to elaborate, and he continues:

> Er ist auf Ausgleich bedacht. Er meint, die Widerkräfte, in der Welt wirken, ließen sich teilen in zwei Zweige der Vernunft—er nennt sie Gut und Böse—, die letzten Endes beide zur Fortentwicklung der Menschheit beitragen müssen. (107)
>
> [He is concerned with harmony. He believes that those contrary forces which are active in the world can be divided into two branches of reason—he calls them good and evil—both of which, ultimately, make an essential contribution to the progress of mankind (83–84).]

Kleist then distinguishes himself from Goethe:

> Ich kann die Welt in gut und böse nicht teilen; nicht in zwei Zweige der Vernunft, nicht in gesund und krank. Wenn ich die Welt teilen wollte, müßt ich die Axt an mich selber legen, mein Inneres spalten, dem angeekelten Publikum die beiden Hälften hinhalten, daß es Grund hat, die Nase zu rümpfen: Wo bleibt die Reinlichkeit. Ja, unrein ist, was ich vorzuweisen habe. (107)
>
> [I am unable to divide the world into good and evil, into two branches of reason, into healthy and sick. If I wanted to divide the world, I should have to turn the ax on myself, cleave my inner self in twain and offer the two halves to the disgusted public so that they would have good cause to wrinkle up their noses and say: Whatever has happened to wholesome entertainment? Yes indeed, what I have to put on display is unclean. (84)]

Kleist alludes here to Goethe's statement in a letter to Eckermann, dated April 2, 1829: "Das Classische nenne ich das Gesunde, und das Romantische das Kranke" (I call the classical healthy, and the romantic sick). This is a statement that Georg Lukács frequently used to legitimate his dichotomous paradigm of literature, which declared Kleist, for example, to be unhealthy. This paradigm is at the heart of the literary heritage of the GDR and is disrupted by works such as *Kein Ort. Nirgends.*

In this passage, furthermore, the fictional Kleist indicates a connection between suicide and a disruption of the paradigm created by the later Goethe and maintained by Lukács. Kleist, often viewed as a bridge between classicism and romanticism, implies both that such a division destroys him, forces him into two parts, and that the way to counter such a destructive, dichotomous paradigm is through transformative self-destruction. The logic here is that representations of suicide demonstrate just how destructive such paradigms are. The situation here of Kleist and Günderrode parallels that of writers in the GDR such as Christa Wolf, who did not fit easily into such a paradigm. Both sets of writers, furthermore, struggle to reappropriate ancient Greek literature away from the view that the Greeks consistently represent the rational, the healthy, and the beautiful. In a different passage, Kleist fortifies this argument: "Muß die Menschheit durch diese Einöde, um ins Gelobte Land zu kommen? Ich kann's nicht glauben. Ach, wie traurig ist diese zyklopische Einseitigkeit." (102; Must mankind pass through this desert in order to arrive at the Promised Land? I cannot believe that it is so. Alas, how sad it is, this unilateral, cyclopean view of things!, 79–80.) In addition to indicating that such paradigms of literature are one-sided, Kleist implies here that there is, in fact, monstrosity in Greek literature, as he alludes to the cyclops, the one-eyed giant described by both Hesiod (in the *Theogony*) and Homer (in the *Odyssey*). This passage, furthermore, strengthens the parallel with the GDR situation of invented literary heritage, as Kleist questions the use of a dichotomous paradigm of literature. Here again, Kleist mentions the destruction inherent in such a paradigm, this time, using again both a gruesome image from Greek mythology and an image of the destruction of his own body. The former is an allusion to Ixion, who killed his father-in-law and was later bound to a spinning wheel for eternity. The latter emerges as Kleist bangs on his head and tells the doctor, Georg Christian Wedekind, that if the problem is in his (Kleist's) head, that he (Wedekind) should prove the efficacy of his beloved science by dissecting his (Kleist's) head and finding it.

Kleist and Günderrode deride Goethe's later classicist work. They maintain, further, that "der Alte in Weimar" (129; the old man in Weimar, 102) that is, Goethe, is not capable of writing a tragedy. Kleist comments that Goethe "hat . . . lange nichts Poetisches hervorgebracht" (126; has . . . not produced any real poetry for a long time, 99). At this remark Günderrode laughs. This "lange" refers apparently to the time since Goethe's Sturm und Drang works, indeed about thirty years. Kleist goes on to suggest that Goethe is "lebensfremd" (126; out of touch with real life, 102). Kleist and Günderrode then criticize Goethe's *Torquato*

Tasso. Earlier Kleist grows jealous as Clemens Brentano explains that he has dreamed that Goethe died. All of this suggests an attempt on the part of Kleist and Günderrode to wrestle away Greek mythology and literary historical legitimacy from Goethe and the Weimar classicists. Likewise, Wolf is wrestling literary history away from the Lukácsian paradigms of heritage. By questioning multiple layers of the official literary heritage—from Lukács's dichotomy of the healthy versus the sick, through Goethe and the Weimar classicists and Kleist and Günderrode, through to the ancient Greeks—Wolf is able to reveal that literary history cannot be entirely molded into literary heritage. While Lukács looks to Ancient Greece as a great, healthy rationalist society,[65] Wolf indicates that the Greeks might just as easily be viewed as irrational, self-destructive, and anything but static.

The fact that the two main transtextual nodes under examination here—Günderrode's allusion to Kleist's *Penthesilea* and Kleist's allusion to Günderrode's Adonis poems—are dreams provides further insight into their transformative nature. Yuri Lotman sees the dream as "a semiotic mirror and each of us sees in it the reflection of our own language. A fundamental property of this language lies in its extreme unpredictability," which makes it "extremely well suited to the generation of new information." Such unpredictability leads to possibilities and to the transformation of stories. In the dream, furthermore, there is, according to Lotman, often confusion between the third-person and the first-person. Such is certainly the case in *Kein Ort. Nirgends*, as Günderrode and Kleist each dream of being someone else. In modernity, the dream, Lotman goes on to explain, provides "a way into the self."[66] The connection between the dream of being someone else and the dream as a way into the self might be explained in that the self, at least in part, is constructed out of the dynamic stories of others. The dream passages in *Kein Ort. Nirgends* create a window into the dynamic nature of those stories. They allow the reader to witness stories changing as they enter the mind of a different person. Dreams, Lotman further explains, inhabit space, and this space has changed over time. With the advent of modernity, dreams transformed from being religious to being psychological. "From the external it became internal" (144). Likewise, literary heritage, as a shaper and transformer of stories, is related to space.

Spatial Transvaluation

Kein Ort. Nirgends utilizes spatial metaphors to express the dynamic nature of literary reception, which stands in opposition to the restrictive rules of literary heritage. In the novel, space, like literary history, is turned inside out. There are at least two spatial binary pairs at work in *Kein Ort. Nirgends*. The first involves a spatial semantic opposition between inside and outside: inside the salon (that is, inside bourgeois society) versus outside the salon, in the forest, for example, which is partly depicted as a space of utopian possibilities. The second pair, the seed and the coffin, also involves the opposition of inside and outside. But with this pair it is the inside that embodies the positive, the possible, the utopian. The first pair has been aptly described. But it can be turned on its head by reading the work in terms of the second pair.

Mechthild Quernheim has described the first spatial semantic binary pair well. She illustrates the pair by creating two opposing lists and placing them side by side.[67] At the top of the lists, she places the terms "Salon" and "Natur" in opposition. Underneath those terms come "bürgerliche Welt" and "Utopie," respectively. In the first list, underneath "salon" and "bürgerliche Welt," follows a list of characters who remain in the physical and metaphorical space of the salon: Savignys, Esenbecks, Merten, Wedekind, C. u. P. Servière, and C. Brentano. In the second list, underneath "Natur" and "Utopie," follows the opposing list of characters, those who venture into nature: Kleist, Günderrode, and, in parentheses, B. Brentano. Underneath those oppositions follows a plethora of semantic oppositions. With these spatial semantic oppositions, Quernheim has done much to explain space in the novel, but there is still more to be done.

The other spatial semantic binary pair inverts the semantics of the outside and the inside, implying that in order to flee oppression, one must enter into the discourse that makes that oppression possible. Regarding literary heritage, one must delve deeply into that heritage in order to loosen its grip. This spatial semantic binary comes largely from the epigraph at the beginning of *Kein Ort. Nirgends.*

> Ich trage ein Herz mit mir herum, wie ein nördliches Land den Keim einer Südfrucht. Es treibt und treibt, und kann nicht reifen.
>
> [I carry around a heart the way a Northern land carries within it the germ of a semitropical fruit from the South. It sprouts and sends forth shoots, but it cannot grow ripe.]
>
> —Kleist
>
> Deswegen kömmt es mir aber vor, als sähe ich mich im Sarg liegen und meine beiden Ichs starren sich ganz verwundert an.
>
> [But for this reason I fancy that I am seeing myself lying in the coffin, and my two selves stare at each other in wonderment.]
>
> —Günderrode[68]

The Kleist quotation is taken from a letter written by Kleist to Adolphine von Werdeck on July 29, 1801.[69] The Günderrode quotation is taken from a letter written by Günderrode to Clemens Brentano, probably in 1803, in which Günderrode compares letters to corpses and explains that seeing a letter that she wrote is like seeing her own corpse in a coffin. Ripped from their respective contexts and read together, these two statements complement each other, and the word "Deswegen" at the beginning of the second statement begs the reader to read the two statements together. Here Günderrode provides a spatial antidote to Kleist's spatial problem. The coffin, perhaps the most claustrophobic space imaginable, is the semantic opposite of the wanderer's open space. However, it is, of course, not that simple. The coffin also represents death. Günderrode's desirous contemplation of the coffin points, at least implicitly, to her wish to die. The book's epigraph foreshadows the suicide at the end of the book, as Kleist and Günderrode wander away from the bourgeois parlor and kill themselves as an act of transformation. However, this is only one of the book's epigraphs.

Kleist's seed, furthermore, is not such a simple matter either. Although it has not yet sprouted, it remains a source of potential energy. Such potential energy lies in narratives as they are passed down and as readings change based on changing situations. Walter Benjamin also used the image of the seed in this manner. At the end of the seventh section of his essay "Der Erzähler: Betrachtungen zum Werk Nikolai Lesskows," Benjamin compares stories—as opposed to information—to unsprouted seeds. "Sie ähnelt den Samenkörnern, die jahrtausendelang luftdicht verschlossen in den Kammern der Pyramiden gelegen und ihre Keimkraft bis auf den heutigen Tag bewahrt haben" (It resembles the seeds of grain which have lain for centuries in the chambers of the pyramids shut up airtight and have retained their germinative power to this day).[70] The seeds do not expend their energy at once but have lasting power. Likewise stories have lasting powers. They do not expend all their energy on instant explanation, but rather they allow for a multitude of interpretations as contexts change. Kleist's stories—and his biography and suicide—allow for such a multitude of interpretations.[71]

Günderrode's coffin, furthermore, is, like the pyramid chambers described by Benjamin, a way of insuring that the energy of the stories is extended. The coffin does not, however, lock away the story or make it inaccessible. It allows the story to become richer. It allows the story to travel and to evolve. Similarly, for Kleist and Günderrode death and enclosure in a coffin does not stop the story but rather allows it to flourish and take on multiple layers of meaning. Death is not the end. Death, when its potential energy is realized, is transformative. "Wandeln ist unsterblich Sterben": that turns out to be a statement that is as much about the dynamic nature of literary reception as it is about utopia through death. Transformative death and the transvaluation of literary texts are precisely what is at stake in *Kein Ort. Nirgends* as well as in several of Wolf's works after *Kein Ort. Nirgends.*

Suicide and Transvaluation in Wolf's Oeuvre

Christa Wolf with *Kein Ort. Nirgends* adopts the technique of transvaluation from Kleist and Günderrode. Kleist, especially with *Penthesilea*, as Genette indicates, creates astonishing transvaluations. Much of the transvaluation in Kleist's works, furthermore, presents rereadings of Greek myths. Günderrode also presents transvaluations of Greek myths. Both Kleist and Günderrode are working against the Enlightenment, Goethean readings of Greek myths. With Wolf's fictional meeting between Kleist and Günderrode, Wolf brings these transvaluations into the context of the literary heritage of the GDR. Although Wolf's Kleist and Günderrode are diegetically located in the year 1804, the work is inevitably read in the context of the GDR, as Ute Brandes makes clear.[72] Wolf's novel emphasizes the transvaluations inherent in the works of Kleist and Günderrode, which upset the Lukácsian dichotomous view of the literary heritage of the GDR not only regarding Kleist and Günderrode but also regarding the ancient Greeks.

Kein Ort. Nirgends represents a caesura in Christa Wolf's oeuvre. Astrid Köhler makes this point by grouping *Kein Ort. Nirgends* together with Wolf's later works *Sommerstück* and *Was bleibt*.[73] Köhler argues that these three works deal with writers and are much less affirmative of the GDR project.[74] Her assessment is accurate, but there is still more to the watershed nature of the novel in Wolf's works. *Kein Ort. Nirgends* is also Wolf's work with the most explicit reference to suicide. As the narrator states, "Wir wissen, was kommt" (151; We know what is coming, 119). Wolf achieves this direct mention of suicide, in part, because the Kleist and Günderrode figures are diegetically in 1804. They are what Eberhart Lämmert calls "Die 'reale Folie' der Geschichte"[75] (the "actual foil" of the story). Still, *Kein Ort. Nirgends* engages the taboo topic of suicide in the wake of Honecker's declaration that there are no taboos in GDR literature, as long as the author is grounded in socialism. The novel, then, surely represents a caesura in Wolf's oeuvre on these grounds.

Kein Ort. Nirgends, however, in addition to making the theme of suicide explicit, is also the first work by Wolf with heavy transtextual elements, a characteristic that appears in several of her later works, especially *Kassandra* and *Medea: Stimmen*, works that continue Wolf's push toward rereading ancient Greek myths against the grain of both the Enlightenment and the literary heritage of the GDR. Although it takes place in 1804, *Kein Ort. Nirgends* has much to do with the GDR. Whereas Wolf's earlier works are subversive via their psychoanalytically oriented reappraisal of communist family narratives, coming-of-age stories, and father and mother figures—as Julia Hell skillfully argues[76]—these works by Wolf starting with *Kein Ort. Nirgends* are subversive in their transvaluations of GDR literary heritage. They probe into Lukács's dichotomy of realism versus modernism. They dig deeply into the archive of German and Western literature, as Wolf writes about Kleist and Günderrode writing about Homer and others writing about Greek history, for example. They thereby reevaluate multiple layers of the literary heritage of the GDR.

Christa Wolf, in *Kein Ort. Nirgends*, establishes a place where one can watch stories transform and epochs communicate. Yuri Lotman, in explaining what he calls "dialogue mechanisms," describes how cultures and even parts of cultures communicate in dialogue.[77] While one people or subculture produces culture, another is receiving culture. When the culture producer recedes into a lull, the culture receiver begins to produce culture. This is, in part, what is at work between classicism and romanticism. Earlier in the same work, Lotman writes: "Romanticism occupies only a part of the semiosphere in which all sorts of other traditional structures continue to exist, some of them going way back into antiquity."[78] Wolf's work illustrates how romanticism awoke elements of the classical that classicism had ignored, and it also awakens elements of literary history that GDR cultural authorities had ignored.

While Wolf's *Kein Ort. Nirgends* used the trope of suicide to transvaluate GDR literary heritage rather methodically, a couple of other works published around the same time engage suicide in ways that cause the literary heritage to spin completely out of control.

5: Suicidal Voices: Heiner Müller's *Hamletmaschine* and Sibylle Muthesius's *Flucht in die Wolken*

THESE TWO WORKS SEEM, on the surface, to counter my claim that suicide in East German literature of the 1970s and 1980s is primarily fictional and imaginative; both of them, however, are wildly transtextual. Moreover, they are an unlikely pair. Heiner Müller's play *Hamletmaschine* (1977/78) and Sibylle Muthesius's *Flucht in die Wolken* (1981) are both inspired, in part, by real suicides. Although each of these two works is extraordinarily rich on its own, they also become even more interesting when they are placed alongside the other literary representations of suicide in the GDR in the 1970s and 1980s. Both works also employ a large number of hypotexts that at times run counter to one another, and both use some combination of hypertextuality, paratextuality, metatextuality, and Kristevan intertextuality. Indeed, Genette's taxonomy of transtextuality, as useful as it is, is not entirely equipped to describe these two works. The wealth of transtextuality functions in both works to resist interpretation and simplification, constituting what Jeff Todd Titon calls "intertextual overload"[1] or what Georgina Paul, writing specifically about *Hamletmaschine*, calls "cultural overload."[2] Whereas Plenzdorf's *Die neuen Leiden des jungen W.* and Wolf's *Kein Ort. Nirgends*, for example, employ the trope of suicide to instigate a shift in literary historiography, causing literary heritage to be rewired, *Hamletmaschine* and *Flucht in die Wolken* short-circuit the idea of literary heritage altogether. Muthesius's *Flucht in die Wolken* uses literary history primarily to cope with the loss of a loved one through suicide. And while Müller's *Hamletmaschine* alludes to real suicides, among many other things, it does not constitute a coming-to-terms with suicide. Instead, it is a dramatic, comparative exploration of suicidal voices and various intellectual strands of self-destruction. In short, in *Hamletmaschine* Müller uses the theme of suicide in an attempt to explore the failures and impossibilities of co-opting literary heritage in the GDR, and in *Flucht in die Wolken* Muthesius uses allusions to literature in an attempt to make some sense of the author's daughter's suicide and the GDR context in which it happened.

Suicidal Polyphony in *Hamletmaschine*

Although no character in *Hamletmaschine* explicitly commits suicide during the action of the play, suicide and self-destruction are the primary themes in the work. Indeed, the play consists largely of a polyphony of suicidal voices. Scholarship on *Hamletmaschine* tends to fall into one of two categories. Scholars typically either claim that the play is a statement about the nature of the GDR, or claim that it is a post-dramatic play about post-dramatic theater. I believe that both of these positions are correct. However, I also believe that both of them can be further reduced to a single description that includes both positions: the play is about suicide and self-destruction. That is, both sets of readings imply that something is self-destructing: either the GDR or the institution of theater. While both sets of reading are entirely valid, I offer a third variant: the play suggests that literary heritage is also self-destructive.

Self-destruction is ubiquitous in the play. Hamlet is self-destructive. Ophelia has already killed herself. Suicide, indeed, is what links Hamlet and Ophelia in the play. The two characters represent two different types of self-destruction. There is also an allusion to Ulrike Meinhof, a leader of the leftist urban guerilla group Red Army Faction, who was found dead in her prison cell in May 1976, allegedly a case of suicide. And there is much destruction in the play, in addition to the self-destruction: the destruction of a photograph of Heiner Müller and the busts of Marx, Lenin, and Mao, not to mention the destruction involved in the suppressed 1956 uprising in Budapest to which the play alludes. Further, the play hints at the self-destructive nature of capitalism with lines such as "Heil COCA-COLA" and "Mit den Narben der Konsumschlacht Armut" (with scars from the battle of consumerism Poverty). Even basic dramaturgical functions self-destruct in *Hamletmaschine.* The actor playing Hamlet stops playing Hamlet, preferring to play a woman instead. Ophelia claims to be Electra. And the play contains little dialogue. Theater itself self-destructs here, as the play seems more like a prose-poem than a traditional play. And the play also points toward the self-destructive nature of the GDR, of course. But, above all, the play illustrates the self-destructive potential of literary heritage.

It should be stated preliminarily that Müller's second wife, Inge Müller, killed herself in 1966 by putting her head in a gas oven. Before that, she had attempted suicide several times. She suffered from severe depression, having had the traumatic experience of spending three days buried under rubble in Berlin in 1945 and then having to recover her parents' corpses.[3] However, *Hamletmaschine* is no simple reflection on her suicide. Müller stated that his wife's suicide provided him with dramatic material to work with, but that the play is not directly about her.[4]

In a 1987 interview, when Müller was asked about the influence of Inge Müller's suicide on *Hamletmaschine*, he replied:

> Ist denn das von Belang? Der Selbstmord meiner Frau hatte ursächlich mit mir nichts zu tun. Sie war im Krieg dreimal verschüttet. Ihre Eltern wurden getötet. Sie hat die Leichen in Einzelteilen aus dem Luftschutzkeller geborgen und auf den Friedhof getragen. Daraus ist ein Kriegstrauma entstanden. Das ging nicht weg. Wenn ich so etwas als Motiv verwende, wird es Literatur und existiert nur noch in diesen Texten. Alles andere ist uninteressant. Es zeugt von einem tiefen Kulturverfall, daß man sich heute, statt die Texte zu lesen, nur noch für das interessiert, was dahintersteckt.[5]
>
> [But is that important? The cause of my wife's suicide had nothing to do with me. She was trapped in rubble three times during the war. Her parents were killed. She retrieved their corpses, piece by piece, from the air-raid shelter and carried them to the cemetery. That led her to have trauma from the war. It wouldn't go away. If I use something like that as a theme in my work, it becomes literature and only exists in these texts. Everything else is uninteresting. It's evidence of a huge cultural decline that people today don't want to read the texts; instead, they only want to know what's behind them.]

I find Müller's response satisfying. It supports my contention that East German literature ought to be read as literature rather than as simplistic biographical documents reflecting Cold War politics. However, the connection between Inge Müller's suicide and the representations of self-destruction in *Hamletmaschine* is an easy one to make—although emphasizing that connection too strongly certainly leads to a misunderstanding of the play—because the horrific events that led to Inge Müller's suicide are, in part, similar to the ones in which the Hamlet and Ophelia figures in *Hamletmaschine* find themselves: Europe destroyed. Right at the beginning of Müller's play the phrase "im Rücken die Ruinen von Europa" (the ruins of Europe to my back) alerts the audience that the play takes place in rubble-covered postwar Europe. Furthermore, the fact that Müller himself appears in the play in the form of a photograph could lead some viewers to assume that the play has some autobiographical elements, although a careful consideration of the photograph, which is destroyed during the play, could also support Müller's claim that the author's life has little directly to do with the play. That is, not only is the specific, biographical author, Heiner Müller, destroyed, but authorship as an institution is also destroyed, an interpretation that supports Müller's literary savvy insistence that people read the text. While Inge Müller's suicide may have influenced the genesis of *Hamletmaschine* in some way, it is not a major feature of the play, and it is not explicitly mentioned in the text. While describing suicide in the context of Müller's biography, it should be noted too that Müller rejected suicide for himself even as he experienced a painful deterioration toward death. He saw nothing heroic in suicide, writing in the final line of a late untitled poem: "sterben kann ein Idiot" (even an idiot can die).

The figure of Hamlet in *Hamletmaschine* represents the self-destruction of melancholic intellectuals. In Shakespeare's *Hamlet*, Hamlet contemplates suicide in the famous "To be or not to be" soliloquy:

> Whether 'tis Nobler in the mind to suffer
> The Slings and Arrows of outrageous Fortune,
> Or to take Arms against a Sea of troubles,
> And by opposing end them. To die, to sleep—
> No more—and by a sleep, to say we end
> The Heart-ache, and the thousand Natural shocks
> That Flesh is heir to? 'Tis a consummation
> Devoutly to be wished. To die . . .[6]

The indecision and melancholy of Shakespeare's Hamlet are also characteristic of Hamlet in *Hamletmaschine*. This Hamlet is even melancholic to the point of paralysis. In act 1 he already perceives everything to be decaying: "Ich legte mich auf den Boden und hörte die Welt ihre Runden drehen im Gleichschritt der Verwesung"[7] (I threw myself on the ground and heard the world rotate in lockstep with decay). However, he cannot do anything about it. His intellect hinders him more than it helps him. He compares his brain to a humpback. He implies that he wishes he had never been born, saying he wishes that his mother had no vagina. He goes on to state that vaginas ought to be sewn shut. Without mothers, he claims, human beings could kill each other into extinction without being bothered. The extent of his melancholy escalates in act 4: "Ich will nicht mehr essen trinken atmen eine Frau lieben einen Mann ein Kind ein Tier. Ich will nicht mehr sterben. Ich will nicht mehr töten" (I no longer want to eat drink breathe love a woman a man a child an animal. I no longer want to die. I no longer want to kill). This statement about not wanting to do anything is made directly before the stage directions indicate that a photograph of Heiner Müller is to be ripped up on stage. Then Hamlet claims that he wants to return to his bowels and live in his shit.

The suicidal Hamlet of *Hamletmaschine* also represents failed revolutions. Act 4 is titled "Pest in Buda Schlacht um Grönland" (Pest in Buda Battle for Greenland) and opens with Hamlet saying "Der Ofen blakt im friedlosen Oktober" (The oven smokes in the violent month of October) ". . . JUST THE WORST TIME OF YEAR FOR A REVOLUTION." Both the title and Hamlet's line allude to the quashed Hungarian uprising of October 1956. It should also be noted, however, that the part of the Russian Revolution involving the overthrow of the provisional government by Lenin's Bolsheviks took place in October 1917 and is often referred to as the October Revolution. Other allusions to revolution, especially to Hungary 1956, are strewn around act 4. The word "Aufstand" (uprising) appears several times, and Hamlet claims: "Mein Drama, wenn es noch stattfinden würde, fände in der Zeit des Aufstands statt" (My drama, if it were still to take place, would take place in the time of the uprising). That is, Hamlet's thinking centers around rebellion, but he may never take action. He speaks of sweeping the police off the streets, throwing rocks at political figures, taking weapons away from the police, and storming buildings. But these actions remain hypothetical. Furthermore, he posits that he would be on both sides of such a clash, destroying himself. At the end of act 4 he splits open the heads of Marx, Lenin, and Mao. *Hamletmaschine* grapples with the question of how a revolutionary-minded intellectual should perceive the Hungarian uprising against a Soviet system backed by Warsaw Pact tanks, a Soviet system that came about through revolution and claimed to support workers and peasants.

While Müller's play criticizes the Soviet treatment of Hungary in 1956, the figure of Hamlet in the play also seems to be an ironic criticism of intellectuals who are unable to bring themselves to act, plagued by indecision or the paralysis of melancholy. His criticism of melancholy partially parallels that of Walter Benjamin, a thinker who both claimed to be melancholic and criticized a certain strain of melancholy. In the Weimar Republic, Benjamin coined the term "linke Melancholie" (leftist melancholy) in the title of a critical review he wrote of a collection of poems by Erich Kästner.[8] Benjamin's criticism was that certain leftists such as Kästner and Kurt Tucholsky were dwelling—emotionless under the banner of *Neue Sachlichkeit*—on lost leftist traditions, thereby rendering themselves useless to their own progressive cause. As Wendy Brown puts it, "Left melancholia, in short, is Benjamin's name for a mournful, conservative, backward-looking attachment to a feeling, analysis, or relationship that has been rendered thinglike and frozen in the heart of the putative Leftist."[9] This sort of melancholia, according to Benjamin, leads to passivity and resignation, which is what seems to have bothered him so much.[10] Ironically, however, Benjamin himself suffered from melancholia, albeit it perhaps another type. In his short esoteric text "Agesilaus Santander" he admits to being "born 'under the sign of Saturn.'"[11] And in 1940 he killed himself, having just crossed into Spain while trying to escape from Nazi-occupied Europe to the United States, and seeing that he would be unable to cross to Portugal where he had planned to set sail, that the Spanish fascists would return him to France where he would be handed over to the Nazis.[12] Max Pensky appropriately sums up Benjamin's dualistic relationship to melancholy: "The author of the *Ursprung des deutschen Trauerspiels*, the expert on the history and phenomenology of the occult history of saturnine melancholia, and the savage critic of the 'tortured stupidity' of the 'newest' phase of melancholia's 'two-thousand year history' are one and the same."[13] Saturnine melancholia, however, is somewhat different from the so-called "linke Melancholie," in that it has a sort of potential energy stored within it. It is this potential energy that turns ostensible melancholia into the dialectic that Pensky describes. Benjamin also wrote about *Hamlet*; indeed, in his *Ursprung des deutschen Trauerspiels* he describes the character of Hamlet in terms of melancholy.[14] Müller, furthermore, was certainly familiar with Benjamin's work, and there is a subtle allusion to Benjamin's well-known passage on the angel of history, which looks backward at the ruins of history but cannot do anything about it, from his "Über den Begriff der Geschichte" in act 3 of *Hamletmaschine*: "Ein Engel, das Gesicht im Nacken" (An angel, breathing down his neck), a line that appears after the character of Hamlet puts on Ophelia's clothes and lets her put makeup on his face. The line appears directly following the line "Hamlet in Hurenpose" (Hamlet strikes a whore's pose). The juxtaposition of Müller's Hamlet with Benjamin's notion of leftist melancholy does much to explain the character of Hamlet in *Hamletmaschine*, but Hamlet is only a part of the play.

Hamletmaschine is as much about Ophelia as it is about Hamlet. While Hamlet (both in Shakespeare's *Hamlet* and in Müller's *Hamletmaschine*) is self-destructive in an indecisive, melancholic, intellectual sense, Ophelia, at least in Shakespeare's *Hamlet*, really does kill herself. It is not entirely clear whether Ophelia, in *Hamletmaschine*, is speaking from the dead or whether she has been revivified or whether she repeatedly kills herself. But she is no stranger to suicide. Most of act 2 consists of Ophelia identifying herself with suicide: "Die Frau am Strick Die Frau mit den aufgeschnittenen Pulsadern Die Frau mit der Überdosis . . . Die Frau mit dem Kopf im Gasherd" (The woman in the noose. The woman with slashed wrists. The woman with the overdose . . . The woman with her head in the gas oven). But she also claims to have stopped killing herself. "Gestern habe ich aufgehört mich zu töten" (Yesterday I stopped killing myself). Somehow, this Ophelia has learned something from her suicide and has moved beyond it. Furthermore, she describes herself as an Ophelia, "die der Fluss nicht behalten hat" (whom the river didn't keep), a line that recalls the main character Beckmann from Wolfgang Borchert's play *Draußen vor der Tür* (1946/1947), who returns home from the Second World War and tries to kill himself by jumping into the Elbe River, only to be told by a feminine personification of the river that she does not want his life, calling him a "Rotznase von einem Selbstmörder" (a snotnose of a suicide) and stating "ich scheiß auf deinem Selbstmord" (I shit on your suicide).[15] In Borchert's play, furthermore, the river Elbe, in mocking Beckmann's suicide attempt, accuses him of wrongfully romanticizing suicide and having visions of Ophelia.[16] Comparing Müller's Ophelia with Beckmann also makes sense because both characters move beyond suicide. Beckmann still exists in the end, suspended between life and death, even though he attempts and then further contemplates suicide. Similarly, Ophelia in *Hamletmaschine* has killed herself but stops killing herself and continues to exist. The fact that she stops killing herself does not mean that she is optimistic or healthy. At the end of the play, act 5, she is in a wheelchair, and doctors are wrapping bandages around her body, although the stage directions also state that she is at sea and that fish are swimming around her. However, she ceases to kill herself, which seems to allow her to make more of a difference in the world than Hamlet is capable of. At the end of act 2 she claims to set fire to her prison (presumably a metaphorical prison) and take to the streets. In act 5 she claims to reject all semen from her body (perhaps achieving what Hamlet suggested ought to be the case when he says that vaginas should be sewn shut). She also claims to turn her breast milk into a lethal poison. She says that she unbirths the world that she gave birth to, strangling it with her thighs. She salutes hatred, contempt, rebellion, and death. While all the men leave the stage, Ophelia remains. While both Hamlet and Ophelia are self-destructive, they are so in very different ways. Hamlet does not physically kill himself. He is incapable of creating change, even though he wants change. His attempts at revolution are unsuccessful. And his self-destruction continues. Ophelia, on the other hand, has physically killed herself, but her suicide redeems her. Because she killed herself, she is now no longer capable of killing herself. However, the self-destruction of Hamlet and Ophelia is far from being the only self-destruction in the play.

Hamletmaschine also represents the self-destruction involved in Brechtian theater, which so heavily influenced Müller or, more precisely, represents Müller's Brecht-influenced destruction of Brecht. As Michael D. Richardson points out, with *Hamletmaschine* Müller takes Brecht's *Verfremdungseffekt* (alienation effect or distancing effect) to its logical conclusion and thereby allows it to destroy itself.[17] *Hamletmaschine* destroys more remnants of Aristotelian theater than Brecht's plays ever did, and in doing so, *Hamletmaschine* also destroys Brecht's project. Not only does the actor playing Hamlet slip out of character momentarily to speak directly to the audience; he also plays a character who was an actor playing Hamlet, who no longer wishes to play the role of Hamlet. He tries to play the role of Ophelia, putting on her clothes and makeup. The opening line of the play, spoken by Hamlet, presumably while he is still in the role of Hamlet, is "Ich war Hamlet" (I was Hamlet). The audience is left wondering whether he is or ever was Hamlet, why he is no longer playing Hamlet, and whether he briefly plays the role of Ophelia or whether he is playing the role of an actor who wishes to play the role of

Ophelia. The play also raises the question of what the difference between a character and an actor even is, and to what extent the difference matters. Furthermore, Ophelia also presumably switches roles, as she claims in act 5, “Hier spricht Elektra” (This is Electra speaking). Again, it is not clear whether Ophelia becomes Electra, or whether the actress playing Ophelia slips into the role of Electra, or whether Electra’s voice speaks transtextually through the character of Ophelia. The post-dramatic implication is that theater has been playing tricks on us all along. The stage directions indicate that a photograph of Müller must be destroyed on stage in act 4. In the 1990 production of *Hamletmaschine*, directed by Müller, the characters of Hamlet and Ophelia were both played by multiple actors on stage at the same time, speaking the same lines simultaneously to break any Aristotelian identification of the audience with the characters and also to highlight the fact that the characters in the play are polyphonic types rather than realistic representations of human beings.[18] While Brecht used the *Verfremdungseffekt* didactically to provide enough distance from the characters to lead the audience toward a certain interpretation of the actions on stage, Müller’s *Hamletmaschine* alienates the audience so much that it inhibits interpretation.

To be sure, Müller consciously pushed Brechtian theater toward its own self-destruction and found doing so to be productive. In the late 1970s and early 1980s, some literary critics accused Müller of killing the Brechtian project. In 1978, Hellmut Karasek declared: “Brecht ist tot” (Brecht is dead) and implied that Müller had killed him.[19] In 1982, Müller argued that the way to continue the Brechtian project was to destroy it, stating: “Brecht gebrauchen, ohne ihn zu kritisieren, ist Verrat”[20] (To use Brecht without criticizing him is betrayal). In 1984, a headline in *Theater heute* called Müller a “Brecht-Killer,” but in the interview to which the caption belongs, Müller, responding to the criticism that he had killed Brecht, explained that his murder of Brecht was a case of patricide (*Vatermord*).[21] The implication is that Müller’s proverbial murder of Brecht is not the murder of an enemy but rather the murder of his major influence. Indeed, it is difficult to overstate the influence of Brecht on Müller. Jonathan Kalb goes so far as to write that “other than Brecht, Müller had no literary fathers,”[22] a statement that is both astonishing, given the extremely broad range of literary allusions that appear in Müller’s works, and supported by Müller in several statements. Müller’s destruction of Brechtian theater (and arguably his destruction of theater in general) is closer to self-destruction than it is to any sort of malevolent or self-serving destruction.

Brechtian theater, however, is not the only theater-related movement that Müller’s *Hamletmaschine* destroyed by instigating self-destruction. The play also changed Shakespeare reception in the GDR by pushing the official heritage of Shakespeare in the GDR to self-destruct.[23] Shakespeare had long been accepted in the GDR as the predecessor of bourgeois humanism, to which socialist realism was the heir. This teleological literary history, known as the *Vollstreckertheorie*, lauded Shakespeare, but it also petrified him. In the 1950s and 1960s Shakespeare's works were often performed in the GDR, and Hamlet was a primary focus in the GDR reception of Shakespeare. The character of Fortinbras was key in early GDR performances of *Hamlet*, as he offers a message of hope at the end of the play after most of the main characters are dead. In such performances Fortinbras offered a socialist messenger in the wake of German fascism. In the 1950s, such performances of *Hamlet* provided a powerful, progressive political message. By the 1970s, however, that conception of *Hamlet* had become stale. Müller's *Hamletmaschine*, then, transforms the GDR reception of *Hamlet* radically.

Using Genette's taxonomy of transtextuality to pin down the ways in which Müller's *Hamletmaschine* transforms *Hamlet* is useful up to a point. It provides a solid starting point, but it ultimately cannot fully describe such transformation. *Hamletmaschine* is simultaneously a proximation (bringing the story into a contemporary context)[24] and a supplement (a continuation of the story, a narrative postscript or sequel)[25] of Shakespeare's *Hamlet.* Like Plenzdorf's *Die neuen Leiden des jungen W.*, Müller's *Hamletmaschine* brings the original text, in this case *Hamlet*, into the context of the GDR. Müller's Hamlet and Ophelia, that is, are not characters living in the Elizabethan era; they are living in the 1970s, or at the earliest in the 1950s. Hamlet knows about Budapest 1956. Ophelia applies twentieth-century cosmetics to Hamlet's face. Hamlet splits the heads of Marx, Lenin, and Mao, figures that did not exist in the early modern period. The play involves tanks and mentions Coca-Cola. There is a photograph of Heiner Müller on stage, while neither photography nor Müller existed in Shakespeare's age. However, the transformation consists not merely of proximation. It also involves supplement, that category of Genette's that involves adding something to an existing story. *Hamletmaschine*, that is, may be seen as a sequel to Shakespeare's *Hamlet.* Ophelia has stopped killing herself, something that can happen only once she has killed herself in Shakespeare's play. Similarly, Hamlet, although he too dies in Shakespeare's play, seems to exist here in a time after the end of Shakespeare's *Hamlet.* He claims to want to stop dying and killing. He even wants to stop being Hamlet, which leads to a different kind of transformation, a sort of trans-characterization. Hamlet becomes Ophelia, and Ophelia becomes Electra. Part of the reason why Genette's taxonomy begins to break down in relation to *Hamletmaschine* is that Genette distinguishes individual types of transformations, creating a sterile (albeit useful) model—that is, the strength of Genette's model is also its weakness—while *Hamletmaschine* involves multiple types of transformation simultaneously. As Günther Klotz writes, "The relation of *Hamletmaschine* to *Hamlet* is not that of an appropriated heritage but that of a sign to a referent from a different continuum."[26] Müller, who translated Shakespeare's *Hamlet* for director Benno Besson, knew Shakespeare and the GDR reception of Shakespeare well. *Hamletmaschine* allows potential energy already at work in *Hamlet* to counter the GDR petrification of Shakespeare and *Hamlet* in particular. And *Hamlet* is far from the only work transformed by *Hamletmaschine*.

Müller's play involves so many hypotexts that it allows for the self-destruction of the notion of literary heritage in general. *Hamletmaschine* alludes to (and deals with), for example, the Red Army Faction, Ulrike Meinhof, Inge Müller, the Second World War, the Cold War, the Hungarian uprising of 1956, consumerism, Stalinism, the Berlin Wall, Hamlet, Karl Marx, Ernst Bloch, Elektra, Sophocles, Euripides, Ophelia, Medea, Shakespeare, Macbeth, Joseph Conrad, Walter Benjamin, e. e. cummings, Hölderlin, the Manson family, Bertolt Brecht, Boris Pasternak, Doctor Zhivago, Aschenputtel, Jakob and Wilhelm Grimm, Wolfgang Borchert, and Heiner Müller himself. Without its hypotexts, both historical and literary, it could not exist as a text. It is, indeed, difficult to locate more than two or three words in a row in the text that are not either an unmarked quotation or an allusion. Attempts to unpack the ramifications of all these allusions at once can only lead to the thwarting of the transformative potential of each. In a sense, they cancel each other out, but this canceling out is not so much a failure as it is Müller's act of revealing the extent to which literary heritage is itself a construction, and a potentially self-destructive one. Not only does the actor who plays Hamlet stop playing Hamlet, creating a hyper-Brechtian distantiation, but the transtextuality also steps out of its role to show that it has been a trick all along.

Reading to Comprehend the Incomprehensible in *Flucht in die Wolken*

Sibylle Muthesius's *Flucht in die Wolken* (1981), like Müller's *Hamletmaschine*, contains a confusing wealth of allusions to other works, many of which seem to contradict one another. And, like *Hamletmaschine*, it also reveals that the project of literary heritage was both a necessity and a failure. *Flucht in die Wolken*, however, shows the inadequacy of literary heritage in a very different way. It documents—albeit it in a highly literary fashion—the story of a young woman in the GDR, who really killed herself in 1971, at the age of eighteen, by way of a gas oven, a bottle of wine, and a sleeping pill.[27] It is edited by the girl's mother under the pseudonym Sibylle Muthesius, who refers to the girl as Pony, with commentary by the mother and a number of epigraphs and other materials also added by the mother.[28] The book contains a number of documents and artifacts, including, for example, Pony's diary entries, letters written by and to Pony, poems and songs by Pony, color prints of Pony's paintings, photographs, extended commentary by Pony's mother, comments written by Pony's teacher, and an afterword written by a psychotherapist. While Pony's suicide was not fictional, it was also not—as the common discourse on GDR suicides would imply—politically motivated. It was not a protest against communism. On the contrary, Pony is a proponent of communism. For example, she serves as FDJ secretary at school, supports Angela Davis, wants to send aid to North Vietnam, and celebrates the birthday of Friedrich Engels. Instead, her suicide—to the extent that it can be understood at all—stemmed from a complex combination of some psychiatric condition, medical malpractice, a problematic amorous relationship, rejection from acting school, and other factors. As Udo Grashoff points out, Muthesius's primary intention seems to be to find out whether her daughter's suicide might have been preventable.[29] However, *Flucht in die Wolken* is neither a standard historical biography nor a psychiatric case study. It is not merely concerned with listing facts in chronological order. Instead, it is a highly literary work of mostly non-fiction and includes an astonishing wealth of allusions to other texts. It is, on the one hand, a document that records the ways in which Pony and Muthesius struggle with Pony's mental health issues in the context of the GDR from 1966 until Pony's death in 1971,[30] and, on the other hand, a highly mediated artistic work that employs works of literature among other things both in the struggle toward expression and in the process of healing. Indeed, polyphonic literary allusions in *Flucht in die Wolken* are propelled by the fact that both Pony and Muthesius struggle to understand.

As Christine Cosentino wrote in a review of *Flucht in die Wolken*, "Das Buch ist umfangreich"[31] (The book is comprehensive). Forty-nine of the book's fifty-one chapters begin with an epigraph (the two that do not being the prologue and the afterword), and those quotations are employed more or less without concern for the literary heritage of the GDR as propagated by the cultural functionaries of the SED. Literary histories constructed in the GDR presumably influenced the selection of the epigraphs indirectly, as the GDR program of literary heritage must to some extent have affected which texts Muthesius had been able to read. However, the selections seem rather inconsistent and apolitical. There can be no doubt, however, that Muthesius was well read. She had an affinity for French literature, poetry, and modernism, judging by the choice of epigraphs. However, she was also familiar with works sanctioned as GDR literary heritage and GDR writers contemporary with her. Of the forty-nine epigraphs, eleven are from Charles Baudelaire, six from Arthur Rimbaud, four from Friedrich Hölderlin, four from Heinrich Heine, four from Friedrich Schiller, three from Johann Wolfgang von Goethe, two from Sully Prudhomme, and one each from Georges Rodenbach, Charles Vildrac, Andreas Reimann, Agostinho Neto, Paul Eluard, Joochen Laabs, Bertolt Brecht, Henri Michaux, Hans Thyriot, Hermann Hesse, Karl Marx, Stephan Hermlin, Alexander Pushkin, Emile Verhaeren, and Rainer Maria Rilke. However, the epigraphs—paratexts in Genette's taxonomy—are not the only allusions to literature and philosophy in the text. Within the body of the text there are also allusions to thinkers and writers such as Marx, Nietzsche, Freud, Goethe, Tolstoy, Brecht, Anne Frank, Gerhart Hauptmann, Carl Jung, Pavlov, Alexander Mitscherlich, Vladimir Levi (a Soviet psychologist), Richard d'Ambrosio (a psychotherapist who wrote a book called *No Language but a Cry* about one of his patients, an abused child who literally never spoke), and others. Muthesius does not seem to discriminate; she looks to poetry and prose, modernism and realism, philosophy and psychology, Marxism and psychoanalysis: whatever might help her understand Pony's situation better. Indeed, these myriad allusions neither maintain nor destroy any programmatic literary history. However, as in *Hamletmaschine*, there are so many references to so many different kinds of hypotexts that it is difficult to locate the boundaries of Pony's and Muthesius's texts.

Similarly, the notion of authorship of *Flucht in die Wolken* is problematic. On the one hand, it is similar to Goethe's *Die Leiden des jungen Werther* or Plenzdorf's *Die neuen Leiden des jungen W.* or Werner Heiduczek's *Tod am Meer* in that it consists of a collection of edited documents with some commentary by the editor. On the other hand, however, *Flucht in die Wolken* constantly lays bare the extent to which those documents and the commentary are always intermingling. In the texts by Goethe, Plenzdorf, and Heiduczek just mentioned (and dealt with earlier in this book), the editor sets up the editorial situation, explaining a limited number of documents, and then mostly stays out of the way to allow the documents to tell the story. In *Flucht in die Wolken*, however, Muthesius intervenes frequently, so much so that the book tells her story nearly as much as it tells Pony's story. Moreover, the range of documents far exceeds that in those works by Goethe, Plenzdorf, and Heiduczek. They include (besides the quotations and allusions to famous thinkers) letters, poems, songs, report cards, drawings, paintings, photographs, captions for those visual materials, handwritten notes, collages, mind maps, fragments of plays, postcards, marginalia, and math problems, for example. Needless to say, Pony was extremely creative (as was her mother) and created a large amount of literary and visual art. On top of that, Muthesius adds a level of creative editing. Pony and Muthesius, it seems, share authorship of the book. And their writing mostly shares the same authorial motive: the will to understand.

Pony's mother pursues a strained hermeneutic to make sense of Pony's situation, both after the suicide and while Pony is still alive but dealing with psychological issues. The mother is desperate to find some source that explains Pony's behavior. "Da ich selbst keine Erklärungen für all das finden konnte, suchte ich danach in der Fachliteratur"[32] (Since I couldn't find any explanation for all of that on my own, I searched in the scholarly literature). In this quotation, Pony's mother is talking specifically about psychological literature. However, the statement also describes her general mode of operation regarding a wide range of texts, including poetry, philosophy, Pony's diaries, Pony's paintings, and so on. As she feels increasingly hopeless, well before Pony's death, she asks herself what she could possibly do. Then she declares: "Ich gehe in die Staatsbibliothek" (331; I go to the Berlin State Library.) And later she writes: "Ich weiß nicht mehr, was und wem ich glauben soll. Viel habe ich zu den Problemen in den Bibliotheken gelesen." (I don't know any more what or whom I should believe. I've read much in the libraries about those problems.)[33] Because she cannot understand what happened to Pony—indeed, because it may not be understandable—she tries to make sense of it largely by reading.

Of all the many texts that Pony's mother reads, many of which contradict one another, she revisits the works of one author in particular and finds some solace in that author: Sigmund Freud. Freud's texts are largely the only ones besides those created by Pony that offer her any satisfactory answers. "Eigentlich finde ich das, was mir weiterhelfen, mir beängstigende Verhaltensweisen erklären kann, immer wieder bei Freud, ohne daß ich auf ihn stoßen will" (331–32; Actually, again and again I find something that helps me and explains the alarming behavior to me in Freud without even meaning to look to him). Indeed, she begins to seem obsessed with Freud. She makes her husband Georg put down his Rosa Luxemburg volume and start rereading Freud (250). While her reading of Freud at times seems to be a wildly speculative forced application to Pony's situation, it is Freud's invitation to speculation, his substratum hermeneutics, that she finds helpful. She understands that her attempts to understand are speculation. "Wenn ich Psychoanalyse sage, bekomme ich zur Antwort: 'Ist doch alles nur Spekulation!'" (311; Whenever I say the word psychoanalysis, people say: "But that's all just speculation"). She resists the belittling of such methods. She wants to understand her daughter's situation in human terms. Of Pavlovian psychology, she retorts: "Mein Kind ist kein Hund" (332; My child is not a dog). Freudian analysis is able to offer her more insight into her daughter's condition because, among other reasons, it invites interpretation. In the words of Michel Foucault, Freud—along with Marx and Nietzsche—puts thinkers "into the presence of a new possibility of interpretation," allowing for "the possibility of a hermeneutic."[34]

Just as Muthesius attempts to understand the case of Pony, Pony also seeks answers about her own life story and mental health issues. Pony even reads her own diary entries, just as her mother later does, in order to try to understand what is happening to her and to try to discover at what point in began to happen. She notes herself that she has a "Tagebuchlese-Komplex" (187–88; diary-reading complex). She writes in a letter to her boyfriend that she needs something constant in her life "da sie alles anzweifelt, außer dem Zweifel" (187; as she doubts everything except doubt), and she promises him that her next letter will involve more "Ponyanalyse" (187; analysis of Pony). Such analysis is ongoing for Pony. As Muthesius writes: "Sie kramt in ihren alten Tagebüchern und Schulheften, um sich mit früher zu vergleichen" (188–89; She rummages through her old diaries and school notebooks, in order to compare herself to her earlier self). Some of those documents are included in the volume, and the reader gets to see both Pony and Muthesius analyze them. Further, Pony keeps writing and analyzing beyond her old papers. As Muthesius tells us: "Sie philosophiert: Auf vielerlei Zetteln analysiert sie ihren Zustand, mal biochemisch, mal physikalisch-kybernetisch, aber immer mit Humor" (442; she philosophizes: she analyses her condition on all kinds of scraps of paper, sometimes biochemically, sometimes physically-cybernetically, but always with humor). However, Pony's investigation does not end there. She also has a faith in literature.

Just as Pony's mother reads broadly to understand Pony's situation, Pony—while still alive—does much the same thing. She is a voracious reader. She writes of her earlier self: "Besonders gern habe ich mich vor Muttis Bücherregal herumgedrückt" (190; I especially liked to hang around mommy's bookshelf). That interest in books never faded. In order to prepare for an audition for acting school, she studies *The Diary of Anne Frank* and interprets many of the passages as relevant to her own situation, and she does much the same with Gerhart Hauptmann's play *Rose Bernd*. However, the author Pony returns to most often is Bertolt Brecht, the literary dialectician whose works she compares to the Bible (185). She sings Brecht/Weill songs such as the "Bilbao Song." She wants to organize a Brecht Evening at the local youth club. As FDJ secretary, she wants to organize a trip for her class to the Berliner Ensemble to see a production of Brecht's *Mann ist Mann* (Man Equals Man). She writes that she is "verbrechtet" (185; Brechtified).

Brecht's sonnet "Lob des Kommunismus" (In Praise of Communism) may be—perhaps alongside *The Diary of Anne Frank*—the most important text that Pony reads in *Flucht in die Wolken*. She recites it as part of her audition for acting school, having chosen it herself, despite her mother's warning that other Brecht poems might make a better impression on the committee (170). The poem describes the self-evident appeal of communism in the first twelve lines, and then in the final couplet—in the spirit of a Shakespearean sonnet—counters that communism is also difficult to implement: "Er ist das Einfache / Das schwer zu machen ist"

(It's something simple / That's difficult to do).[35] That final couplet is prophetic for Pony. In describing Pony's preparation for her audition, her mother recalls how Pony compared the poem to *The Diary of Anne Frank*. For Pony, the phrase "Das Ende der Tollheit" (the end of madness) is reminiscent of Anne Frank's hope that "Vielleicht macht die Welt auch eine Art Entwicklung durch!" (174; Perhaps the world will also experience a kind of progress!). Pony, like Anne Frank, wants the world to become a better place. Unfortunately, as the Brecht poem indicates, such a development is difficult. If we replace the word "communism" with "love" or "health" or "happiness," it would also aptly describe Pony's situation in the world. Things that she thinks ought to be simple remain nonetheless out of her reach. Further, the word "Tollheit" (madness) suggests a relevance to Pony's struggle with her condition, even without needing to insert a word such as "health" in the text. Like the speaker of the poem, Pony wants her condition to end. The poem is also relevant to the work of literary and philosophical allusions in the book, because it is a poem about the incomprehensible. The poem itself questions—yet cannot explain—the state of human existence. Like Pony and her mother, the speaker of the poem seeks an answer to a riddle and cannot find it.

Both Müller's *Hamletmaschine* and Muthesius's *Flucht in die Wolken* rely on a chaotic constellation of literary and philosophical allusions, pushing against the boundaries of any theory of intertextuality or transtextuality. Both works also center around the theme of suicide and self-destruction. Whereas *Flucht in die Wolken* explores many texts to try to understand and explain what led to Pony's suicide, *Hamletmaschine* uses the theme of suicide to problematize transtextuality and highlight the self-destructiveness inherent in any programmatic construction of literary heritage. Although these two modes of alluding to contradictory texts seem rather different, the two works highlight both the therapeutic potential of allusion and the impossibility of any absolute construction of literary lineage.

While the self-destruction of literary heritage seems to have run its course with these two works, this story is not over yet. While *Hamletmaschine* destabilized Shakespeare reception in the GDR, it was not the final literary work in the GDR to transform Shakespeare's *Hamlet*. And while *Flucht in die Wolken* examines the powerful constellation of suicide, memory, and allusion, it was not the final work in the GDR to show how suicide instigates memory. Christoph Hein's *Horns Ende* ties all these issues together.

6: Specters of Suicide: Christoph Hein's *Horns Ende*

WHY MIGHT A HISTORIAN KILL HIMSELF? And what would his ghost tell us? These questions are at the core of Christoph Hein's *Horns Ende*. In 1985, fourteen years after Honecker's "No Taboos" speech, and following two years of struggle with the censors, Christoph Hein's second major prose work appeared. *Horns Ende* deals with difficult issues of history and memory, asking, for example, what became of the Nazis who previously dwelt in the territory that became East Germany, and evoking memories of Stalinist show trials in the GDR in the 1950s. The presence of such issues in the novel delayed its publication. Aufbau and Luchterhand publishers, the former in the East, the latter in the West, had worked out a deal to publish the novel in East and West simultaneously.[1] This is the same deal negotiated between the same two publishers that led to the publication of Wolf's *Kein Ort. Nirgends* in 1979. The Ministry of Culture, however, temporarily inhibited publication. Klaus Selbig, one of three censors who screened the novel, wrote a letter to Klaus Höpcke, the Minister of Culture from 1973 until 1989, dated May 10, 1984, in which he provided the following reason, among others, for halting publication of the book: "The impression remains that the story carries over into the present as a history of human cruelty. To be sure, the dialogues which precede the individual chapters and the concluding dialogue provide a kind of contrapunkt, but it requires an extremely thorough reading and a great deal of good will not to interpret this novel in the aforementioned sense."[2] The censors were correct in noting that the novel presents a "history of human cruelty," part of which "carries over into the present," that is, into the GDR. They were mistaken, however, in their reading of the dialogues between chapters, which include the posthumous voice of Horn, as a counterpoint to that history. Their misreading of those dialogues is further evident in the fact that they persuaded Hein to change the original title, *Horn*, to the title under which the work was later published, *Horns Ende*, because they thought that emphasizing Horn's death would demonstrate a disconnect between the histories of fascism and Stalinism, on the one hand, and the contemporary situation in the GDR, on the other. Their mistake lies in the fact that they read the ghost of Horn as belonging entirely to the past. His haunting relies on a transtextual borrowing from Shakespeare's *Hamlet*, and has everything to do with the GDR present.

History and memory are vital to the novel, and scholars have often read the novel in those terms, but they struggle to pinpoint precisely the subversive nature of those elements in the novel. The key to reading it in terms of subversive memory are found in the ghost's dialogues with the character Thomas. These ghostly dialogues resemble the communication between the ghost of Hamlet's father and Hamlet in Shakespeare's play. The hypertextual relationship between Hein's *Horns Ende* and Shakespeare's *Hamlet*, furthermore, is complex. It is, in part, one of proximation, that transformation that occurs when the hypertext juxtaposes the hypotext with a contemporary setting. It is also prosafication, that transformation that occurs when the narrative of a dramatic text is portrayed in prose. The proximation in *Horns Ende* is not as obvious as that in Plenzdorf's *Die neuen Leiden des jungen W.* It does not juxtapose *Hamlet* with crass youth culture. Nor does it present *Hamlet* in a way that appears to parody it. Instead, it utilizes a type of haunting that is, upon examination, remarkably similar to the haunting that occurs in *Hamlet*. It employs such haunting as subversive memory.

Memory and History

Horns Ende consists of five characters' accounts of the time surrounding Horn's suicide in the 1950s in the GDR. In addition to the disjointed and interspersed narrative accounts, there is a dialogue in eight sections (one for each chapter) between Thomas and the long-dead Horn, who demands that Thomas not forget the long-past events. The titular character, Horn, who is not one of the narrators, except in the dialogue, is the director of the museum in Bad Guldenberg, the small town where the novel is set. Horn is reprimanded for creating a museum display that some of the authorities find to be opposed to the project of socialism. Without the consent of the mayor, several governmental figures investigate Horn and find out that his sister has fled to West Germany. Neither the museum display nor any punishment is described in detail. It is made clear, however, that Horn is being threatened by legal and social measures. Eventually Horn hangs himself. His body is found by Paul, a mischievous adolescent who shows the hanging body to his friend, Thomas, one of the narrators and characters whom Horn's ghost later haunts. Again, this haunting, and its similarity to the haunting in Shakespeare's *Hamlet*, is key for my reading of the novel.

Many critics who have written about *Horns Ende* examine it, at least in part, by describing the ways in which different characters in the novel see history differently. Reading the novel in this way is no doubt worthwhile, as history and memory are certainly key elements in the novel. Hein himself has made this point repeatedly.[3] Important as history and memory are in *Horns Ende*, the point has been, if not overstated, stated too often without leading anywhere new. The main two thrusts of such criticism are first, that different characters in the novel represent different philosophies of history and memory, and second, that Walter Benjamin's influence upon Christoph Hein can be seen in the novel, especially through the character Horn.

It may be that Bernd Fischer first set up this paradigm of criticism on *Horns Ende* in the chapter on this novel when he writes, "Die Schwierigkeiten, die die vielstimmigen Erzählinstanzen des Romans mit dieser Nachkriegsgeschichte einer Kleinstadt haben und vermitteln, werfen zugleich fundamentale Fragen nach der Möglichkeit von Geschichte und Geschichtsschreibung"[4] (The difficulties that the polyphonous narrative instances of the novel have with this postwar, small-town story also posit fundamental questions about the possibility of history and the writing of history). Fischer's taxonomy of narrators in the novel vis-à-vis the writing of history consists of three categories.[5] The first of these three categories groups together the two narrators who are consciously writing some form of history, Spodeck and Kruschkatz. Fischer's second category consists of the characters who narrate without being conscious of historical theory, yet are psychologically stable, Gertrude Fischlinger and Thomas. The third category is reserved for Marlene Gohl, who has a serious mental illness. Marlene's narration, Fischer argues, represents irrational, romantic memory. At the end of the chapter Fischer comes to the character of Horn, who is not a narrator, although he may be the main character. For Horn, Fischer emphasizes, history is all-important. On this point Fischer is correct. However, Horn has another relationship to history that Fischer has overlooked, namely the way in which Horn's ghost deals with history.

Many critics also see Horn's view of history as being similar to that of Walter Benjamin, a figure who has deeply influenced Christoph Hein. Bernd Fischer and Joachim Lehmann especially emphasize the parallels between Horn's view of history and that of Benjamin. Fischer, between his chapters on *Horns Ende* and *Passage*, writes an excursion to Walter Benjamin in which he attempts to explain why Benjamin is important for Hein's writings, especially for *Horns Ende*. Fischer points to selections from Benjamin's *Passagenwerk* as well as from his "Über den Begriff der Geschichte." He argues that *Horns Ende* follows at least some of Benjamin's ideas about the writing of history, in that it emphasizes the dangers of deterministic philosophies of history and highlights the losers of history, that is, the victims of deterministic philosophies of history. These two branches of Benjamin's influence on *Horns Ende*, then, are actually two sides of the same coin. A third branch of influence that Fischer sees is Benjamin's inversion of Marx's metaphor of revolutions as the locomotives of history into revolutions being the emergency brakes of history. Fischer's point here is that the narrators in *Horns Ende* imply that nothing about Bad Guldenberg, if not the GDR as a whole, performed that emergency-brake function, just as Benjamin lamented the lack of any emergency brake in the nineteenth and early twentieth century. Yet a fourth branch of influence is Benjamin's insistence that history, for the historical materialist, is best seen as a snapshot, a flicker of light. It is through these snapshots, as Fischer reads Benjamin, that redemption becomes a possibility for perceivers of history, such as the adult Thomas in *Horns Ende*. Horn's suicide, Fischer correctly points out, is a powerful example of such a snapshot of history. The ghost of Horn, however, also insists that the past is persistently relevant for the present. Such haunting may be seen as the core of Benjamin's project.

Along these lines, Joachim Lehmann points out four related phenomena that he sees in *Horns Ende* and other works by Hein: first, the portrayal of a major political event that plays a role in an anecdote about a minor figure; second, the presence of the dead in the present; third, the leap of the past into the present through memory; and fourth, the compulsion of the living to remember the dead.[6] Lehmann goes on to place Hein's prose under the rubric of Benjamin's concept of the historical materialist. To do so, he compares Benjamin's notion of the chronicler with that of Hein. Lehmann cites Benjamin's statement about the chronicler from "Über den Begriff der Geschichte," in which Benjamin writes that the chronicler documents events without distinguishing between those that are important and those that are unimportant, so that readers of the chronicles may use any moment of history as a point of redemption. Hein, Lehmann argues, works in this vein. To back up this claim in the case of *Horns Ende*, Lehmann—in a move similar to that of Fischer—argues that Marlene, with her mental handicap, comes closer to the "Benjamin/Hornschen Wahrheit" (Benjaminian/Hornian truth) than other narrators.[7] Like Fischer, Lehmann also claims, correctly, that Horn's suicide functions as a catalyst for the other narrators to remember Bad Guldenberg in the 1950s.

Memory and history are no doubt important issues in the novel. Furthermore, Benjamin's influence on Hein is, indeed, present in the novel, and Benjamin-informed approaches to *Horns Ende* are useful in understanding the novel. However, such criticism—useful and accurate as it is—misses two key points that are related to each other as well as to memory and history: the ghost and the space of Bad Guldenberg. Horn's ghost has been largely ignored and needs to be examined in order to understand fully the way that history and memory function in the novel, as well as the degree to which the novel is subversive. Reading the space of Bad Guldenberg in *Horns Ende* then further demonstrates just how subversive haunting is in the novel.

Further, the haunting in *Horns Ende* is propelled by Horn's suicide, and the nature of that fictional suicide needs to be examined as well. Michael Douglas Schleihauf Zimmermann argues, accurately but imprecisely, that Horn's suicide is a matter of egression.[8] That is, Horn has little human contact, as he is alienated and rejected by GDR society. Zimmermann also sweeps Horn's suicide into Durkheim's broad category of egoistic suicide, a suspicious categorization, since—although egoistic suicides involve a low degree of integration of the individual into society—egoistic suicides have no moral implications, that is, the individual does not kill himself for a cause.[9] Horn carries an enormous moral burden. He is fighting for a cause. Although his suicide may arguably fit better into the category of egoistic suicides than into any of the other three of Durkheim's categories, it is far from a perfect fit, and there is no reason to squeeze his suicide into one of Durkheim's categories. Zimmermann's main point, however, is the lack of integration, which makes up half of the criteria for egoistic suicides. This point is accurate, but not entirely precise. Zimmermann's attempt to define Horn's suicide in terms of Durkheim's categories, furthermore, causes him to forget that the fictional suicide is a narrative event with narrative consequences. Horn's suicide leads to subversive memory through haunting.

The Ghost of Horn

Horn's ghost is remarkably similar to that of Hamlet's father in Shakespeare's *Hamlet*. Christoph Hein, too, has been influenced by *Hamlet*. The transtextual role of Shakespeare's play in Hein's novel, however, has yet to be extrapolated. A reading of *Horns Ende* that is informed by *Hamlet* adds to scholarship on memory in the novel by emphasizing the role of the ghost in both works. In other words, it needs to be read with *Hamlet* in mind because of the nature of the man, and later ghost, around whom the novel centers. "Erinnere dich" (remember), the ghost of historian and museum director Horn commands Thomas, the boy who sees Horn's body, in the first two words of the novel. These are nearly the same words that the ghost of Hamlet's father utters to his son: "Remember me."[10] What remains to be clarified, however, is the nature of such memory.

Stephen Greenblatt comes close to answering this question in *Hamlet in Purgatory*: "*Prosopopoeia*—personification, the making of what is absent to speak—is the rhetorical device behind all haunting."[11] That is, the ghost not only commands one to remember but is itself (unorthodox) memory personified. Indeed, *Horns Ende* has long been read as a text about memory in the GDR. However, a reading of the novel with *Hamlet* in mind allows for a more thorough connection among memory, communication, and the ghost in *Horns Ende*. Who is remembering? What is being remembered? Most importantly, what role does the ghost play in the remembering? My reading of the novel sees Horn's ghost as a vessel of subversive, intergenerational memory, a way of disturbing, not dissimilar to that of the ghost of Hamlet's father. For that reason, I pay particular attention to the passages in which the ghost speaks. In other words, the main question of this chapter is: What does the posthumous voice of a historian who killed himself in the 1950s in the GDR have to say? Examining the ghost's speech by drawing on theories of spectrality and space, this chapter hands Horn's ghost an interpretive open mic and comes to the conclusion that the historian's haunting loosens the retracting, claustrophobic, politico-cultural space of the GDR represented largely by the town of Bad Guldenberg.

The ghost of Hamlet's father is a natural model for such haunting in the context of East Germany. Shakespeare was received positively in the GDR, and productions of his plays were often staged there.[12] For Georg Lukács, Shakespeare was a revered model for theater. He particularly praised the historicism of that playwright's dramas.[13] That Shakespeare ought to be received positively is also a rare point on which Lukács and Brecht agreed. They disagreed, however, on how to receive him. In 1951, for example, Brecht staged a production of *Coriolanus*[14] and was lambasted for his modernization of the piece.[15] Following Brecht, Heiner Müller staged a version of *Macbeth* in 1972 that likewise differed from Lukács's historicist Shakespeare.[16]

Lukács was especially fond of *Hamlet*, and there were ample productions of the play in the GDR. Lukács saw in that play an example of how various characters can reveal comprehensive worldviews. Hamlet's contrast with Laertes, Horatio, and Fortinbras, Lukács contends, demonstrates the historical typicality of Hamlet.[17] Lukács, however, does not appear ever to mention the ghost of Hamlet's father. While Lukács is interested in the historicism of the play, the ghost deals with history quite differently. Writers such as Christoph Hein and Heiner Müller, however, confront the ghost in ways that Lukács never did.

There is no doubt that Shakespeare is also an important figure for Hein. He says as much himself in an interview with Klaus Hammer in the context of defining his notion of chronicling: "Chronist ist für mich ein Homer wie ein Shakespeare wie ein Kafka"[18] (For me, a chronicler is a Homer or a Shakespeare or a Kafka). In addition to this explicit statement of the influence of Shakespeare on Hein, there are at least two instances where Hein declares the influence specifically of *Hamlet* on his own thought. In his 1978 essay, "Hamlet und der Parteisekretär," Hein implicitly points toward *Hamlet*, in order to argue that theater should do two things: examine the past for the sake of understanding the present (that is, using twelfth-century Denmark to comment on England around 1600) and make the private public (as in the play within the play, "The Mousetrap").[19] The importance of *Hamlet* for Christoph Hein, however, is again evident in his 1989 essay "Die Zeit, die nicht vergehen kann oder Das Dilemma des Chronisten:

Gedanken zum Historikerstreit anlässlich zweier deutscher vierzigster Jahrestage," in which Hein recalls that the German national character, in a previous century, was summed up by the statement: "Deutschland ist Hamlet"[20] (Germany is Hamlet). Hein reminds his audience of some of the similarities: both are young, philosophically minded, lonely, misunderstood, morbid, and so forth. Although Hein concurs that no one would use the image of Hamlet to describe the Germany of 1989 and goes on to explore other possibilities from Western literature, the image of Hamlet implicitly reemerges at the end of the essay, as Hein insists that history will not simply disappear. In short, Hein argues that, despite (or perhaps even because of) attempts at normalization, German history will continue to haunt the German people. These two essays, together with the fact that Hein learned much about theater under the direction of Benno Besson and was an accomplished playwright a decade before he wrote *Horns Ende*, indicates at the very least that Hein was familiar with *Hamlet* and was aware of some uses of the image of Hamlet.

There is a long tradition of ghosts in Western literature. In antiquity, ghosts were associated with the underworld: one need only to think of Seneca's *Thyestes*.[21] There are many ghosts in renaissance drama, especially in Shakespeare. In the nineteenth century, there are ghosts in Dickens's novels. Modernist ghosts abound in works by authors such as Beckett and Joyce.[22] Later, there are postcolonial ghosts in the works of authors such as Toni Morrison and Luisa Valenzuela.[23] But what is a ghost? And how have ghosts evolved over time?

One of the sharpest caesuras in the lineage of ghosts in Western literature comes with the ghost of Hamlet's father in *Hamlet* (1601). Before Shakespeare's *Hamlet*, ghosts tended to "let loose a high-pitched blood-curdling shriek" and have a "bloody appearance" and a "slightly hysterical diction."[24] In other words, pre-*Hamlet* Western ghosts were intended to startle in a physical sense and to seek revenge. There is relatively little change in the role of ghosts from Ancient Greece and Rome to Shakespeare's 1597 play *Richard III*. E. Pearlman elaborates on the shift in Shakespeare's ghosts from the "old-style ghosts" in *Richard III* through the ghost of Caesar in the 1599 play *Julius Caesar* (which see some change in the form of Brutus's brooding and Anthony's attempt to make amends for Caesar's death) to the ghost of Hamlet's father, the nature of which, Pearlman indicates, the theatergoing Londoner at the time could not have predicted.[25] The ghosts that visit Richard III are the ghosts of those he has murdered, and they come to him to curse him with revenge. The ghost of Hamlet's father—in Shakespeare's 1601 version of the play—does not insist upon revenge but rather on remembrance. It may be argued, then, that the ghost of Hamlet's father is the first ghost to haunt, in Avery Gordon's sense of giving a voice to the voiceless, a topic to which we must return later.[26]

Stephen Greenblatt shines much light on *Hamlet* as well as on the history of European ghostdom in his monograph *Hamlet in Purgatory*. He examines the history of the theological notion of purgatory, in order to understand better the nature of the ghost of Hamlet's father. He argues that the (largely medieval) Catholic doctrine of purgatory, a place in between heaven and hell where souls may be sent after corporeal death in order to clear away their sins through finite—if lengthy—punishment, collapses during the Renaissance into the notion of the ghost who returns to Earth to right a wrong. Protestants tended to view ghosts either as frauds or as demons, a view that often led them to deride or condemn the notion of ghosts.[27] Shakespeare, Greenblatt ultimately argues, catholicizes the Ur-*Hamlet*, in which the ghost screeches for revenge (which is in line with both the ancient, underworld ghosts and the Protestant, demonized ghosts), by staging the ghost of Hamlet's father as a purgatorial ghost (the ghost himself states that he has come from purgatory)[28] in the form of a "deep psychic disturbance."[29] In other words, the main command that the ghost of Hamlet's father gives to Hamlet—rather than startling him or demanding revenge—is that he remember. Greenblatt turns to a historical document that indicates, to the surprise of many, that Shakespeare's father, if not Shakespeare himself, had been a closet Catholic, and this in a time and place in which being Catholic was illegal.

Although the topic of religion in Elizabethan England is quite distant from the GDR, Greenblatt's thesis has much to do with *Horns Ende*. It would indubitably be a dubious argument—as well as a useless one—to argue that Christoph Hein is Catholic. In fact, he is the son of a Lutheran minister and has stated in an interview that he sees himself as a spiritually inclined pantheist.[30] However, Greenblatt's emphasis on the role of the ghost as a purgatorial "deep psychic disturbance" is quite important for understanding the nature of Horn's ghost. A reading of Horn's ghost that is informed by Greenblatt's reading of the ghost of Hamlet's father illuminates the nature of haunting in *Horns Ende*, which is otherwise not readily apparent.

Some critics of *Horns Ende* have struggled to define the nature of Horn's posthumous voice. Christl Kiewitz compares it to the resurrected Christ. David Clarke calls the voice "what may be Horn's ghost, or perhaps an invention of Thomas's own imagination."[31] Phillip McKnight more precisely describes it as "an apparition which continually admonishes and exhorts him to remember what had happened—even to remember, if he can, some things which he hadn't seen."[32] Bernd Fischer points out how Gertrude, somewhat superstitiously, opens the windows and burns incense in Horn's room in order to keep out "schlechte Geister"[33] (evil spirits). David Robinson gets even closer to the matter, writing that Thomas "is prodded into remembering by the ghostly exhortations of Horn" and that Thomas is "haunted by the ghost of memory."[34] Finally,

Robinson calls the apparition "Horn's ghost" and later labels the dialogues between the dead Horn and the adult Thomas the "the ghost prologues."[35] Furthermore, Robinson insists—and rightly so—upon the importance of Horn's ghost's command that Thomas remember. It is, indeed, this point that defines the ghost. David Clarke's concern that the ghost is a figment of Thomas's imagination—that Thomas does not actually see the ghost—is beside the point. In other words, Clarke fails to acknowledge fully the nature of literary ghosts. Theatrical and cinematic ghosts are often transparent or silhouette-like, not only for an uncanny effect but because the director wants to make the point that ghosts are not (entirely) visual figures.[36] Perhaps the most famous literary ghost ever, the ghost of Hamlet's father, for example, cannot be seen by Gertrude. That is, ghosts *are* figments of the imagination. Or more precisely—and this is the thrust of Alice Rayner's argument—ghosts exist, but they exist in a way that leads one to think that they are imaginary. In short, ghosts are not clearly visible, corporeal entities.

Joachim Lehmann mentions in passing the possibility of a comparison between the ghost of Horn and that of Hamlet's father.[37] Lehmann, however, mentions several possibilities for the nature of Horn's posthumous voice and does not elaborate on the comparison with the ghost of Hamlet's father. This comparison, however, allows for a reading of the novel that pinpoints its subversive nature. A return to Lehmann's essay will prove relevant later in the explication of the relationship between ghosts and chronicling. First, however, it is necessary to follow up on a reading of Horn's ghost through the lens of Greenblatt's reading of the ghost of Hamlet's father.

The question here is this: Is Horn's ghost a "deep psychic disturbance" for Thomas? The answer lies in the conversation between Thomas and the ghost. Not only does the ghost command Thomas to remember: "Erinnere dich."[38] Thomas does not want to remember, but the ghost insists: "Du mußt dich erinnern . . . Du kannst es nicht vergessen haben . . . Alles hast du gesehen" (5; You must remember . . . You cannot have forgotten it . . . You saw everything). The ghost personifies this unremitting memory. Thomas attempts to repress the memory, but it will not go away. This struggle between wanting to forget and being forced to remember repeats itself. Again, the ghost commands: "Erinnere dich" (31). And again Thomas attempts to repress the memory: "Ich weiss es nicht mehr" (31; I can't remember). But the ghost does not let up: "Du kannst es nicht vergessen haben. Du mußt dich erinnern" (31; You can't have forgotten it. You must remember). And again: "Streng dich an. Du hast viel gesehen. Mehr als du weißt . . . Dein Gedächtnis hat alles festgehalten . . . Was war? Sprich!" (145; Try really hard. You saw a lot, more than you know . . . Your memory held onto everything . . . What happened? Speak!). The exclamation point demonstrates the ghost's aggressive insistence. The aggressive punctuation continues, as does the ghost's insistent command: "Ach, was du verstehst! Denk nicht nach. Erinnere dich. . . . Erzähl! Was war dann?" (217; Oh, what you understand! Don't think about it. Remember . . . Tell! What happened?). Even as Thomas has begun to remember and is growing tired, the ghost chants that Thomas should keep remembering. "Erinnere dich. . . . Weiter, Junge. Weiter. Weiter. Du mußt dich erinnern" (249; Remember . . . Keep going, boy. More. More. You must remember). The memory of Horn and the events surrounding Horn's death, all personified by the ghost of Horn, cannot be repressed. It emerges again and again, a "deep psychic disturbance" indeed.

Not only is the emergence of Horn's ghost unremitting; it also frightens Thomas, as Horn's hanging corpse had already frightened him before. "Sie haben mich erschreckt. Damals als ich Sie fand . . . wie Sie gestorben sind . . . Sie waren völlig verändert. Ihre Zunge, Ihre Lippen. . . ." (59; You scared me back then when I found you . . . how you died . . . you were completely changed. Your tongue, your lips. . . .) Even before Horn's death Thomas is afraid of him. "Ich hatte Angst vor Ihnen . . . Sie waren mir unheimlich. Ich verstand so wenig und fürchtete mich." (31; I was afraid of you . . . You freaked me out. I understood so little and was afraid.) Thomas recalls the extent to which the hanging corpse had disturbed him.

> Dann sah ich zu dem Toten hoch. Er sah mich mit offenen Augen an, und ich trat so schnell zur Seite, daß ich über die eigenen Füße stolperte.
> Es war tatsächlich Herr Horn, wenn ich ihn auch kaum wiedererkannte. Die Augen waren hervorgetreten, und die Zunge quoll breit und verfärbt aus dem Mund. Ich blickte zu Paul, um den Toten nicht ansehen zu müssen. (252)
>
> [Then I looked up at the dead body. He looked at me with open eyes, and I moved to the side so quickly that I tripped over my own feet.
> It really was Mr. Horn, even if I hardly recognized him. The eyes were bulged out, and the tongue stuck out of the mouth, wide and discolored. I looked over at Paul, so that I didn't have to look at the corpse anymore].

At his first sight of the corpse, Thomas is startled. Then the gore of the corpse overwhelms him. He looks away, but he will not forget Horn and his corpse. For the adult Thomas, the memory of the living Horn is just as disturbing as the hanging corpse of Horn. Thomas tells Horn's ghost: "Sie quälen mich" (99; You are torturing me). But Horn's ghost gets to the crux of haunting as a "deep psychic disturbance" when he replies: "Nicht ich bin es, der dich quält. Du bist es, du selbst" (99; I'm not the one who's torturing you. You're doing it to yourself). Thus Horn's ghost is the personification of Thomas's unremitting, deeply disturbing memory of Horn.

Greenblatt's history of purgatory provides not only an approach to *Hamlet*, but also a term for a space where it is possible to work through the past. The ghost of Hamlet's father reports that he is

> Doomed for a certain term to walk the night
> And for the day confined to fast in fires
> Till the foul crimes done in my days of nature
> Are burnt and purged away.[39]

When we have acknowledged the similarities between the ghost of Hamlet's father and that of Horn, it is possible to regard Horn as a figure from a secular purgatory. Furthermore, Horn's purgatory may even be less secularized than that of Hamlet's father, since, as David Clarke notes, the priest prays for Horn,[40] even though he is buried in the "ehemaligen Selbstmörderecke" (261; former suicide corner) where atheists (and, unofficially, suicides) are buried. Horn's haunting creates memory and instigates a working through of the past in a town that is symbolic for repression. Just as the ghost of Hamlet's father purgatorially returns to insist that Hamlet remember, Horn's haunting creates a space where critical, unorthodox remembering is possible. Furthermore, it creates the possibility—or rather the necessity—of giving the past relevance for the present. Thus it is possible to see the realm of Horn's ghost as purgatory. He must appear and command that Thomas remember until the crimes of Bad Guldenberg, like those of Hamlet's Denmark, are purged away.

Before, during, and after the *Wende* of 1989/1990, Hein has described himself as a "Chronist" (chronicler)—a writer who narrates, through literary and subjective means, what he sees without including explicit commentary on how the events at hand ought to be interpreted. In a 1986 interview with Krzysztof Jachimczack, when asked about his role as a chronicler, Hein explains "Ich bin nicht klüger als mein Publikum, ich kann keine Richtung angeben. Ich bin so unberaten wie mein Publikum. Ich kann ihm nur etwas über den Weg sagen, den wir gegangen sind." (I'm not any smarter than my audience. I can't provide any direction. I'm just as uninformed as my audience. I can only tell the readers something about the path that we've been down.)[41] This recounting of the path that has been walked down is what Hein means by chronicling. According to Hein, this method of writing is not new, but rather has existed for quite a while. In a March 1990 interview with Sigrid Löffler, Hein places himself within a tradition of literary chroniclers: "Ja ich verstehe mich als Chronist, der mit großer Genauigkeit aufzeichnet, was er gesehen hat. Damit stehe ich in einer großen Tradition von Johann Peter Hebel bis Kafka." (Yes. I see myself as a chronicler, who plots out, with great precision, what he has seen. As such, I stand in a great tradition stretching from Johann Peter Hebel to Kafka.)[42] In an interview a year later with Klaus Hammer, Hein, in further explaining what he means by the term "Chronist," traces this tradition back somewhat further:

> Ich benutze das Wort weniger im Sinne des Buchhalters als des wirklichen Chronikschreibers etwa des 14. und 15. Jahrhunderts, wo die kleinen Fürsten einen Schreiber hatten, der wirklich tagtäglich aufzeichnete, was da passierte, und dies mit ein bißchen Rückgrat machte. Er berichtete also auch über Dinge, die nicht berichtet werden sollten.
>
> [I use the word less in the sense of a bookkeeper and more in the sense of the chronicler of the fourteenth and fifteenth centuries, when the regional princes had a scribe, who really wrote down what happened on a day-to-day basis, and did it with a bit of backbone].[43]

These things about which the chronicler reports—things that are not meant to be mentioned—may also be seen as "ghostly matters."[44] It makes sense, then, that the figure in *Horns Ende* who forces both the reader and the narrators of the novel to focus on taboo matters in the GDR—suicide, the Stalinist show trials, the Nazi past—is a ghost. Without using the word ghost or highlighting the connection to *Hamlet*, Klaus Hammer describes this process of haunting in an early review of *Horns Ende*, as he writes:

> Der Tod Horns lastet auf der Seele der Kleinstädter wie ein Alpdruck. Er spült Vergangenes, Unbewältigtes hoch, weckt gegen alle subjektiven wie objektiven Widerstände die Erinnerung, das Ringen um Gedächtnis, um Seele und Vernunft, Bewußheit und Mündigkeit.[45]
>
> [Horn's death weighs on the soul of the small-town inhabitants like a nightmare. It stirs up past events that have not been dealt with. Working against all subjective and objective resistance, it awakens the memory, the struggle of remembering, the struggle for soul and reason, consciousness and enlightenment.]

This involuntary excavation of and wrestling with memory is what Horn subversively instigates.

The chronicling in the case of *Horns Ende* comes about not through a third-person narrator with overview focalization,[46] but rather through multiple first-person narrators with more or less internal focalization.[47] It may seem counter-intuitive that such a narrative situation allows for chronicling. However, the subjectivity of such narrators allows for the percolation of the "deep psychic disturbance" manifest in Horn's ghost. The multiplicity of narrators offsets the potential lopsidedness of a single subjective narrator. Rather than being a single narration that claims to be objective, the narrations in *Horns Ende* create a more or less objective view of Horn, and the focalization of the narrators allows for the addition of personal details to the narration. Consider Thomas's memory of seeing Horn's corpse.

> Wir gingen zu dem Toten. Neben ihm lag ein umgestürzter Hocker, der mit Farbflecken bedeckt war. Der Hocker war aus der Burg, ich kannte ihn, Herr Gohl hatte ihn manchmal bei der Arbeit benutzt . . . Ich dachte den ganzen Weg über an den beschmierten Hocker aus dem Museum. Ich hatte auch schon auf ihm gestanden, wenn ich Herrn Horn half, die tiefen Schautische einzurichten. (252–53)
>
> [We went over to the corpse. Next to it, there was a stool that was knocked over. The stool was covered in paint stains. It was from the museum in the castle. I knew it. Mr. Gohl had used it at work sometimes . . . The whole way over, I thought about the stained stool from the museum. I had stood on it as well, when I had helped Mr. Horn arrange the display cases, which were deep].

In Thomas's mind, the fact that he recognizes—and had himself even stood on—the stool with which Horn had used to hang himself, reinforces Thomas's connection to Horn and deepens the impression that seeing Horn's corpse makes on him. Such details, scattered throughout the narrations of the five narrators, combine to create a chronicling of Horn in Bad Guldenberg.

At this point, it may be useful to bring in another theorist of ghosts and haunting. Avery Gordon examines the sociological role of ghosts and haunting in two literary works: Luisa Valenzuela's *He Who Searches* and Toni Morrison's *Beloved*.[48] Gordon, however, achieves something well beyond the scope of these two novels. She defines ghostdom and haunting at the intersection of sociology and psychology. She gets there via literature, but she does so for the sake of sociology. Gordon has two main (interrelated) theses: First, "Sociology needs a way of grappling with what it represses, haunting, and psychoanalysis needs a way of grappling with what it represses, society."[49] This first thesis indicates the complex methodological contraption needed to deal with ghosts and haunting. It also indicates what traditional social-science disciplines cannot do alone and correctly highlights that literature can do something that the social sciences cannot. After all, ghosts, as Greenblatt points out, are a type of personification. That is, literature is capable of giving haunting a face, or, at least, a voice. Second, through the ghost, furthermore, literature can recognize (that is, imagine) and "reckon with haunting as a prerequisite for sensuous knowledge and . . . ponder the paradox of providing a hospitable memory for ghosts *out of a concern for justice*" [italics are Gordon's].[50] If haunting is, as Greenblatt insists, "the making of what is absent to speak,"[51] then it makes sense that someone like Gordon, who has "a concern for justice," will attempt to listen to the voice of the absent. Others have also provided images of the absent that speaks.

According to Robert Shandley, postwar (more specifically post-Holocaust) German representations of catastrophe morph, around the 1960s, into two different metaphors of catastrophic history in the present.[52] The first, deriving largely from Benjamin's Ninth Thesis on the Philosophy of History and finding later prominent expression in Wim Wenders's film *Himmel über Berlin*,[53] is the angel, a voyeuristic, yet largely inactive (or rather not interactive) figure. In contradistinction to the angel, Shandley posits another metaphor of catastrophic history in the present: the ghost, an interactive, at times even threatening, figure. Shandley goes on to call *Hamlet* "the hegemonic spectral trope,"[54] a statement that once again leads back to Greenblatt. The posthumous voices of Hamlet's father and Horn are both clearly ghosts according to Shandley's categorization. They are both interactive. They do not merely observe history passing by, but rather engage with figures in the present.

It makes sense, then, that Gordon should choose the ghost, the interactive figure, to interact with. However, Gordon, the sociologist, is less interested in ghosts than in what she calls "ghostly matters," that is, the thing that the ghost represents, the historical injustice that the ghost brings to the present. In the case of Valenzuela's *He Who Searches*, the ghostly matter is Argentine state-sponsored terror, that is, torture and disappearances. In the case of Morrison's *Beloved*, the ghostly matter is slavery in the United States. These ghostly matters do not exist as such in the present, but they affect the present. Their shadows linger over the present. To return to Greenblatt, purgatory is a ghostly matter in two senses. It is a medieval matter that casts its shadow over Elizabethan England, and arguably still projects a shadow today. It is also ghostly, however, in the sense that all ghosts come from a sort of purgatory, Catholic or otherwise. It will be necessary to return to the concept of ghostly matters and purgatory in the conclusion. At this point, however, it is in order to read Horn's ghost in Gordon's terms.

Gordon's sociological interest in welcoming ghosts "*out of a concern for justice*" and Greenblatt's contention that haunting is "the making of what is absent to speak" are related points. Allowing the absent to speak is a move toward justice. In fact, Gordon, echoing Greenblatt almost exactly, writes: "The ghost or the apparition is one form by which something lost, or barely visible, or seemingly not there to our supposedly well-trained eyes, makes itself known or apparent to us, in its own way, of course."[55] The question is then: What is the absent that speaks through Horn's ghost, and how is it related to justice? It is difficult to pin this down. Horn wants Thomas to remember all the events and circumstances surrounding his death in the mid-1950s in Bad Guldenberg, and they are many: the Stalinist show trials of 1955–56; the persecution of Roma and Sinti and the mentally handicapped in Nazi Germany; the refusal of officials in the GDR to come to terms with the fact that such persecution occurred in the territory that became the GDR, in some cases by those very officials; the censorship of historians and museum directors in the GDR; and the general environment of fear in the GDR. This constellation of circumstances was censored in Bad Guldenberg and in the GDR. Censorship, again, is part of the constellation, rendering it even more difficult to define the constellation as a single point. And the censorship of the constellation points back to Greenblatt's definition of haunting, "the making of what is absent to speak." Horn, as history professor, as museum director, and as ghost, wanted to allow the absent to speak. In a sense, then, Horn was trying to haunt all along. His posthumous voice, however, is probably the most successful of these acts of haunting. But how is Horn's haunting related to justice?

According to Horn's ghost, counter-memory acts against injustice. The ghost tells the adult Thomas: "Sterben versöhnt nicht. Nicht, wenn die Erinnerungen unversöhnlich geblieben sind . . . der Tod ist nicht das Ende der Mühsal. Die Ruhe wird dir nicht geschenkt." (Dying doesn't reconcile anything. Not if the memories remain irreconcilable . . . death is not the end of the plight. Peace isn't just given to you.)[56] Death, then, according to the ghost, does not end the injustice or remove the memory of it. Horn's corporeal "Ende" is rather the beginning of the work of memory for Thomas and the other narrators. This work of memory confronts the constellation of "ghostly matters" in Bad Guldenberg and the GDR. In order to confront these matters, however, Thomas must not only remember things that he perceived first-hand. He must also engage what Marianne Hirsch has called post-memory, "a form of memory" whose "connection to its object or source is mediated not through recollection but through an imaginative investment and creation,"[57] as the ghost commands: "erinnere dich an das Ungesehene"[58] (remember the unseen). Thomas replies that such an act of remembering is impossible, but the ghost, using a metaphor of memory as network, insists. Memory, the ghost explains, is an "unendliche[s] Netz" (infinite net), which has to be "weiter[ge]knüpf[t]" (145; continuously knotted together). The notion of memory as an infinite net creates the possibility of post-memory, as the associative work of memory digs deeper and deeper into the subconscious archive of events past. This associative work, the ghost argues, is not so much important for the (un)dead Horn, but rather for

Thomas, for the living. This memory work by the living and for the living is the work of justice that concerns Gordon. Furthermore, the word "Netz" that the ghost uses to describe memory has a second meaning, which becomes apparent when looking at a larger segment of the passage. "Dein Gedächtnis hat alles festgehalten. Nur wenn du dich nicht erinnerst, wenn du das unendliche Netz nicht weiterknüpfst, dann falle ich ins Bodenlose. Aber dann wird auch dich keiner halten können" (145; Your memory has held onto everything. Only if you don't remember, if you don't keep knotting the infinite net together, then I'll fall into the bottomless abyss. But then no one will be able to hold you up either). Not only is memory a network, but it is also a safety net that catches the dead and stops them from falling into oblivion. But the net of memory catches not only the remembered but also the rememberer.

The relationship between ghosts and justice is further illuminated by Gordon's major source for a theory of justice: Jacques Derrida, namely his essay "Force of Law: The Mystical Foundation of Authority"[59] and his monograph *Specters of Marx: The State of the Debt, the Work of Mourning, and the New International.*[60] In distinguishing between law (*loi*) and justice, Derrida does much to define the slippery term "justice." Justice is a complicated matter, for, as Derrida tells us "aporetic experiences are the experiences, as improbable as they are necessary, of justice."[61] For Derrida, justice links past, present, and future. Derrida's justice might be understood as a trinity of these three levels of time. Another way of understanding Derrida's concept of justice might be to think about the three ghosts that haunt Ebenezer Scrooge in Dickens's *A Christmas Carol* and then to rename them justice past, justice present, and justice future. In describing how justice interlinks the past and the present, Derrida tells us that justice is both a memory and a responsibility toward memory.

> One must [il faut] be *juste* with justice, and the first justice to be done is to hear it, to try to understand where it comes from, what it wants from us, knowing that it does so through singular idioms . . . This responsibility before memory is a responsibility before the concept of responsibility that regulates the justice and appropriateness [justesse] of our behavior, of our theoretical, practical, ethicopolitical decisions." (248)

Here Derrida already sounds like Horn's ghost. In Horn's ghost's conversation with Thomas, the ghost is both a personification of memory and a commentary on how Thomas should respond to that memory, namely that Thomas should keep on remembering. Justice, however, is not merely a memory and commentary on that memory. For Derrida, justice is also the present: "Justice, however unpresentable it remains, does not wait. It is that which must not wait" (255). Horn's ghost's speech is urgent. Justice is both past and present. Such is the ghostliness of justice: it is, at the same time, present and not present-able. It is something from the past that demands present urgency.

From the relationship of the past to the present in his concept of justice, Derrida moves to the relationship of the present to the future. Here Derrida explores the word "avenir": "a 'to come' [à-venir]" (256). Derrida writes: "Justice . . . opens up to the *avenir* the transformation, the recasting or refounding [la refondation] of law and politics" (256–57). In short, justice opens up possibilities for a different future. Justice is also defined partly in terms of the future in the speech of Horn's ghost.

> Du darfst mich nicht vergessen, mein Junge. Wenn du mich vergisst, erst dann sterbe ich wirklich. Aber dann wird die Hölle die Toten erwecken.
>
> . . . der Tod ist nicht das Ende der Mühsal. Die Ruhe wird dir nicht geschenkt.
>
> Nur wenn du dich nicht erinnerst, wenn du das unendliche Netz nicht weiterknüpfst, dann falle ich ins Bodenlose. Aber dann wird auch dich keiner halten können.
>
> So lange es ein menschliches Gedächtnis gibt, wird nichts umsonst gewesen sein, ist nichts vergänglich.
>
> Wenn ihr schweigt, dann werden die Steine schreien. (59, 99, 145, 145, 249)

> [You are not allowed to forget me, my boy. If you forget me, that's when I'll really die. But then hell will awaken the dead
>
> . . . death is not the end of the plight. Peace isn't just given to you.
>
> Only if you don't remember, if you don't keep knotting the infinite net together, then I'll fall into the bottomless abyss. But then no one will be able to hold you up either.
>
> As long as there is a human memory, nothing will have been in vain, nothing is transient.
>
> If you all are silent, then the stones will scream.]

Here the ghost uses the future tense. Taken as a whole, these passages boil down to the following: if you do not remember, there will be no justice. Or to place the ghost's speech back into Derrida's terms: if you do not remember, there will be no "to-come."

There is one last image in *Horns Ende* that is relevant to the haunting and has been overlooked: Horn's hanging corpse. This image, morbid as it may be, is similar to both Greenblatt's and Gordon's ghosts and

Benjamin's torso. Indeed, Gordon has already made the link between the ghost and Benjamin's "profane illuminations," pointing out that Benjamin himself once wrote of "ghostly signals."[62] The image is of Horn literally suspended above Thomas's head. The suspension of the corpse is key, as it represents the suspension of memory in Thomas's mind. To knead in Greenblatt's argument, purgatory is suspension. However, it is not only Horn's corpse and Thomas's memory that hang, suspended in air. *Hamlet* was suspended in the cultural memory in the GDR. More importantly, however, suicide, along with the cultural baggage that accompanies it, was suspended in the literary imagination of the GDR. Suicide in the GDR is what Gordon would call a "ghostly matter."

Suicide is a ghostly matter, but it is also a way into other ghostly matters. Here Stephen Greenblatt, Avery Gordon, and Christoph Hein are all on the same page. Haunting is chronicling. Stephen Greenblatt tells us, after his elaborate history of purgatory, that the ghost from purgatory can be, in the end, a rhetorical device: "*Prosopopoeia*—personification, the making of what is absent to speak—is the rhetorical device behind all haunting."[63] That is, the ghost not only commands one to remember, but it is itself unorthodox memory personified. In a similar, if less literary-informed, definition, Avery Gordon writes: "The ghost or the apparition is one form by which something lost, or barely visible, or seemingly not there to our supposedly well-trained eyes, makes itself known or apparent to us, in its own way, of course."[64] Both theorists define the ghost as an unapparent, unorthodox, un-"stated" memory, which uncannily finds its way to the surface of consciousness, whether as a literary device or as part of the unorthodox sociological imagination. Both of these definitions tie in to Christoph Hein's oft-mentioned notion of chronicling. Horn, the historian and the ghost, seems to be conscious of all of this. He wishes to communicate about the past for the purposes of the present and the future. When his post as history professor in Leipzig fails to provide him with this opportunity—or rather when this opportunity is taken away from him by the Party—he tries to seize such an opportunity through the provincial museum that he is sent to Bad Guldenberg to direct. When he is denied this opportunity as well, he takes advantage—consciously or unconsciously—of suicide as a method of haunting and, therefore, insistent communication about the past for the sake of the present. Horn's haunting, his act of forcing people in Bad Guldenberg, especially Thomas, to interpret and make relevant the events of the 1950s for the 1980s is radically subversive.

Bad Guldenberg

The town of Bad Guldenberg represents ever more restrictive political space. But what can transcend borders more easily than a ghost? Indeed,

Horn's haunting loosens such restrictive political space. In order to begin such a reading, it is in order to ask: How do we imagine the geography of cultural repression in the German Democratic Republic? Many works of fiction, from Christa Wolf's 1963 novel *Der geteilte Himmel* to Thomas Brussig's post-Wende novels *Helden wie wir* and *Am kürzeren Ende der Sonnenallee*, focus on the Berlin Wall, a construction that no doubt symbolizes containment and repression, not only for the GDR but also for the entire Eastern Bloc. However, the image of the Berlin Wall simplifies the matter to a certain degree. It encourages an image of the GDR as one homogenous space. Moreover, it focuses only on the static borders. David Bathrick examines two metaphors of repression related to Stasi activity in the GDR: the panopticon and the many-tentacled octopus.[65] Since the panopticon implies an outside, unaffected viewer, the image of the octopus seems to win out for Bathrick. The aim here is to point toward an imagining of restrictive space with retracting borders. Such borders are seen in *Horns Ende*, which, for the most part, takes place in Christoph Hein's fictional provincial town of Bad Guldenberg, a small town near Leipzig in Saxony, which Hein himself says may resemble his own hometown of Bad Düben.[66] Three of Hein's works are set in Bad Guldenberg: *Horns Ende* (1985), *Von allem Anfang an* (1997), and *Landnahme* (2004).

Spatiality is important in the works of Christoph Hein in general, and the space of Bad Guldenberg is an important part of *Horns Ende* in particular. David Clarke describes how ideological contradictions are reflected in architectural spaces in two of Christoph Hein's works, namely in *Der fremde Freund* (1982) (published in the Federal Republic under the title *Drachenblut*) and *Willenbrock* (2000). Clarke maintains that Claudia's socialist Plattenbau apartment comes to represent not community but rather a breakdown in community, while Bernd Willenbrock's large house and accumulation of wealth brings about not freedom but rather a restriction of freedom, as his security systems end up locking him into his own house.[67] Clarke mentions in passing that Thomas and Gertrude Fischlinger, two of the narrators in *Horns Ende*, experience Bad Guldenberg in terms of "asphyxia and claustrophobia."[68] He does not, however, elaborate on the point, nor does he mention that other characters in the novel also experience the town in terms of claustrophobia, nor does he tie it in with his discussions of space and ideology in *Der fremde Freund* and *Willenbrock*. Christl Kiewitz claims that "Bad Guldenberg ist eine Metapher für die Kontinuität des alltäglichen Faschismus in der neuen sozialistischen Gesellschaft"[69] (Bad Guldenberg is a metaphor for the continuity of quotidian fascism in the new socialist society). Kiewitz is correct in noting that Bad Guldenberg is a fictional place where there is some continuity from the Third Reich into the 1950s in the GDR, a continuity that no doubt also existed in reality. Andrea Hilbk and Uwe

Wittstock have also hinted toward reading Bad Guldenberg in a negative manner, but without elaboration and without reading the town explicitly in terms of claustrophobia.

Most critics who have written about *Horns Ende* focus rightly on issues of history and memory but fail to connect those issues to issues of space in the novel. Critics who write about the space of Bad Guldenberg—with the exception of Kiewitz—seem to do so merely to point out that three of Hein's works take place there. Simon Bevan mentions the town to argue that, although *Horns Ende* and *Von allem Anfang an* both take place in Bad Guldenberg, the two texts are actually quite different.[70] Astrid Köhler uses the town to group together *Horns Ende*, *Von allem Anfang an*, and *Landnahme*, arguing that together these three texts provide a relatively holistic view of the Saxon province in the 1950s.[71] Although Köhler's grouping of these three texts is appropriate, she does not go out of her way to describe the town or what it means for the characters in the book or the reader's imagining of repression in provincial East Germany.

In order to explore the space of Bad Guldenberg, I engage the help of three narratologists who have dealt with space.[72] Mieke Bal has made the following distinction between place and space: "The concept of *place* is related to the physical, mathematically measurable shape of spatial dimensions . . . These places seen *in relation to their perception* are called space" [italics are Bal's].[73] Lubomir Dolezel, in his 1998 monograph *Heterocosmica*,[74] expands upon Bal's distinction and broadens narratology by zooming out to examine the fictional worlds in which narratives take place and the relationships that the fictional characters in the narratives have with those fictional worlds. Yuri Lotman engages narratologically with space by redefining the narratological building block, the event (sujet, Ereignis), in spatially oriented terms, namely that an event involves movement across a semantically charged border.[75] I contend that Bad Guldenberg is perceived as an ideological space similar to those described by David Clarke and that the town might be related to the images explored by David Bathrick. In order to analyze Bad Guldenberg as a narratologically meaningful space, it is worth showing how various characters in the novel perceive the town.

First, for Gertrude Fischlinger, Bad Guldenberg reflects what she perceives as failure in her life. Her husband lives with a younger woman in Leipzig, while she remains in Bad Guldenberg. Despite her condition of phlebitis, she stands on her feet all day working in the town's general store to support herself and her delinquent son Paul. Her husband later takes Paul to the city, a move that she finds problematic, since she believes her husband to be anything but a role model for her son. Thus two of the people most important to her have abandoned her for Leipzig. Finally, her quiet, but nonetheless present, renter Horn kills himself, and she is left all alone.

Second, Bad Guldenberg represents restrictive childhood space for Thomas. Not only does he experience the pains and confusion of puberty but he also has the feeling of being held back from his dreams, a feeling he strongly associates with Bad Guldenberg. He hints at this relatively early in the novel, when he describes the spatial experience of walking through town with his parents on Sundays. "Diese Sonntagsspaziergänge . . . waren wie drohende Grabsteine, die meine wild wuchernden Träume zurückhielten, ihnen irdische Schwerkraft aufdrängten"[76] (These Sunday walks . . . were like threatening gravestones, which held back my wildly growing dreams, forced earthly gravity onto them). These images, gravestones and gravity, both indicate that Thomas feels that Bad Guldenberg is preventing his dreams from coming true. Furthermore, it is the act of walking through the town that gives him this feeling. Later, Thomas reveals more about this feeling as he thinks to himself:

> Mein Wunsch war es allein, mich von dieser Stadt und den schlimmen elf Jahren meines bisherigen Lebens vollständig zu lösen. Ich wollte sie vergessen, austilgen, so gründlich, als seien sie nie gewesen. Ich fürchtete, dass diese Stadt und meine Kindheit mir immer anhängen und nie mehr auszulöschen sein werden (65)
>
> [My only wish was to free myself completely from this city and from the bad eleven years of my life up to that point. I wanted to forget them, obliterate them so thoroughly that it would be as though they had never existed. I feared that this city and my childhood would always cling to me and never disappear.]

Here again, Thomas associates the town of Bad Guldenberg with containment. He wants to leave the town and his childhood behind, but he fears that this is impossible.

Dr. Spodeck also experiences Bad Guldenberg as restrictive space, although in a somewhat less political way than for some of the other characters. Spodeck is financially trapped in Bad Guldenberg. His father, a wealthy man who had multiple children by multiple women without marrying any of them, saw intellectual potential in Spodeck and paid for him to study medicine at the University of Leipzig, and later Munich. Although Spodeck is much more interested in psychiatry, his father forces him to study medicine, stating that he is to make a living from the sick, not the crazy. When Spodeck completes his studies, his father buys him a practice, under the agreement that he must stay in Bad Guldenberg and practice general medicine there for at least twenty-five years. After the twenty-five years are over, he cannot leave, because he is too old and tired. Spodeck comes to see nearly every aspect of the town as a trope of paternal suppression. He fantasizes about treating the mayor of the town,

Kruschkatz, one day as a dying patient, saying that he will keep the dying, vegetating man alive as long as possible, so that he will suffer as much as possible. He then realizes the real cause of his hatred.

> Es ist diese Stadt an der ich sterbe. Ich habe sie verabscheut, seit ich hier lebe, seit ich auf der Welt bin. Und ich hasse sie, seitdem mein Vater mir hier eine Praxis kaufte und mir sagte, dass er mich nur für diese Stadt hat ausbilden lassen. (8)
>
> [This city is what I'm dying of. I've hated it as long as I've lived here, as long as I've been on this planet. And I've hated it ever since my father bought a practice for me here and told me that he only educated me for this city.]

For Spodeck, then, Bad Guldenberg represents a claustrophobia that is at once spatial, economic, and oedipal.

Fourth, the town of Bad Guldenberg is a restrictive space for Mayor Kruschkatz in a political, but also familial way. As an apparatchik, Kruschkatz came to Bad Guldenberg from Leipzig thinking that his tenure as mayor of the small town would be simply a rung up the Party ladder. In the end, however, he must remain there. It may even be the case that the Party has sent him there to keep him from ascending the Party ladder. In any case, Bad Guldenberg proves to be a space of isolation for Kruschkatz. His wife never wanted to go there in the first place and made him promise her that she would not be buried in Bad Guldenberg. After she realizes that they will remain in the town indefinitely, she ceases to interact with him in any meaningful way. In fact, she tells him, "Ich habe nie geglaubt, daß es einmal möglich wäre, aber ich ekle mich vor dir" (53; I never believed that it would ever be possible, but I'm disgusted by you). He manages to uphold his promise to her that she wouldn't be buried in Bad Guldenberg, but not in the way she intended. Instead, he sends her back to Leipzig to stay with her family, as she falls ill with cancer. She dies in Leipzig three months later and is buried there. Kruschkatz, however, knows that he had, for all practical purposes, lost her much earlier, as he notes: "Schon lange bevor sie an Krebs starb, war sie von mir gegangen" (52; long before she died of cancer, she had already left me). Thus Bad Guldenberg isolates him from the person he loves the most. Moreover, Kruschkatz is strongly isolated from any possibility of contact with other members of the intelligentsia in Bad Guldenberg. Dr. Spodeck hates him, as noted earlier. Horn also avoids contact with Kruschkatz, because Krutschkatz was involved in reprimanding Horn earlier in Leipzig.

Fifth, Bad Guldenberg is one of a series of restrictive spaces for Horn. The more Horn attempts to communicate about these spaces, the tighter they become. He is sent to be the director of a museum in Bad

Guldenberg as a punishment after he taught something at the University of Leipzig that the Party in its paranoia deemed inappropriate. The town of Bad Guldenberg, where the bulk of the novel takes place, proves even more metaphorically narrow than the already tight space of the University. At the museum in Bad Guldenberg he creates an exhibit about an ancient Sorbian people who murder those who do not fit into the societal hierarchy. As Horn's allegorical intentions are discovered, he loses his position at the museum. After two failed attempts at communicating about these claustrophobic spaces—each attempt leading to narrower space—Horn communicates in a different manner: he kills himself and thereby haunts the memories of the narrators, especially that of Thomas.

Furthermore, as Bärbel Lücke briefly points out, the name of the town Bad Guldenberg (golden mountain) is ironic. As Lücke puts it, "Dort ist nichts Gold, und es glänzt auch nicht"[77] (Nothing is gold there, and it doesn't shine either). Indeed, Bad Guldenberg is a place of stillborn hopes. This can be seen also in Kruschkatz's description of the train station in Bad Guldenberg as he recounts the day his wife Irene first arrived there from Leipzig:

> Vor Jahrzehnten wurde es als Denkmal einer großen lokalen Hoffnung in solchen Ausmaßen errichtet, einer Hoffnung auf Prosperität, die allzu sorglos die künftige Entwicklung des Kurbades sah. Und nun, da Wirtschaftskrise und Kriege die weitgespannten Pläne mit Rotstift und ausgebrannten Ruinen zunichte gemacht hatten, stand das Bahnhofsgebäude, unversehrt und überflüssig, als grauer Gedenkstein unerfüllter, vergilbter Wünsche. (50)
>
> [Decades ago it was erected as an enormous monument to the great local hope for prosperity, given the intended development of the spa. And now—since economic crisis and wars had nixed the broad plans with a red pen and turned them into burnt out ruins—the train station stood there, intact and superfluous, as a gray memorial to unfulfilled, yellowed wishes].

Here the train station serves as a metonym for the entire town. The large, ornate building is ironic, given its lack of use and its dilapidated state. Another image of Bad Guldenberg as a place of stillborn hopes emerges as Kruschkatz calls the town a "Sackgasse" (49; a blind alley or dead-end), providing the image of a street that leads nowhere. Indeed, Bad Guldenberg serves, in part, as a trope not only for the hopelessness of the individual characters in the novel but also for the stillborn hopes of the German Democratic Republic itself.

Returning to David Clarke's description of the ironic use of space in Hein's *Der fremde Freund*, we can see how Bad Guldenberg is similar to the Plattenbau in which Claudia lives. Both the building and the town are designed as spaces for providing a sense of community, but both function as spaces in which a sense of community breaks down. In describing this phenomenon in the case of Claudia's building, Clarke writes: "Claudia's apartment block, as a microcosm of GDR society, is characterized either by the indifference of individuals to their neighbours . . . or a suspicion encouraged by the state security services."[78] Just as the relations among people who live in Claudia's apartment block range from indifference to suspicion, so do the relations among people living in Bad Guldenberg: Horn is suspicious of Kruschkatz. Spodeck is suspicious of Kruschkatz. Kruschkatz, at first indifferent toward Horn, eventually comes to blame Horn for the loss of his wife. Spodeck is suspicious of his father, and so on.

If Bad Guldenberg is—as Clarke claims Claudia's apartment block is—a microcosm of GDR society, then it is worthwhile to ask whether the fictional world of Bad Guldenberg allows for a more complicated imagining of the geography of cultural repression in the GDR. In other words, how does the fictional town stack up against other spatial images of GDR society? It may seem odd to compare or contrast the image of Bad Guldenberg with that of the Berlin Wall, since *Horns Ende*—as well as the other two novels that take place there—take place during the 1950s, before the Berlin Wall was constructed. *Horns Ende*, however, was written in the 1980s, when the Berlin Wall certainly existed. More importantly, Bad Guldenberg points toward more complicated mechanisms in cultural repression in the GDR. The illusion of hope combined with mass hopelessness as well as the breakdown of communication and community—not to mention that the majority of GDR citizens did not live in Berlin—are not easily portrayed by the image of the Berlin Wall. Bad Guldenberg, moreover, can be seen as fortifying David Bathrick's assertion that the image of the octopus may be appropriate. In Bad Guldenberg, there are no good guys and no bad guys, nor is there an outside voyeur. Instead, the tentacles of the octopus are everywhere, squeezing spaces—as we have seen, especially in the case of Horn—into an unbearable restriction.

In order to translate Bathrick's tentacle metaphor into narratological terms, it is appropriate to return to Lotman's definition of event (sujet, Ereignis). For Lotman, an event requires the crossing of a semantic border. In *Horns Ende*, the borders move; they retract, and when they do, they cross semiotic borders. We have seen how Gertrude Fischlinger, Thomas, Dr. Spodeck, and Mayor Kruschkatz feel contained. Two more cases of the effect of retractable borders of human beings remain to be fleshed out. The Roma people—who have created problems not only for Mayor Kruschkatz but also for many readers and critics of *Horns Ende*—represent the effects of the retractable political borders in a concrete, spatial sense. The limitation of their movement is not abstract. It is not only that they are not promoted, or that they feel lonely. They physically do not return to Bad Guldenberg. Many critics have asked what hides behind the relationship between the disappearance of the Roma people and the death of Horn. The answer is that both are contained—to the point of disappearance—by the retracting space of Bad Guldenberg. Horn, the ghost, however, loosens this retracting space by asking people to remember.

Suicide and Haunting

Before concluding, it is worthwhile to outline other suicides in Hein's works, in order to further illuminate what is at work in Horn's suicide in *Horns Ende* and to further demonstrate the connection between suicide and haunting. Suicide is a prominent theme in the oeuvre of Christoph Hein. At least nine of his works deal to some degree with suicide. Six of these works were written and published in the GDR. The other three were written and published in the reunited Germany. How do these nine works dealing with suicide connect with one another? Are there parallels? Can a typology of suicide in Hein's works be drawn? What is it about *Horns Ende* that deems it more relevant for this study than Hein's other works dealing with suicide?

Chronologically, Hein's other works dealing with suicide are *Schlötel, oder Was solls* (1974, Schlötel, or What's the Use), "Die Familiengruft" (1979, The Family Burial Place), "Frank, eine Kindheit mit Vätern" (1979, Frank, a Childhood with Fathers), *Der fremde Freund* (1982, The Distant Lover), *Horns Ende* (1985, Horn's End), *Passage* (1987), *Landnahme* (2004, Settlement), *In seiner frühen Kindheit ein Garten* (2006, In His Early Childhood, a Garden), and *Frau Paula Trousseau* (2007). They are divided here into works written in the GDR and works written in the twenty-first century. *Schlötel, oder Was solls* is a play that premiered in 1974, in which an overachieving sociology student from Leipzig is sent to Schwedt to work in a production brigade. Although (or perhaps because) Schlötel has "revolutionary" ideas about working, he does not get along with his coworkers. One night he is assaulted, and eventually he kills himself, it is assumed by characters in the play, as his body in found in the Baltic Sea (although audience members may assume this to be a case of homicide). In "Die Familiengruft," one of the short stories included in Hein's *Ein Album Berliner Stadtansichten*, the narrator tells how his uncle, a Jewish actor, hid with his family in their family crypt in order to escape Gestapo violence during the Second World War, how the uncle poisoned his wife, his three children and himself there in the crypt, and how the narrator reads the uncle's suicide note decades later and goes to visit the family crypt. "Frank, eine Kindheit mit Vätern," another short story from the same collection, describes the unrealized desire of Frank's great-grandfather, grandfather, and father that their sons receive a university education. Frank's grandfather and father could not attend university because of various volatile turns in world history. Frank, however, has severe learning disabilities. Conscious of the disappointment his condition causes his family, Frank fatally flings himself out of a fifth story window onto a cement sidewalk. The mention of suicide in *Der fremd Freund* is brief but important and will be further dealt with below. *Horns Ende*, the object of this chapter, needs no further summary. *Passage* is a play that premiered in 1987, in which German Jews in the 1930s are trying to flee across the Pyrenees Mountains into Spain in order to avoid persecution by the Nazis. One character, who remarkably resembles Walter Benjamin, does not make it to freedom and kills himself.

Suicides in Hein's works do not cease with the collapse of the GDR, although they take a hiatus during the 1990s. *Landnahme* (2004) tells the story of Bernhard Haber, who along with his parents is forced after the Second World War to migrate from their home in Silesia to the fictional town of Bad Guldenberg. Haber's father, a one-armed carpenter, dies and is reported to have committed suicide. In the end, however, the reader finds out that Haber's father, as Haber insists throughout, has been murdered. Although the death of Haber's father is not a case of suicide, the novel nonetheless provides a contribution to the discourse on the taboo of suicide in the GDR. *In seiner frühen Kindheit ein Garten* (2005) tells the story of an elderly couple, Richard and Friederike Zurek, who are mourning the death of their son, Oliver, a left-wing terrorist in West Germany, who according to the police and court system shot himself during a shoot-out with the police. The father believes he has evidence proving that the son was shot by a police officer. In the end, the reader never finds out for sure whether the death is a case of suicide or murder. Nonetheless, the novel provides a (perhaps West German) take on the taboo of suicide. *Frau Paula Trousseau* (2007) is the story of an artist who grows up in the GDR, later lives in France, and eventually kills herself and leaves her paintings to an old friend who has not seen her for years. In a way, it can be seen as a mystery novel in that the friend spends much of the novel trying to figure out why Paula killed herself.

Hein's first major work of narrative fiction, the novella *Der fremde Freund* (1982), illuminates the subversion in all of Hein's fictional suicides, particularly that in *Horns Ende*, and the link between suicide, memory, and haunting. Claudia, the novella's main character, ponders suicide. In examining her life after the death of her lover, Henry, Claudia, a medical doctor, thinks to herself: "In der Klinik gelte ich als robuste Person. . . . Würde ich Selbstmord begehen, stünden sie vor einem Rätsel." (In the clinic, I am deemed to be a stable person . . . If I were to commit suicide, they would see it as a riddle.)[79] Claudia does not commit suicide in the novella. What is important about Claudia's suicidal thought is her idea that her suicide would cause her coworkers to be puzzled. That is, it would force them to interpret the events surrounding her hypothetical suicide. Thinking about suicide in this way illuminates the suicide carried out by Horn. Suicide, at least in the case of *Horns Ende*, causes people to ask why. It sets in motion a hermeneutic process, just as Pony's suicide does in Muthesius's *Flucht in die Wolken*. This "why" triggers interpretation, an attempt at solving the mystery,[80] and, ultimately, "the making of what is absent to speak."[81] To hark back to Derrida, suicide demands justice. Yuri Lotman lends insight into this as well. For Lotman, the approaching of the puzzle that Claudia describes is explained by unpredictability in history, that is, questioning what might have been.[82] Such questioning allows for change in the present. "Or in other words, the content of memory is the past, but without memory we cannot think 'here' and 'now': memory is the deep-seated ground of the actual process of consciousness. And if history is culture's memory then this means that it is not only a relic of the past, but also an active mechanism of the present."[83] Suicide, in Hein's works, then, appears to be a catalyst for haunting and establishing memory as "an active mechanism of the present." With this link between suicide and haunting in mind, the analysis of Horn's ghost becomes a relevant point of entry into Hein's other suicides. Horn's ghost personifies what is at work in the other suicides in Hein's oeuvre. That is, while those suicides all haunt, Horn really is a ghost.

Horns Ende is about memory and history, as many critics have suggested. However, it is about memory in a way much richer than they have implied. Not only do different narrators in the novel have different philosophies of history and different ways of remembering, as Fischer and others have noted, but their memories are rich and potentially subversive. Horn's suicide, which left his corpse suspended from a tree in a Guldenberg forest instigated unorthodox memory. In the end, then, Horn, through his suicide and spectrality—as well as through the greater cultural and literary discourse on suicide and ghosts—is able to break free from the restrictive, claustrophobic, even retracting space of Bad Guldenberg and communicate un-"stated" memory. Just as the retracting space of Bad Guldenberg haunts the people of Bad Guldenberg, Horn's ghost, in turn, haunts that space, loosening, if not exploding, those retracting borders.

Horns Ende utilizes haunting, an element from *Hamlet*—a play that was well received in the GDR—that was overlooked by GDR cultural authorities, in order to force readers to remember both fascism and Stalinism and the extent that those ideologies remain influential on the GDR of the 1980s. The censors, furthermore, overlooked the importance of haunting in the novel. They thought that the death of Horn and the emphasis on his death via the novel's title indicated a break with that unsavory past. Such was not the case. They perhaps also thought that Horn's suicide shows that he and his attempts to remember such past events were irrational. This was also not the case. Horn's suicide and his haunting are precisely the subversive instigators of memory that the censors feared. The element that they feared least turned out to be the most subversive element.

Conclusion: The Reality of Fictional Suicides

Und käm es heraus übers Jahr
Daß der Selbstmord kein Selbstmord war

[And what if it comes out over the years
That the suicide was no suicide]

—Wolf Biermann

Slavoj Žižek begins his monograph *Welcome to the Desert of the Real* by relating a joke from the GDR in which a person who is sent to Siberia promises to write to his friend and tells him that if the letter is written in blue ink everything in it is true. If the letter is written in red ink the statements made in the letter are false. The letter arrives in blue ink and explains how wonderful Siberia is and lists many nice things that are readily available in Siberia. In conclusion, the friend writes that the only thing not available in Siberia is red ink. Žižek asserts that the punchline of the joke indicates that the friend in Siberia found a way to communicate the incommunicable. The letter-writer, lacking the language needed to express his discomfort, finds an alternative way of communicating.[1] While Žižek relates the joke in order to describe matters at work in twenty-first century, Western capitalism, it can be reapplied to the GDR to describe literary works from the GDR that make use of the theme of suicide. That is, fictional suicide in GDR narrative fiction is a literary theme that communicates ideas that are otherwise difficult to communicate. This study demonstrates that those suicides allude to suicides from canonical works of literature in the wrong color ink, as it were. Unlike the letter written in blue ink, however, these works are not merely tricks to fool the censors (suicide would likely not have been the best way to do that)—they are rich in interpretive potential. Above all, they are literary. Not only do they broach the taboo topic of suicide, but they perform transformative readings of GDR literary heritage, revealing the slippery power of literature, and leading the sclerotic literary heritage of the GDR to destroy itself.

Read narratologically, the fictional suicides examined in this study together comprise a literary historical trajectory. The ways in which those fictional suicides transform earlier texts that deal with suicide become increasingly abstract. Before the 1970s they are richly literary, but not primarily transtextual. After Honecker's "No Taboos" speech in 1971,

Plenzdorf's *Die neuen Leiden des jungen W.* (1973) tests Honecker's statement by having Edgar Wibeau read Goethe's *Die Leiden des jungen Werther* without its GDR-constructed, literary historical context and killing himself with an electric paint sprayer, thus proximating Goethe's text to the context of GDR youth culture of the early 1970s. In Plenzdorf's work it is unmistakable from the work's title, from Edgar's readings of *Werther*, from Edgar's constant commentary on the parallels between Werther and himself, from the Charlotte figure being named Charlie, and from Edgar's suicide that the work is an explosive reworking of Goethe's *Werther*. Its semiotic explosion, furthermore, lies in its proximation of that text. Werner Heiduczek's *Tod am Meer* (1977) confronts the GDR reception of Thomas Mann's *Der Tod in Venedig* by having the Aschenbach figure, Jablonski, narrate his own story. Such vocalization allows for the detection of Jablonski's memory, revealing how intertwined his life has been with self-destructive Stalinism. Christa Wolf's *Kein Ort. Nirgends* (1979) reads Kleist and Günderrode reading ancient Greek literature against German classicism and against prescribed GDR notions of ancient Greek literature. It does so by adopting Kleist's and Günderrode's technique of transvaluation, creating a parallel between their reevaluation of German classicism and Wolf's reevaluation of GDR literary heritage. Heiner Müller's *Hamletmaschine* (1979) and Sibylle Muthesius's *Flucht in die Wolken* (1981) are overloaded with transtextual (and paratextual) chaos, the former in an intellectual exercise in taking literary heritage to its logical—and disturbing—conclusion, the latter in an attempt to make sense of the world in light of unspeakable tragedy. Finally, Christoph Hein's *Horns Ende* (1985) establishes counter-memory with its use of Shakespearean haunting. Although this text represents a subtle proximation, it is its architextual haunting that is truly subversive. If Plenzdorf's *Die neuen Leiden* bombastically opens up the can of worms regarding suicide and literary heritage, Hein's *Horns Ende* somberly provides the *coup de grâce*.

The official literary heritage of the GDR was itself suicidal. It was invented and contrived, largely dictated by Georg Lukács. The fact that it was dictated at all indicates that it was a construction. And its very constructedness made it self-destructive. That is, the notion of literary heritage itself wants readers to notice the relationships among texts, but the more readers examine those relationships, the more the whole prescriptive heritage breaks down. The more it was probed, the less logical it appeared, and the more potential it bore for subversion. *Die neuen Leiden des jungen W.* and *Kein Ort. Nirgends* make this especially clear. The former, by proximating Goethe's *Werther* into the context of early 1970s East Germany, shows just how staid Goethe reception in the GDR had become. The latter gives a voice to Kleist and Günderrode, so as to take their concerns and readings seriously, thereby portraying a perspective that radically counters the literary historical tradition constructed by GDR cultural authorities.

Fictional suicides in the GDR also tended to instigate counter-memory. This is especially the case in *Horns Ende*, as Horn haunts Thomas, forcing him to remember the events surrounding Horn's suicide. Horn speaks on behalf of memories that have been suppressed. Similarly, Edgar Wibeau, in Plenzdorf's *Die neuen Leiden des jungen W.* haunts. His friends and family attempt to inform themselves about the events surrounding his death. Only Edgar's hauntings, both his ghostly voice and his tape recordings, have the answers for them. Also, characters try to find out why Jablonski kills himself in *Tod am Meer*. The autobiographical fragment that Jablonski leaves behind is the best explanation available, and it contains horrific memories of both German fascism and German communism.

Even if one were to point toward the biographies of suicidal figures associated with East German communism—and this has certainly not been my method or primary intention—it would become clear that many of the suicidal figures were not so much the dissidents but rather the founders of East German communism themselves. Perhaps that is yet another reason why suicide was such a taboo topic in the GDR. During the First World War Johannes R. Becher, who would later become the first Minister of Culture of the GDR, attempted suicide by purposely getting shot. In 1918, Becher's younger brother committed suicide, after which Becher himself frequently attempted suicide. Becher was also dependent on morphine and consumed an abundance of cocaine, despite understanding, as a doctor, the detrimental effects that these substances had on his body.[2] Georg Lukács pondered the prospect of committing suicide to the extent that he composed a suicide note. In 1911, his first wife, Irma Seidler, committed suicide by leaping from a Budapest bridge into the Danube. Lukács then spent much of his life contemplating suicide.[3] As mentioned in the chapter on Heiduczek in this study, Stalin's wife committed suicide, and Montefiore even thinks that Stalin committed suicide. Slavoj Žižek, describing the show trials of Bukharin, provides plenty of evidence that the Communist Party of the Soviet Union was self-destructive.[4]

As demonstrated in the chapter on Heiduczek in this study, *Tod am Meer* points toward such self-destruction. Jablonski self-destructs. He writes himself to death. He detects his biography—and that of Stalin—and abjects the elements that he finds unpleasant until there is nothing left of him. Several other characters in the novel are also self-destructive, including Imme and Schippenschiß. The other three works examined in this study can also be viewed as indicating the self-destruction in the context of East German communism, especially Plenzdorf's *Die neuen Leiden des jungen W.* Edgar Wibeau, in a sense, works himself to death. He kills himself while trying to assemble an electric painting machine to help his construction brigade. Horn, in Hein's *Horns Ende*, is reprimanded to the point that he commits suicide, a matter that literally haunts the town of Bad Guldenberg.

Studies of GDR literature tend to focus on history, power, and resistance, a logical approach given the historically peculiar and politically charged nature of that country. Purely historicist views of GDR literary history, however, inevitably fall flat. Reading GDR literature *qua* literature allows not only for close readings of some astonishingly artistic texts but also allows a more focused lens for viewing resistance at work in those texts, and it allows for a literary history that takes into account the literary texts themselves, rather than their mere position in political history. Reading fictional suicides in GDR literature only as a historicist reflection of suicide in GDR society cannot precisely describe what is at work in those texts. Further, such readings risk making the same mistakes that the GDR censors and apparatchiks made in their own pseudo-historicist readings.

With the GDR now dead and gone, with its literature perhaps a matter for specialists, it might seem that the trope of suicide in the context of the GDR is now irrelevant; such is not the case. To the contrary, suicide continues to inform the way people think about the GDR well after reunification. It remains a dominant trope for understanding life in the GDR. The social-science-oriented conviction—one that not even social scientists such as Grashoff and Matussek believe any more—that the GDR was full of real suicide cases as political protest has dominated the view of suicide in the GDR. For that reason, it is now well worth turning briefly to a problematic fictional film that falsely portrays suicide in the GDR.

In March 2006, Florian Maria Georg Christian Graf Henckel von Donnersmarck's film *Das Leben der Anderen*,[5] a dramatic movie about the horrors of the Stasi and about suicide in East Germany, appeared in cinemas in Germany. The following year it was released in the United States as well, where it received mixed reviews. Many moviegoers enjoyed the film. Indeed, it won an Oscar for Best Foreign Language Film in 2007. But the film is highly problematic for several reasons. As filmmaker Andreas Dresen put it: "Dieser Film [hat] mit der DDR so viel zu tun wie Hollywood mit Hoyerswerda"[6] (This film has about as much to do with the GDR as Hollywood has to do with Hoyerswerda). Historians have criticized the film for containing historically inaccurate details.[7] As Wendy Westphal points out, there is an irony to the film's historical inaccuracies, because some media reviews lauded the film as being highly authentic, and because the director intended the film to be historically accurate.[8] Udo Grashoff—who wrote a history of suicide in the GDR—a book that in part led me to ask some of the questions behind this book, was sought out by the production team of *Das Leben der Anderen* as an expert on the topic of suicide in the GDR. However, they failed to ask him the right questions, and perhaps they also failed to listen to him. Grashoff rightly criticizes the film because it misleadingly implies that most suicides in the GDR were politically motivated, which was in fact rarely the case.[9] Grashoff's assessment of the film is in line with my own, but the problems with the film do not end there.

In another critical account of the film, Slavoj Žižek notes that the film fails to portray the horror of GDR state security, even though it attempts to do exactly that.[10] Here Žižek's position is similar to that of Westphal. Žižek observes that such horror is represented in the film by a mere personal betrayal, something that could happen in any society. He also observes that Dreymann, the young playwright in the film, is only reprimanded because of personal affairs. That is, the melodrama of the film gets in the way of showing that state surveillance in the GDR was systemic. Žižek goes on to demonstrate the problem with Dreymann with a joke from the East Bloc: "Of the three features—personal honesty, sincere support of the regime and intelligence—it was possible to combine only two, never all three."[11] Dreymann, however, possesses all three of these features, a matter that makes his character utterly unconvincing.

While those points are certainly correct, Žižek takes a further step that I find particularly relevant; he asks what kind of a writer Dreymann would have been in the context of the GDR. He asks questions such as the following: What would the regime have thought about Dreymann's literary works, about which the viewer knows nothing? Why did Dreymann not run into trouble with the regime sooner, if he were such a powerful writer? Did Dreymann have international fame? Where was Dreymann during the Biermann affair of 1976? The answers to these questions are not provided in the film. However, it is clear that the questions cannot be answered, as the film has fundamentally misunderstood East German literature.

While the film is—as Žižek and others correctly maintain—historically inaccurate and unconvincing, it also fundamentally misunderstands the role of suicide in the GDR imagination. The two suicides in the film are atypical, according to Grashoff's historical assessment, and, frankly, unrealistic. The film detaches suicide from the rhetorical role that it often played in the GDR in the seventies and eighties. (Most of Donnersmarck's film takes place in 1984.) The suicide of actress Christa-Maria is performed on the spur of the moment and is narratively simplistic. The aging playwright, who commits suicide because he can no longer publish in the GDR, in addition to possibly using suicide to commit an act of protest, might have been writing something that disrupts the official literary heritage of the GDR, but this information does not exist in the text, and his character remains largely unexplored. Instead, the suicide of the actress shifts the focus of the film to the love story between her and the young playwright, Georg Dreymann. That is, by passing over the suicide of the older playwright, the film overlooks the rich history of suicide stories in the GDR. Moreover, the playwright Dreymann, rather than writing a play about suicide, writes a journalistic essay on suicide rates in the GDR, which he submits to the West German news magazine *Der Spiegel.* The fact that the only piece the playwright composes in the film is a journalistic essay implies that writers in the GDR were merely journalistically reflecting the society around them. Such was not the case. GDR writers who dealt with suicide did so with complex literariness, using suicide in ways that were much more subversive than merely stating that people in the GDR killed themselves. What the film ignores entirely is the relationship between suicide, literary heritage, and literariness in the GDR.

Wolf Biermann's lyrics from the song "Mich traf ein Mädchen" (1977), cited in the epigraph of this chapter, pose the same question that this study has pondered.[12] If, as historian Udo Grashoff has convincingly demonstrated, the suicide rates in the territory that became the GDR were not higher during the forty-year communist tenure and that most of the real suicides in the GDR were not politically motivated, as is commonly assumed and recently propagated by Donnersmarck's melodramatic film, what do the suicides in GDR narrative fiction represent? The answer to this question lies in the fact that fiction often contains more truth than simple, realistic reflections of society. The fact that there was no great number of protest-oriented suicides in the GDR, however, does not mean that the fictional suicides in GDR literature are not subversive. Suicides in GDR narrative fiction of the 1970s and 1980s perform functions that are much more subversive than merely suggesting that people commit suicide under communist regimes. Among other subversive functions, these rich fictional suicides disrupt the official literary heritage of the GDR and suggest that such literary heritage is self-destructive.

Epilogue: The Literariness of East German Literature

REINER KUNZE'S three-line, twelve-word poem "Selbstmord" (Suicide) was composed in 1971, the year that Erich Honecker gave his "No Taboos" speech, and the poem was published in 1972, the year that Ulrich Plenzdorf first published *Die neuen Leiden des jungen W.* Kunze's poem compares suicide to a door, states that it is the last door, but then counters that no one has ever knocked on all of the other doors.[1] On the surface, it is an inspirational poem concerned with suicide prevention. At first glance, it concretizes suicide as a "way out" and then gives the hope that there is another, less violent way out. Implicit in this reading of the poem is also the idea that no one should ever reach for the door of suicide, an idea that may strike some as condescending and moralistic. Jean Améry, for example, deplored both psychological and sociological approaches to suicide, because they take the volition away from the person who commits suicide.[2] Michel Foucault, furthermore, defends one's right to take one's own life.[3] In other words: Who is Reiner Kunze to say that there are always other open doors? Such a debate, however, is about real, historical suicides. But such readings are not the only possible ones. After all, this is a poem.

Read somewhat differently, Kunze's poem provides an appropriate image for this study. The poem does not indicate where the door of suicide leads, nor does it indicate whether it is an exit, as most readers might assume, or whether it might be an entrance. Each door has two sides. For the study of GDR literature, fictional suicides are not only a way out but also a way in. The poem indicates, furthermore, that there are a myriad of such doors. Fictional suicides allow the scholar, as well as the writer and the reader, to enter into issues of memory and transtextuality in the GDR, as much as transtextuality provides a way into the idea of suicide. Suicide is one of many doors into GDR literature, but it is one that has, until now, remained largely shut.

This study has opened a door into suicide in GDR literature, but it has not knocked on all possible doors of suicide in GDR literature. There is no shortage of such texts. There are also GDR films that deal with suicide. There are GDR works of literature that contain suicide attempts. In short, suicide in GDR literature deserves much more examination. It is my hope not only that such work may be completed but also that it will take into account the fact that GDR literary suicides are more than mere historicist reflections of suicide in GDR society. Paying attention to the literariness of such literature allows for close readings that reveal rhetorically powerful literary devices that may be much more subversive than simply stating that GDR citizens killed themselves.

Further, my plea is that GDR literature in general should be read as literature, with literary methodology and an honest appreciation of the human imagination. Suicide in GDR literature is but one case study in an expansive body of rich texts. As Christa Wolf insisted in 1968: "Literatur und Wirklichkeit stehen sich nicht gegenüber wie Spiegel und das, was gespiegelt wird"[4] (Literature and reality do not stand directly across from one another in the way that a mirror and its reflection do). Literature and reality correlate, to be sure, but not as mirror images, not as simple reflections. Literature is complex, mediated, and rhetorical. Scholars studying East German literature will do well to keep this in mind, not despite the highly politically and rhetorically charged nature of the GDR but precisely because of it.

Notes

Introduction

[1] Michael Douglas Schleihauf Zimmermann, "Suicide in the German Novel, 1945–1989" (PhD diss., University of Waterloo, Canada, 1997), 62; Michael Rohrwasser, "Das Selbstmordmotiv in der DDR-Literatur," in *Probleme deutscher Identität: Zeitgenössische Autobiographien; Identitätssuche und Zivilisationskritik*, ed. Paul Gerhard Klussman and Heinrich Mohr (Bonn: Bouvier, 1983), 209–32; Fritz J. Raddatz, "Mein Name sei Tonio K," *Der Spiegel*, June 2, 1969.

[2] Ulrich Plenzdorf, *Die neuen Leiden des jungen W.* (West Berlin: Suhrkamp, 1978). Originally published in the journal *Sinn und Form* in 1972 and in the form of a book the following year by Hinstorff in the East and by Suhrkamp in the West.

[3] Johann Wolfgang von Goethe, *Die Leiden des jungen Werther*, in *Sämtliche Werke*, series 1, vol. 8, ed. Waltraud Wiethölter (Frankfurt am Main: Deutscher Klassiker, 1985), 9–267.

[4] Invocation of the Central Committee of the German Communist Party to the German people on June 11, 1945, in the *Deutsche Volkszeitung* on June 13, 1945. Appears in Matthias Judt, ed., *DDR-Geschichte in Dokumenten: Beschlüsse, Berichte, interne Materialien und Alltagszeugnisse* (Berlin: Christoph Links, 1998), 45. All translations in this volume are my own, unless otherwise noted.

[5] Wilhelm Pieck, *Zur Bildungspolitik der Arbeiterbewegung: Reden und Schriften*, ed. Rudi Schulze (Berlin: Volk & Wissen, 1981), 212.

[6] Anton Ackermann, cited in *Dokumente zur Kunst-, Literatur-, und Kulturpolitik der SED*, ed. Elimar Schubbe (Stuttgart: Seewald, 1972), 55.

[7] Wolfgang Emmerich, *Kleine Literaturgeschichte der DDR* (Berlin: Aufbau, 2000), 86; Theo Honnef, *Heinrich von Kleist in der Literatur der DDR* (New York: Peter Lang, 1988).

[8] Honnef, *Heinrich von Kleist in der Literatur der DDR*, 19.

[9] Ibid.

[10] Ibid.

[11] See "Erbe" in the index to Schubbe, *Dokumente zur Kunst-, Literatur-, und Kulturpolitik der SED*, 1806.

[12] Udo Grashoff, *"In einem Anfall von Depression . . .": Selbsttötungen in der DDR* (Berlin: Christoph Links, 2006), 269–70.

[13] Edwin S. Shneidmann, *Definition of Suicide* (New York: Wiley, 1985); Antoon A. Leenaars ed., *Suicidology: Essays in Honor of Edwin S. Shneidman* (Northvale, NJ: Aronson, 1993); Danuta Wasserman and Camilla Wasserman, eds., *Oxford Textbook of Suicidology and Suicide Prevention: A Global Perspective* (Oxford: Oxford University Press, 2009).

[14] Udo Grashoff, *"In einem Anfall von Depression. . . ."*

[15] Matthias Matussek, *Das Selbstmord-Tabu: Von der Seelenlosigkeit des SED-Staates* (Reinbek bei Hamburg: Rowohlt, 1992).

[16] Christa Wolf, *Nachdenken über Christa T.* (Halle: Mitteldeutscher Verlag, 1968).

[17] Fritz J. Raddatz, "Mein Name sei Tonio K," 153. Raddatz claims that 27 out of every 100,000 citizens of the GDR killed themselves.

[18] Michael Rohrwasser, "Das Selbstmordmotiv in der DDR-Literatur."

[19] Udo Grashoff, *"In einem Anfall von Depression . . . ,"* 448–69; Dieter Sevin, *Textstrategien in DDR-Prosawerken zwischen Bau und Durchbruch der Berliner Mauer* (Heidelberg: C. Winter, 1994), 88–89.

[20] Magdalene Mueller, "Alltagserfahrung? Bemerkungen zur Darstellung des Todes in der neueren DDR-Literatur," in *Studies in GDR Culture and Society* 8, ed. Margy Gerber (Lanham, MD: University Press of America, 1988), 127–40. Mueller lists the following works: Jurij Brezan's *Bild des Vaters* (1983), Egon Richter's *Der Tod des alten Mannes* (1983), Uwe Saeger's *Noehr* (1980), Günter de Bruyn's *Neue Herrlichkeit* (1984), Charlotte Worgitztky's *Heute sterben immer nur die andern* (1986), and Christoph Hein's *Der fremde Freund* (1982).

[21] Ernst Bloch, *Das Prinzip Hoffnung* (Frankfurt am Main: Suhrkamp, 1982).

[22] For more on Bloch's influence on Christa Wolf, see Andreas Huyssen, "Traces of Ernst Bloch: Reflections on Christa Wolf," in *Responses to Christa Wolf: Critical Essays*, ed. Marilyn Sibley Fries (Detroit: Wayne State University Press, 1989), 233–47.

[23] *Michael Douglas Schleihauf* Zimmermann, *Suicide in the German Novel.*

[24] Wolfgang Emmerich, "Für eine andere Wahrnehmung der DDR-Literatur: Neue Kontexte, neue Paradigmen, ein neuer Kanon," in *Geist und Macht: Writers and the State in the GDR.*, ed. Axel Goodbody and Dennis Tate, German Monitor 29 (Amsterdam: Rodopi, 1992), 7–22.

[25] David Bathrick, *The Powers of Speech: The Politics of Culture in the GDR* (Lincoln: University of Nebraska Press, 1995).

[26] Julia Hell, *Post-Fascist Fantasies* (Durham, NC: Duke University Press, 1997).

[27] Benjamin Robinson, *The Skin of the System: On Germany's Socialist Modernity* (Stanford, CA: Stanford University Press, 2009).

[28] Gérard Genette, *Palimpsests: Literature in the Second Degree*, trans. Channa Newman and Claude Doubinsky (Lincoln: University of Nebraska Press, 1997), 212. Originally published in 1982 by Edition du Seuil.

[29] Werner Heiduczek, *Tod am Meer* (Berlin: Aufbau, 1999). Originally published in 1977.

[30] Christa Wolf, *Kein Ort. Nirgends* (Darmstadt: Luchterhand, 1979). In English, *No Place on Earth*, trans. Jan Van Heurck (New York: Farrar, Straus & Giroux: 1982).

[31] Heiner Müller, *Die Hamletmaschine*. In Müller, *Werke*, vol. 4, ed. Frank Hörnigk (Frankfurt am Main: Suhrkamp, 2001), 543–54. Sybille Muthesius, *Flucht in die Wolken* (Berlin: Der Morgen, 1981).

[32] Christoph Hein, *Horns Ende* (Darmstadt: Luchterhand, 1985).

Chapter One

[1] Rolf Schneider, "Imagination," in *19 Erzähler der DDR*, ed. Hans-Jürgen Schmitt (Frankfurt am Main: Fischer, 1971).

[2] David Lester, *Suicide and the Holocaust* (New York: Nova, 2005).

[3] Thomas Fox, *Stated Memory: East Germany and the Holocaust* (Rochester, NY: Camden House, 1999).

[4] Anna Seghers, *Das siebte Kreuz* (Hamburg: Rowohlt, 1965). Translations are taken from Anna Seghers, *The Seventh Cross*, trans. James A. Galston (Jaffrey, NH: Verba Mundi, 2004).

[5] Anna Seghers, *Transit* (Berlin: Aufbau, 1993).

[6] Friedrich Albrecht, *Bemühungen: Arbeiten zum Werk von Anna Seghers* (Bern: Peter Lang, 2005), 249.

[7] Anna Seghers, *Der Ausflug der toten Mädchen: Und andere Erzählungen* (Berlin: Aufbau, 1995).

[8] Anna Seghers, *Die toten bleiben jung* (Darmstadt: Luchterhand, 1980), 160–64.

[9] The development of the film adaption and the correspondence between Seghers and Schneider is outlined by Ian Wallace, "Andere Lösung Quatsch: Anna Seghers and the Film of *Die toten bleiben jung*," in *Aliens—Uneingebürgerte: German and Austrian Writers in Exile*, ed. Ian Wallace (Amsterdam: Rodopi, 1994), 74–75.

[10] Hans Fallada, *Jeder stirbt für sich allein* (Berlin: Aufbau, 2012).

[11] Jurek Becker, *Jakob der Lügner* (Frankfurt am Main: Suhrkamp, 1977).

[12] Christa Wolf, *Nachdenken über Christa T.* (Halle: Mitteldeutscher Verlag, 1968); and *Kindheitsmuster* (Berlin: Aufbau, 1976).

[13] Heiner Müller, *Der Lohndrücker, Philoktet, Die Schlacht: Textausgabe mit Materialien* (Berlin: Klett, 1986).

[14] Uwe Johnson, *Mutmassungen über Jakob* (Frankfurt am Main: Suhrkamp, 2000).

[15] Uwe Johnson, *Jahrestage: Aus dem Leben von Gesine Cresspahl* (Frankfurt am Main: Suhrkamp, 2000).

[16] Erwin Strittmatter, *Ole Bienkopp* (Berlin: Aufbau, 1977).

[17] Ibid., 375.

[18] Ibid., 404.

[19] Christa Wolf, *Der geteilte Himmel* (Munich: Deutscher Taschenbuch Verlag, 1973). Originally translated as *Divided Heaven*, but a more recent translation has the title *They Divided the Sky.*

[20] Hell, *Post-Fascist Fantasies*, 164.

[21] Fritz J. Raddatz, "Mein Name sei Tonio K.," *Der Spiegel*, June 2, 1969, http://www.spiegel.de/spiegel/print/d-45741041.html.

[22] Ibid.

[23] Rolf Schneider, "Imagination," in *19 Erzähler der DDR*, ed. Hans-Jürgen Schmitt (Frankfurt am Main: Fischer, 1971), 156.

[24] Ibid., 160.

Chapter Two

[1] Dieter Sevin, *Textstrategien in DDR-Prosawerken*, 82.

[2] Gundula Sharman, *Twentieth-century Reworkings of German Literature: An Analysis of Six Fictional Reinterpretations from Goethe to Thomas Mann* (Rochester, NY: Camden House, 2002), 124.

[3] Stephan Hermlin, "Erwiderung auf Friedrich Karl Kaul," *Sinn und Form* 25 (1973): 244.

[4] Friedrich Karl Kaul, Letter, *Sinn und Form* 24 (1972): 219–20.

[5] Monika Sch., "Der neue Werther: Ein Gespräch," *Neue Deutsche Literatur* 21, no. 3 (1973): 139.

[6] Peter J. Brenner, *Plenzdorf's "Neue Leiden des jungen W."* (Frankfurt am Main: Suhrkamp, 1982), 21.

[7] "Ist es denn wirklich so, dass wir jeden Dreck, der vom Westen kommt, nur kopieren müssen? Ich denke, Genossen, mit der Monotonie des Je-Je-Je, und wie das alles heißt, ja, sollte man doch Schluss machen." The allusion "Je-Je-Je" is to the refrain from the Beatles' 1963 song "She Loves You": "yeah, yeah, yeah." Walter Ulbricht, SED Archives (IfGA/ZPA). IV 2.1. 190.

[8] Honecker, speech given on December 15, 1971, reprinted in *Neues Deutschland*, December 18, 1971, 5.

[9] West German critic Dieter E. Zimmer also makes a comparison between *Die neuen Leiden des jungen W.* and *Die Legende von Paul und Paula*. For

Zimmer, both works represent a thaw in the restrictions on GDR cultural production, but he does not mention that suicide occurs in both works. Dieter E. Zimmer, "Nicht mehr so dogmatisch: Ulrich Plenzdorf, sein neuer Film *Paul und Paula* und sein Werther-Roman als Symptome einer neuen Offenheit," *Die Zeit*, April 20, 1973.

10 Genette, *Palimpsests*, 304.

11 Yuri Lotman, *Culture and Explosion*, ed. Marina Grishakova, trans. Wilma Clark (Berlin: de Gruyter, 2009).

12 Plenzdorf, *Die neuen Leiden*, 148.

13 These changes are described at length in Raymond G. Stokes, *Constructing Socialism: Technology and Change in East Germany, 1945–1990* (Baltimore: Johns Hopkins University Press, 2000). Such changes are also mentioned in Dolores L. Augustine, *Red Prometheus: Engineering and Dictatorship in East Germany, 1945–1990* (Cambridge, MA: MIT Press, 2007), 305.

14 For a general overview of both economics in the GDR and the state of scholarship on economics in the GDR, see Corey Ross, "The East German Economy: 'Planned Miracle,' Victim of Circumstance or Fundamentally Flawed?," in Ross, *The East German Dictatorship: Problems and Perspectives in the Interpretation of the GDR* (London: Arnold, 2002), 69–96. For an examination of the influence of the NÖSPL on GDR literature and culture, see Günter Erbe, *Verfemte Moderne: Die Auseinandersetzung mit dem "Modernismus" in Kulturpolitik, Literaturwissenschaft und Literatur der DDR* (Opladen: Westdeutscher Verlag, 1993).

15 As Corey Ross notes, "the entire reform effort [of the New Economic System] was more a political than economic programme; its aim was not a partial liberalization of the economy for its own sake, but rather in order to secure SED power and stabilize the GDR by improving its economic performance. It is hardly surprising, then, that the reforms were hamstrung from the outset by political expediency." Ross, *The East German Dictatorship*. 90.

16 Benjamin Robinson, *The Skin of the System*, 228–39.

17 Raymond G. Stokes, *Constructing Socialism*, 129–76.

18 Plenzdorf, *Die neuen Leiden*, 88.

19 Augustine. *Red Prometheus*, 246.

20 Lotman defines "semiosphere" as the "semiotic space, outside of which semiosis [that is, the creation of meaning] cannot exist." Yuri Lotman, "On the Semiosphere," trans. Wilma Clark, *Sign Systems Studies* 33, no. 1 (2005): 208.

21 Brenner, *Plenzdorf's "Neue Leiden des jungen W.,"* 44.

22 Georg Lukács, *Goethe und seine Zeit* (Bern: A. Francke, 1947).

23 Bruce Duncan and Jürgen Scharfschwerdt also see Lukács as the central figure in shaping GDR literary criticism on *Die Leiden des jungen Werther*. Bruce Duncan, *Goethe's Werther and the Critics* (Rochester, NY: Camden House,

2005), 80–82. Jürgen Scharfschwerdt, "Werther in der DDR: Bürgerliches Erbe zwischen sozialistischer Kulturpolitik und gesellschaftlicher Realität," *Jahrbuch der deutschen Schillergesellschaft* 22 (1978): 238–57. Daniel J. Farrelly, however, while noting Lukács's influence, avoids defining any singular GDR stance on *Die Leiden des jungen Werther*, seeing instead a plurality of stances. Farrelly, *Goethe in East Germany, 1949–1989: Toward a History of Goethe Reception in the GDR* (Rochester, NY: Camden House, 1998), 54–63.

[24] Peter Müller, *Zeitkritik und Utopie in Goethes "Werther"* (Berlin: Rütten & Loening, 1969).

[25] Brenner, *Plenzdorf's "Neue Leiden des jungen W.,"* 82–85.

[26] Hans-Georg Werner. "Peter Müller, Zeitkritik und Utopie in Goethes 'Werther,'" *Weimarer Beiträge* 7 (1970): 193–99.

[27] Kirsten Scherler, *"Wie froh bin ich, dass ich weg bin!": Werther in der deutschen Literatur* (Frankfurt am Main: Peter Lang, 2010), 108–9.

[28] Edgar Wibeau is one of Layne's examples for her claim that postwar Germans have often associated with black culture as a means of rebellion. "The Stranger Within: Black Voices, German Rebels" (PhD diss., University of California, Berkeley, 2011).

[29] Plenzdorf, *Die neuen Leiden*, 19.

[30] Others have made this point: Clayton Koelb, "'The Heavenly Revelation of Her Spirit': Goethe's *The Sorrows of the Young Werther*," in *The Revivifying Word: Literature, Philosophy, and the Theory of Life in Europe's Romantic Age* (Rochester, NY: Camden House, 2008), 47–67; Ehrhard Bahr, "Unerschlossene Intertextualität: MacPherson's Ossian und Goethe's Werther," *Goethe-Jahrbuch* 124 (2007): 178–88; Arnd Bohm, "'Klopstock!' Once More: Intertextuality in Werther," *Seminar: A Journal of Germanic Studies* 38, no. 2 (May 2002): 116–33; Martin Swales, *Goethe: The Sorrows of the Young Werther*, Landmarks of World Literature (Cambridge: Cambridge University Press, 1987), 39–44; Bruce Duncan, "'Emilia Galotti lag auf dem Pult aufgeschlagen': Werther as (Mis-)Reader," *Goethe Yearbook* 1 (1982): 42–50; Erdmann Waniek, "*Werther* lesen und Werther als Leser," *Goethe Yearbook* 1 (1982): 51–92; Carol E. W. Tobol and Ida H. Washington, "Werther's Selective Reading of Homer," *MLN* 92, no. 3 (1977): 596–601. However, given the percentage of the novel in which Werther is reading or talking about books, the relationship between Goethe's novel and the works that Werther reads is mentioned surprisingly little in secondary literature on *Werther.*

[31] Duncan, "'Emilia Galotti lag auf dem Pult aufgeschlagen,'" 44.

[32] Bohm. "'Klopstock!,'" 129.

[33] Tobol and Washington, "Werther's Selective Reading," 598–99.

[34] Ibid.

[35] Swales, *Goethe: The Sorrows of the Young Werther*, 40.

[36] Bahr, "Unerschlossene Intertextualität," 183–88. Duncan briefly made this point in "'Emilia Galotti lag auf dem Pult aufgeschlagen,'" 44.

[37] Duncan, "'Emilia Galotti lag auf dem Pult aufgeschlagen,'" 45.

[38] Bahr, "Unerschlossene Intertextualität," 188.

[39] Duncan, "'Emilia Galotti lag auf dem Pult aufgeschlagen,'" 42–43.

[40] Johann Wolfgang von Goethe, *Die Leiden des jungen Werther*, in *Sämtliche Werke*, vol. 1.8, ed. Waltraud Wiethölter (Frankfurt am Main: Deutscher Klassiker, 1985), 16–17.

[41] Genesis 29:1–20.

[42] Goethe, *Werther*, 36–55.

[43] The German original does not mention lightning directly, and may be better translated as "affected by the weather" rather than as "struck by lightning."

[44] Wolfgang Emmerich, *Kleine Literaturgeschichte der DDR*, 168, 171, 233, 371.

[45] Emmerich points out that Braun's 1977 poem "Müggelsee" is a rewriting of Klopstock's "Zürichersee." Emmerich, *Kleine Literaturgeschichte der DDR*, 225, 372–73.

[46] Klopstock, *Werke in einem Band* (Berlin: Bibliothek Deutscher Klassiker, 1971).

[47] Harro Zimmermann, *Freiheit und Geschichte: F. G. Klopstock als historischer Dichter und Denker* (Heidelberg: Carl Winter, 1987), 43.

[48] Ibid., 39–44.

[49] The ellipsis here indicates only an omission of a different narrator, which interrupts Edgar's narration. There is no omission here from Edgar's narration.

[50] Plenzdorf, *Die neuen Leiden*, 145–47.

[51] Ibid., 142–43.

[52] The abject plays an even greater role in the chapter on Werner Heiduczek's *Tod am Meer.*

[53] Julia Kristeva, *Powers of Horror: An Essay on Abjection*, trans. Leon S. Roudiez (New York: Columbia University Press, 1982), 4.

[54] Plenzdorf, *Die neuen Leiden*, 35.

[55] Ibid., 46.

[56] Ibid., 135.

[57] Horn's ghost says something remarkably similar in Christoph Hein's *Horns Ende*, as will become evident in the chapter on that novel: "Nicht ich bin es, der dich quält. Du bist es, du selbst" (99; I'm not the one who's torturing you. You're doing it to yourself. Further, the narrator of Christa Wolf's *Nachdenken über Christa T.* makes the same point before

the works of either Plenzdorf or Hein: "Sie selbst [the deceased Christa T.], natürlich, vergißt oder hat vergessen, sich, uns, Himmel und Erde, Regen und Schnee. Ich aber sehe sie noch" (7; she [the deceased Christa T.], naturally, forgets; she has forgotten herself, us, heaven and earth, rain and snow. But I can still see her." Clearly, discourses of remember and communicating with the dead were important in the East German imagination). *The Quest for Christa T.*, trans. Christopher Middleton (New York: Farrar, Straus & Giroux, 1970), 4.

[58] Yuri Lotman, *Die Struktur literarischer Texte*, trans. Rolf-Dietrich Keil (Munich: Wilhelm Fink, 1993), 338.

[59] Lotman, *Culture and Explosion*, 123.

[60] Brenner, *Plenzdorf's "Neue Leiden des jungen W.,"* 46–51.

Chapter Three

[1] Carsten Wurm, "'Uneigennützige Hilfeleistung': Ein Dokument zu Werner Heiduczeks Roman *Tod am Meer*," *Neue Deutsche Literatur: Zeitschrift für deutschsprachige Literatur* 44, no. 6 (Nov./Dec. 1996): 147.

[2] Ibid., 149.

[3] Ibid., 147.

[4] Michael Hametner, "Die Literatur von heute wird schnell vorbeigehen," interview with Werner Heiduczek, *Kunststoff* 3 (2006): 6–9.

[5] Heiduczek's children's literature, it should be stated, is also rich and merits study in its own right.

[6] Genette, *Palimpsests*, 290.

[7] Werner Liersch, "Wann die Wahrheit," *Neue Deutsche Literatur* 26, no. 3 (1978): 139–44.

[8] Hans Jürgen Geerdts, "Werner Heiduczek: Tod am Meer," *Weimarer Beiträge: Zeitschrift für Literaturwissenschaft*, 24, no. 5 (1978): 143–51.

[9] Achim Trebeß, "Zum Todesmotiv in der DDR-Literatur," *Weimarer Beiträge: Zeitschrift für Literaturwissenschaft*, 47, no. 1 (2001): 82–84.

[10] Grashoff, *"In einem Anfall von Depression*, 456.

[11] Trebeß, "Zum Todesmotiv in der DDR-Literatur," 86. This fits largely into the argument Zimmerman makes in his dissertation, namely that suicides in GDR literature represent a conflict between the individual and society.

[12] Heiduczek, *Tod am Meer*.

[13] Earlier in his manuscript Jablonski explicitly cites *Hamlet* (185).

[14] To my knowledge, this quotation appears nowhere in Rilke's oeuvre.

[15] Bertolt Brecht, *Arbeitsjournal* (Frankfurt am Main: Suhrkamp, 1973), 599.

16 Alfred Kurella, "Gespräch mit Alfred Kurella," *Sinn und Form* 2 (1975): 232.

17 Georg Lukács, "Über Preußentum" in *Internationale Literatur* 13, no. 5 (1943): 36–47.

18 Georg Lukács, "Die deutsche Literatur im Zeitalter des Imperialismus," *Internationale Literatur* 15, no. 3 (1945): 53–65; Georg Lukács, "Auf der Suche nach dem Bürger," *Internationale Literatur* 15, nos. 6–7 (1945): 58–75.

19 Georg Lukács, "Die Tragödie der modernen Kunst," in *Thomas Mann* (Berlin: Aufbau, 1949), 49–113; Georg Lukács, "Das Spielerische und seine Hintergründe," *Aufbau* 11, no. 6 (1955): 501–24.

20 Dorrit Cohn, "The Second Author of *Der Tod in Venedig*," in *Probleme der Moderne: Studien zur deutschen Literatur von Nietzsche bis Brecht; Festschrift für Walter Sokel*, ed. Benjamin Bennett, Anton Kaes, and William J. Lillyman (Tübingen: Max Niemeyer, 1983), 223–45.

21 Matias Martinez, "Choleratod und regressive Transzendenz: Thomas Mann, *Der Tod in Venedig* (1912)," in Martinez, *Doppelte Welten: Struktur und Sinn zweideutigen Erzählens* (Göttingen: Vandenhoeck & Ruprecht, 1996), 151–76.

22 Georg Lukács, "Deutsche Literatur im Zeitalter des Imperialismus," 1945. In *Skizze einer Geschichte der neueren deutschen Literatur*. (Neuwied: Luchterhand, 1963), 190. Inge Diersen, *Thomas Mann: Episches Werk, Weltanschauung, Leben*. 3rd ed. (Berlin: Aufbau, 1985), first published in 1975. Bernhard Böschenstein, "Exzentrische Polarität," in *Interpretationen: Thomas Mann; Romane und Erzählungen*. ed. Volkmar Hansen (Stuttgart: Reclam, 1993), 89–120. Note that both Lukács and Diersen were critics from the East Bloc.

23 Diersen, *Thomas Mann: Episches Werk*, 99.

24 Martinez, "Choleratod und regressive Transzendenz, 151–76.

25 Ernst Bloch, "Philosophische Ansicht des Detektivromans," in *Literarische Aufsätze*, vol. 9 of *Werkausgabe* (Frankfurt am Main: Suhrkamp, 1965): 242–63. The italics are Bloch's.

26 Ibid. Gérard Genette mentions similar aspects of detective fiction in *Narrative Discourse: An Essay in Method*, trans. Jane E. Lewin (Ithaca, NY: Cornell University Press, 1980). Originally published as "Discours du récit," a portion of *Figures III* (Paris: Editions du Seuil, 1972), 77, 196–97. Also, Edgar Marsch explicitly alludes to Bloch as he (Marsch) develops a typology of order in detective fiction in *Die Kriminalerzählung: Theorie, Geschichte, Analyse* (Munich: Winkler, 1972), 82.

27 Heiduczek, *Tod am Meer*, 19. The synagogue in Hindenburg (today Zabrze) was burned down on November 9, 1938, around eight o'clock in the morning by National Socialists as part of "Kristallnacht." "'Reichskristallnacht': Vor 65 Jahren; Rückfall in die Barbarei," *Unser Oberschlesien* 21, no. 13. (November 2003): 5–8.

[28] Julian Symons, *Bloody Murder: From the Detective Story to the Crime Novel: A History* (New York: Viking, 1985).

[29] Cohn, "The Second Author of *Der Tod in Venedig*," 223–45.

[30] Martinez, "Choleratod und regressive Transzendenz," 158.

[31] Monika Ankele, "Begrenzter Raum: Das Bett in der Frauenpsychiatrie um 1900," *Zeitschrift für Kulturwissenschaften* 2 (2008): 61–71.

[32] Ibid., 62.

[33] Ibid., 66–68.

[34] Lotman, *Culture and Explosion*, 121.

[35] Ibid., 121.

[36] Later I point to Kristeva's definition of the abject in order to describe the symbolic value of these symptoms. For now, by abjective symptoms, I mean simply that the body is excreting fluids.

[37] Simon Sebag Montefiore, *Stalin: The Court of the Red Tsar* (London: Phoenix, 2004), 661. (originally published by Weidenfeld & Nicolson, 2003). Montefiore also believes Stalin killed himself.

[38] The allusion here to Oedipus also foreshadows the subversive engagement with ancient Greek literature in Christa Wolf's *Kein Ort. Nirgends*, as is discussed in the next chapter.

[39] Thomas Mann, *Der Tod in Venedig* (Berlin: S. Fischer, 1913), 22.

[40] Julia Kristeva, *Julia Kristeva, Interviews*, ed. Ross Mitchell Guberman (New York: Columbia University Press, 1996), 118. Abjection also plays a role in the chapter on Plenzdorf's *Die neuen Leiden des jungen W.*

[41] Heiduczek, *Tod am Meer*, 187.

[42] The Bitterfelder Weg, initiated in 1959, was a program that encouraged writers to perform manual labor and encouraged laborers to write. It was named after the town of Bitterfeld, where the first conference to plan the program convened on April 24, 1959.

[43] Udo Grashoff, *"In einem Anfall von Depression,"* 456.

[44] Ibid., 456. Grashoff cites Koch from *Neues Deutschland*, April 15–16, 1978, 4.

[45] Heiduczek, *Tod am Meer*, 279. The allusion to Beethoven here also demonstrates how tiresome the official literary heritage of the GDR had become.

[46] Heiner Müller's play *Der Lohndrücker* deals with a similar paradox. The main character of the play, modeled after Hans Garbe, who became a Party propaganda tool because he once rebuilt a furnace while one of the ovens was still on, becomes both a socialist hero and a wage buster, or rather an instigator for the increase in production norms despite a decrease in worker safety.

[47] Slavoj Žižek, "When the Party Commits Suicide," in *Did Somebody Say Totalitarianism: Five Interventions in the (Mis)use of a Notion* (London: Verso, 2002), 88–140.

[48] J. Arch Getty and Oleg V. Naumov, *The Road to Terror: Stalin and the Self-Destruction of the Bolsheviks* (New Haven, CT: Yale University Press, 1999).

[49] Werner Heiduczek, "Statt eines Vorworts," in *Im gewöhnlichen Stalinismus: Meine unerlaubten Texte* (Leipzig: Kiepenheuer, 1991), 8.

Chapter Four

[1] See Anna K. Kuhn, *Christa Wolf's Utopian Vision: From Marxism to Feminism* (Cambridge: Cambridge University Press, 1988), 138; Theresa Hörnigk, *Christa Wolf* (Göttingen: Steidl, 1989), 187; Sonja Hilzinger, *Christa Wolf* (Stuttgart: Metzler, 1986), 106–8; Peter F. Teupe, *Christa Wolfs "Kein Ort. Nirgends" als Paradigma der DDR-Literatur der siebziger Jahre* (Frankfurt am Main: Peter Lang, 1992); and Jörg Magenau, *Christa Wolf: Eine Biographie* (Berlin: Kindler, 2002), 267–84.

[2] Jörg Magenau, *Christa Wolf: Eine Biographie*, 267–84.

[3] The interview was published: Christa Wolf, "Projectionsraum Romantik," interview by Frauke Meyer-Gosau, *alternative* 8 (1981/82), 239. See also Kuhn, "*No Place on Earth*: Revision of the Romantic Heritage," 138.

[4] Magenau, *Christa Wolf: Eine Biographie*, 285–301.

[5] Ann Stamp Miller, *The Cultural Politics of the German Democratic Republic: The Voices of Christa Wolf, Wolf Biermann, and Heiner Müller* (Boca Raton, FL: Brown Walker, 1999), 156.

[6] Ute Brandes, "Quotation as Authentication: *No Place on Earth*," in *Responses to Christa Wolf: Critical Essay*, ed. Marilyn Sibley Fries (Detroit, MI: Wayne State University Press, 1989), 329.

[7] Wolf, *Kein Ort. Nirgends*, 6; in English, *No Place on Earth*, 4.

[8] Genette, *Palimpsests*, 343.

[9] Ibid., 375.

[10] See Theo Honnef, *Heinrich Kleist in der Literatur der DDR* (New York: Peter Lang, 1988), 39–42.

[11] Honnef, *Heinrich von Kleist in der Literatur der DDR*, 41.

[12] Ibid., 58–61, 123–91.

[13] Ibid., 123–91.

[14] Ibid., 62.

[15] David Bathrick underscores this point: "Once linked to the most reactionary historical tendencies, nineteenth-century writers such as Kleist and Hölderlin, E. T. A. Hoffmann and Jean Paul, Günderrode and Bettina von Arnim suddenly [in the 1970s] were looked to not merely as literary models to be emulated but as articulating experiences that spoke directly to the contemporary society." Bathrick, *The Powers of Speech: The Politics of Culture in the GDR* (Lincoln: University of Nebraska Press, 1995), 187. Sture

Packalén also locates a change in the reception of romanticism in the GDR in the 1970s. For Packalén, the change is primarily related to an interest in the biographies of the romantic writers and artists. Packalén, *Zum Hölderlinbild in der Bundesrepublik und der DDR* (Stockholm: Acta Universitatis Upsaliensis, 1986), 58.

16 This description of Kleist also appears verbatim in Günter Kunert's "Pamphlet für K.," *Sinn und Form* 27 (1975): 1093. Theo Honnef cites Kunert citing the passage in *Heinrich von Kleist in der Literatur der DDR*, 123.

17 Günter Kunert, *Ein anderer K.* (Stuttgart: Reclam, 1977). Theo Honnef writes at length about this radio play in *Heinrich von Kleist in der Literatur der DDR*, 123–43.

18 This polyphony of voices ruminating about the mysterious death resembles Uwe Johnson's 1959 *Mutmaßungen über Jakob.* Kunert's radio play, like Johnson's book, reads like detective fiction.

19 Kunert. *Ein anderer K.*, 13.

20 Ibid., 15.

21 Again, the use of the posthumous voice has been used by William Faulkner and, in the context of divided Germany, Uwe Johnson in several works and later by Christoph Hein in *Horns Ende*, as will become evident in the chapter in this study on that work.

22 Kunert, *Ein anderer K.*, 42.

23 Heinrich von Kleist, "Über das Marionettentheater," In *Sämtliche Werke und Briefe*, ed. Helmut Sembdner, vol. 2 (Darmstadt: Wissenschaftliche Buchgesellschaft, 1983), 342; in English, Heinrich von Kleist, "On the Marionette Theatre," trans. Idris Parry, in the *Times Literary Supplement*, October 20, 1978, 1211–12. Also available at http://www.southerncrossreview.org/9/kleist.htm.

24 Wolf makes a similar argument in her 1968 essay "Lesen und Schreiben." Her point can be perceived in part as a response to the realism insisted upon by Georg Lukács. Azar Nafisi, in the Iranian context, makes the same point as she commands: "*do not*, under *any* circumstances, belittle a work of fiction by trying to turn it into a carbon copy of real life."Azar Nafisi, *Reading* Lolita *in Tehran: A Memoir in Books* (New York: Random House, 2003).

25 John Pizer makes a similar argument, namely that the violence and gender-bending in *Kein Ort. Nirgends* can be better understood by thinking of the novel as being influenced in part by Kleist's *Penthesilea*. He does not, however, point to textual examples from *Kein Ort. Nirgends* that allude to *Penthesilea*. John Pizer, "Staging Violence and Transcendence: Reading Christa Wolf through German Romanticism," *German Studies Review* 33, no. 1 (February 2010): 1–22.

26 Heinrich von Kleist, *Penthesilea: Ein Trauerspiel*, Studienausgabe, ed. Ulrich Port (Stuttgart: Reclam, 2012), lines 3025–34; In English, Heinrich

von Kleist, *Penthesilea: A Tragic Drama*, trans. Joel Agee (New York: Harper Collins, 1998), 142.

[27] Christa Wolf, "Kleists 'Penthesilea,'" in *Werke*, vol. 8., ed. Sonja Hilzinger (Munich: Luchterhand, 2000), 261–79. Written in August 1982.

[28] Christa Wolf, *Kassandra*. Frankfurt am Main: Luchterhand, 1983. See also Jean Wilson, "Transgression and Identity in Kleist's Penthesilea and Wolf's Cassandra," in *Women in German Yearbook: Feminist Studies in German Literature and Culture* 16 (2000): 191–206.

[29] Wolf, *Kein Ort. Nirgends*, 9–10; *No Place on Earth*, 6–7.

[30] Kleist, *Penthesilea*, scene 23, lines 41–54. *Penthesilea*, trans. Joel Agee, 127.

[31] Christa Wolf, "Der Schatten eines Traumes: Karoline von Günderrode—ein Entwurf," in Karoline von Günderrode, *Der Schatten eines Traumes: Gedichte, Prosa, Briefe, Zeugnisse von Zeitgenossen*, ed. Christa Wolf (Darmstadt: Luchterhand, 1979), 5.

[32] Fritz Wittels, "Heinrich von Kleist—Prussian Junker and Creative Genius: A Study in Bisexuality," in *Art and Psychoanalysis*, ed. William Phillips (New York: World, 1957), 165–82; Catriona MacLeod, "The 'Third Sex' in an Age of Difference: Androgyny and Homosexuality in Winckelmann, Friedrich Schlegel, and Kleist," in *Outing Goethe and His Age*, ed. Alice Kuzniar (Stanford, CA: Stanford University Press, 1996), 194–214; Joachim Pfeiffer, "Friendship and Gender: The Aesthetic Construction of Subjectivity in Kleist," trans. Robert D. Tobin, in Kuzniar, *Outing Goethe and His Age*, 215–27; Simon Richter, *Missing the Breast: Gender, Fantasy, and the Body in the German Enlightenment* (Seattle: University of Washington Press, 2006), 221–26. Christa Wolf also underscores this point in "Kleists 'Penthesilea,'" 270–71.

[33] Helen Fehervary, "Autorschaft, Geschlechtsbewusstsein und Öffentlichkeit: Versuch über Heiner Müllers *Die Hamletmaschine* and Christa Wolfs *Kein Ort. Nirgends*," in *Entwürfe von Frauen in der Literatur des 20. Jahrhunderts*, ed. Irma von der Lühe (Berlin: Argument, 1982): 132–53; Sara Lennox, "Christa Wolf and the Women Romantics," in *Studies in GDR Culture and Society*, ed. Margy Gerber. (Washington, DC: University Press of America, 1982), 31–44; Anna Kuhn, *Christa Wolf's Utopian Vision*.

[34] Maximilian Harden made this point as early as 1895. See his text in *Schriftsteller über Kleist: Eine Dokumentation*, ed. Peter Goldammer (Berlin; Aufbau, 1976), 452.

[35] Wolf, *Kein Ort. Nirgends*, 56–57.

[36] Christa Wolf, "Kleists 'Penthesilea,'" 269.

[37] This island is today known as Hispaniola and is divided into Haiti and the Dominican Republic. Indeed, the story is largely about the Haitian slave revolution.

[38] Eberhard Lämmert, *Bauformen des Erzählens* (Stuttgart: Metzler, 1972), 40. Originally published in 1955.

[39] Martin Greenberg, ed., "Introduction," in Heinrich von Kleist, *Five Plays* (New Haven, CT: Yale University Press, 1988), ix–li.

[40] Many scholars have noted this. See, for example Joachim Pfeiffer, "Friendship and Gender: The Aesthetic Construction of Subjectivity in Kleist," trans. Robert D. Tobin, in Kuzniar, *Outing Goethe and His Age*, 222; Franz M. Eybl, *Kleist-Lektüren* (Vienna: WUV Facultas (UTB), 2007), 92; Martin Greenberg, ed., "Introduction," xx, xxx–xxxi, xxxviii–xl; Simon Richter, *Missing the Breast*, 227.

[41] Genette, *Palimpsests*, 375.

[42] Theo Honnef indicates this quite explicitly: "Die Romantiker aber blieben von dem offiziell sanktionierten Literaturkanon ausgeschlossen." Honnef, *Heinrich Kleist in der Literatur der DDR*, 27.

[43] David Bathrick underscores this point: "Once linked to the most reactionary historical tendencies, nineteenth-century writers such as Kleist and Hölderlin, E. T. A. Hoffmann and Jean Paul, Günderrode and Bettina von Armin suddenly [in the 1970s] were looked to not merely as literary models to be emulated but as articulating experiences that spoke directly to the contemporary society," *Powers of Speech*, 187. Sture Packalén also locates a change in the reception of romanticism in the GDR in the 1970s. For Packalén, the change is primarily related to an interest in the biographies of the romantic writers and artists. Packalén, *Zum Hölderlinbild in der Bundesrepublik und der DDR*.

[44] Anna K. Kuhn, *Christa Wolf's Utopian Vision*, 142–43.

[45] Christa Wolf and Anna Seghers, *Das dicht besetzte Leben: Briefe, Gespräche und Essays*, ed. Angela Drescher (Berlin: Aufbau, 2003), 43, letter dated June 20,1978.

[46] Ibid., letter dated December 7, 1977.

[47] Karoline von Günderrode, *Der Schatten eines Traumes: Gedichte, Prosa, Briefe, Zeugnisse von Zeitgenossen*, ed. Christa Wolf (Darmstadt: Luchterhand, 1979).

[48] Brigitte Reimann and Christa Wolf, *Sei gegrüßt und lebe: Eine Freundschaft in Briefen, 1964–1973* (Berlin: Aufbau, 1999), 34.

[49] Jörg Magenau, *Christa Wolf: Eine Biographie*, 240.

[50] Wolf and Seghers, *Das dicht besetzte Leben*, 29, letter dated May 10, 1970.

[51] Emmerich, for example, mentions Günderrode only three times in his *Kleine Literaturgeschichte der DDR*, 294, 336, and 338. All three instances are related to Wolf's *Kein Ort. Nirgends.*

[52] Lukács, indeed, speaks of literary history in the metaphorical terms of healthy versus ill. See Ferenc Fehér's exposition of this dichotomy in Lukács's

thought in "Lukács in Weimar," in *Lukács Reappraised*, ed. Agnes Heller (New York: Columbia University Press, 1983): 75–106.

[53] Günderrode, *Der Schatten eines Traumes*, 128.

[54] Ibid., *Ich sende Dir ein zärtliches Pfand: Die Briefe der Karoline von Günderrode*, ed. Birgit Weißenborn (Frankfurt am Main: Insel, 1992), 380.

[55] Ibid., 383–84.

[56] Ibid., 201.

[57] Ibid., 385.

[58] Steven D. Martinson, "'. . . aus dem Schiffbruch des irdischen Lebens': The Literature of Karoline von Günderrode and Early German Romantic and Idealist Philosophy," *German Studies Review* 28, no. 2 (May 2005): 304.

[59] Edith Hamilton, *Mythology* (New York: Mentor, 1969), 90–91. Originally published in 1940.

[60] Ibid., 90.

[61] Lotman, *Die Struktur literarischer Texte*, 338.

[62] Johann Wolfgang von Goethe, *Briefe aus der Schweiz*, in *Weimarer Ausgabe*, ser. 1, 19:323; in English, *Letters from Switzerland, Letters from Italy*, trans. A. J. W. Morrison, ed. Nathan Haskel Dole (Boston: Francis A. Niccolls, 1902), 15–16.

[63] Friedrich Schiller, "Nänie," in *Werke und Briefe*, ed. Georg Kurscheidt, vol. 1 (Frankfurt am Main: Deutscher Klassiker, 1992), 182–83; in English, "Nenia," in *Poetical Works of Friedrich Schiller*, trans. E. P. Arnold-Forster, ed. Nathan Haskell Dole (Boston: Francis A. Niccolls, 1902), 253–54.

[64] Steven D. Martinson, "'. . . aus dem Schiffbruch des irdischen Lebens,' 311; Markus Hille, *Karoline von Günderrode* (Reinbek: Rowohlt, 1999).

[65] See, for example, Lukács, *Die Zerstörung der Vernunft*, vol. 9 of *Werke*, ed. Frank Benseler (Neuwied: Lukács Archive, 1954).

[66] Lotman, *Culture and Explosion*, 144.

[67] Mechthild Quernheim, *Das moralische Ich: Kritische Studien zur Subjektwerdung in der Erzählprosa Christa Wolfs* (Würzburg: Königshausen & Neumann, 1990), 189.

[68] Wolf, *Kein Ort. Nirgends*, 5.

[69] Heinrich von Kleist, *Sämtliche Briefe*, ed. Dieter Heimböckel (Stuttgart: Reclam, 1999), 266.

[70] Walter Benjamin, "Der Erzähler: Betrachtungen zum Werk Nikolai Lesskows," in *Gesammelte Schriften* (Frankfurt am Main: Suhrkamp, 1991), 2.2:446; In English, "The Storyteller: Reflections of the Works of Nikolai Leskov," in *Illuminations*, trans. Harry Zohn, ed. Hannah Arendt (New York: Schocken, 1969), 90.

[71] Indeed, David Wellbery has edited a volume of essays on Kleist's "Das Erdbeben in Chili" that showcase a variety of literary methodologies. Kleist's

story lends itself easily to such a variety of approaches. David Wellbery, ed., *Positionen der Literaturwissenschaft: Acht Modellanalysen am Beispiel von Kleists "Das Erdbeben in Chili}* (Munich: Beck, 1985).

[72] Ute Brandes, "Quotation as Authentication: *No Place on Earth*," in *Responses to Christa Wolf: Critical Essays*, ed. Marilyn Sibley Fries (Detroit: Wayne State University Press, 1989), 329.

[73] Astrid Köhler, *Brückenschläge: Autoren vor und nach der Wiedervereinigung* (Göttingen: Vandenhoeck & Ruprecht, 2007), 22–29.

[74] Ibid., 23.

[75] Eberhard Lämmert, *Bauformen des Erzählens*, 26–28.

[76] Hell, *Post-Fascist Fantasies.*

[77] Yuri M. Lotman, *Universe of the Mind: A Semiotic Theory of Culture*, trans. Ann Shukman (London: Tauris, 1990), 143–50.

[78] Ibid., 126.

Chapter Five

[1] Jeff Todd Titon, "Text," in *Eight Words for the Study of Expressive Culture* (Champaign: University of Illinois Press, 2003), 74.

[2] Georgina Paul, *Perspectives on Gender in Post-1945 German Literature* (Rochester, NY: Camden House, 2009), 192.

[3] *Hamletmaschine* is not the only work of literature that relates to Inge Müller's suicide; Wolf Biermann composed a rather offensive poem titled "Legende vom Selbstmord der Inge Müller im Jahre '66,'" which Müller's fourth wife and widow, Brigitte Mayer, refused to allow to be published in an anthology of works by and about Inge Müller. "Das Veto der Witwe," *Der Spiegel*, June 10, 1996, http://www.spiegel.de/spiegel/print/d-8933790.html.

[4] Jonathan Kalb, *The Theater of Heiner Müller* (Cambridge: Cambridge University Press, 1998), 6–7.

[5] Heiner Müller, "Dichter müssen dumm sein," *Die Zeit*, August 14, 1987, http://www.a-e-m-gmbh.com/andremuller/heiner%20mueller.html.

[6] William Shakespeare, *Hamlet*, act 3, scene 1, lines 57–64.

[7] Heiner Müller, *Hamletmaschine.*

[8] Walter Benjamin, "Linke Melancholie," in *Angelus Novus* (Frankfurt am Main: Suhrkamp, 1966), 457–61.

[9] Wendy Brown, "Resisting Left Melancholy," in *Loss*, ed. David L. Eng and David Kazanjian (Berkeley: University of California Press, 2003), 460.

[10] Max Pensky, *Melancholy Dialectics: Walter Benjamin and the Play of Mourning* (Amherst: University of Massachusetts Press, 1993), 12.

[11] Walter Benjamin, "Agesilaus Santander," in *Gesammelte Schriften* (Frankfurt am Main: Suhrkamp, 1991), 6:520–23. Saturn, the Roman god of

agriculture, after which the planet was named, has long been associated with melancholia. Susan Sontag wrote a collection of essays called *Under the Sign of Saturn*, in which the title essay is about Walter Benjamin. Susan Sontag, "Under the Sign of Saturn," in *Under the Sign of Saturn* (New York: Farrar, Straus, & Giroux, 1980).

[12] Of course, Benjamin killed himself not out of melancholia but because he had no other option besides being captured by the Nazis and taken to a concentration camp, where he likely would have been killed anyway. However, Sontag writes: "Scholem has written that the first of several times Benjamin contemplated suicide was in the summer of 1931. The second time was the following summer, when he wrote 'Agesilaus Santander.'" Sontag further notes: "He [Benjamin] thought that there was a peculiarly modern temptation to suicide . . . Suicide is understood as a response of the heroic will to the defeat of the will. The only way to avoid suicide, Benjamin suggests, is to be beyond heroism, beyond efforts of the will." Susan Sontag, "Under the Sign of Saturn," 131–32.

[13] Pensky, *Melancholy Dialectics*, 14.

[14] Benjamin, *Gesammelte Schriften*, 1.1:334–35.

[15] Wolfgang Borchert, *Draußen vor der Tür* (Hamburg: Rowohlt, 1986), 12–13.

[16] Ibid., 12.

[17] Michael D. Richardson, "Allegories and Ends: Heiner Müller's "Hamletmaschine," *New German Critique* 98 (Summer 2006): 89.

[18] Ibid., 95.

[19] Hellmut Karasek, "Brecht ist tot," *Der Spiegel*, February 27, 1978, 216–17.

[20] Heiner Müller, *Rotwelsch* (Berlin: Merve, 1982), 149.

[21] Heiner Müller, Interview, *Theater heute* 1 (January 1984): 61–62. David Bathrick recounts these developments in his monograph *The Powers of Speech: The Politics of Culture in the GDR* (Lincoln: University of Nebraska Press, 1995),151.

[22] Kalb, *The Theater of Heiner Müller*, 18.

[23] Michael D. Richardson establishes this point as well. Richardson, "Allegories and Ends," 88.

[24] Genette, *Palimpsests*, 303–11.

[25] Ibid., 202–5, 377–81.

[26] Günther Klotz, "Shakespeare Contemporized: GDR Shakespeare Adaptations from Bertolt Brecht to Heiner Müller," in *Redefining Shakespeare: Literary Theory and Theater Practice in the German Democratic Republic*, ed. J. Lawrence Guntner and Andrew M. McLean (Newark: University of Delaware Press, 1998), 93.

[27] Muthesius, *Flucht in die Wolken*, 505.

[28] We now know that Muthesius is Sibylle Boden-Gerstner, founder of the fashion magazine *Sibylle* and costume designer for DEFA films, who died on Christmas Day, 2016. Pony is her daughter Sonja Gerstner. And Pony's sister, called Maja in the book, is Daniela Dahn, an award-winning author and journalist. Their father, Karl-Heinz Gerstner, was a well-connected journalist in the GDR.

[29] Grashoff, *"In einem Anfall von Depression."*

[30] The GDR was not alone in having a mental health crisis. A review of *Flucht in die Wolken* published in *Der Spiegel* in 1982 made it clear that that the Federal Republic also had deficiencies in the way it dealt with mental health issues. "Deutsche Leiden," *Der Spiegel*, July 26, 1982, http://www.spiegel.de/spiegel/print/d-14341949.html.

[31] Christine Cosentino, Review of *Flucht in die Wolken*, *GDR Bulletin* 9, no. 3 (1983): 10.

[32] Muthesius, *Flucht in die Wolken*, 106.

[33] Ibid., 425.

[34] Michel Foucault, "Nietzsche, Freud, Marx," in *Aesthetics, Method, and Epistemology*, ed. James D. Faubion (New York: New Press, 1998), 271–72.

[35] Bertolt Brecht, "Lob des Kommunismus," in *Gesammelte Werke* (Frankfurt: Suhrkamp, 1968), 9.2:463–64.

Chapter Six

[1] Phillip McKnight, *Understanding Christoph Hein* (Columbia: University of South Carolina Press, 1995), 74.

[2] Portions of this letter are provided in English translation by Phillip McKnight in *Understanding Christoph Hein*, 74–76.

[3] For example, see Christoph Hein, "Wir werden es lernen müssen, mit unserer Vergangenheit zu leben," interview with Krzysztof Jachimczak (1986), in *Christoph Hein: Texte, Daten, Bilder*, ed. Lothar Baier (Frankfurt am Main: Luchterhand, 1990). Also, David Clarke provides a good summary of Hein's essays on history-writing and literature in "Mit Kunst der Welt beikommen," chapter 1 of his monograph *"Diese merkwürdige Kleinigkeit einer Vision": Christoph Hein's Social Critique in Transition* (Amsterdam: Rodopi, 2002).

[4] Bernd Fischer, *Christoph Hein: Drama und Prosa im letzten Jahrzehnt der DDR* (Heidelberg: Winter, 1990), 92.

[5] Fischer, *Christoph Hein*, 95.

[6] Joachim Lehmann, "Christoph Hein—Chronist und 'historischer Materialist,'" *Text + Kritik* 111 (July 1991): 44–56.

[7] Ibid., 50–51.

[8] Michael Douglas Schleihauf Zimmermann, *Suicide in the German Novel, 1945–1989* (PhD diss., University of Waterloo, Canada, 1997), 108–27.

[9] Emile Durkheim, *Suicide: A Study in Sociology*, trans. John A. Saulding and George Simpson, ed. George Simpson (Glencoe, IL: Free Press, 1951).

[10] Shakespeare, *Hamlet*, act 1, scene 5, line 91.

[11] Stephen Greenblatt, *Hamlet in Purgatory* (Princeton, NJ: Princeton University Press, 2001), 251.

[12] Wolfram Schlenker, *Das "kulturelle Erbe" in der DDR: Gesellschaftliche Entwicklung und Kulturpolitik, 1945–1965* (Stuttgart: Metzler, 1977), 156.

[13] Arpad Kadarkay, *Georg Lukács: Life, Thought, and Politics* (Cambridge, MA: Blackwell, 1991), 334.

[14] Emmerich, *Kleine Literaturgeschichte der DDR*, 153.

[15] David Bathrick, *The Powers of Speech: The Politics of Culture in the GDR*, 261.

[16] Emmerich, *Kleine Literaturgeschichte der DDR*, 248.

[17] Georg Lukács makes this point at least twice: *The Historical Novel* (Lincoln: University of Nebraska Press, 1983), 96; and *Writer and Critic* (London: Merlin, 1970), 159–60.

[18] Klaus Hammer, "*Horns Ende*: Versuch einer Interpretation" (1987), in *Chronist ohne Botschaft*, ed. Klaus Hammer (Berlin: Aufbau, 1992), 12.

[19] Christoph Hein, "Hamlet und der Parteisekretär," in *Schlötel oder Was solls: Stücke und Essays.* (Darmstadt: Luchterhand, 1986), 21–85. Excerpt from "Christoph Hein antwortet auf Fragen von *Theater der Zeit*," *Theater der Zeit* 7 (1978).

[20] Christoph Hein, "Die Zeit, die nicht vergehen kann oder Das Dilemma des Chronisten: Gedanken zum Historikerstreit anlässlich zweier deutscher vierzigster Jahrestage," in *Der Ort: Das Jahrhundert* (Frankfurt am Main: Suhrkamp, 2003), 140. This is likely a reference to Ferdinand Freiligrath's 1844 poem "Deutschland ist Hamlet." Heiner Müller also quoted Freiligrath's poem in the program for his play *Hamletmaschine.*

[21] Mark Pizzato, "Ancient Specters (Prehistoric, Egyptian, Greek, and Roman)," in *Ghosts of Theatre and Cinema in the Brain* (New York: Palgrave MacMillan, 2006).

[22] Jean-Michel Rabaté, *The Ghosts of Modernity* (Gainesville: University Press of Florida, 1996). See also Alice Rayner, *Ghosts: Death's Double and the Phenomena of Theatre* (Minneapolis: University of Minnesota Press, 2006).

[23] Avery F. Gordon, *Ghostly Matters: Haunting and the Sociological Imagination*, 2nd ed. (Minneapolis: University of Minnesota Press, 2008).

[24] E. Pearlman, *William Shakespeare: The History Plays* (New York: Twayne, 1992), 71, 73.

[25] Ibid., 73. Greenblatt makes the same point in *Hamlet in Purgatory*, 164–65.

[26] Gordon, *Ghostly Matters.*

[27] Greenblatt, *Hamlet in Purgatory*, 158.

[28] "I am thy father's spirit,/Doomed for a certain term to walk the night,/ And for the day confined to fast in fires/Till the foul crimes done in my days of nature/Are burnt and purged away." Shakespeare, *Hamlet*, act 1, scene 5, lines 9–13.

[29] Greenblatt, *Hamlet in Purgatory*, 185, 195, 206.

[30] See Hilary Mimpriss, "'Ohne Hoffnung können wir nicht leben': Christoph Hein's Use of Religious Motifs as an Expression of Resignation and of Hope," in *Christoph Hein in Perspective*, ed. Graham Jackman, German Monitor 51 (Amsterdam: Rodopi, 2000), 95–114.

[31] David Clarke, *"Diese merkwürdige Kleinigkeit einer Vision": Christoph Hein's Social Critique in Transition* (Amsterdam: Rodopi, 2002), 124.

[32] McKnight, *Understanding Christoph Hein*, 40.

[33] Fischer, *Christoph Hein*, 111. The scene that Fischer cites is in Hein, *Horns Ende*, 58.

[34] David W. Robinson, *Deconstructing East Germany: Christoph Hein's Literature of Dissent* (Rochester, NY: Camden House, 1999).

[35] Robinson, *Deconstructing East Germany*, 158, 160.

[36] Alice Rayner, "Introduction: Doubles and Doubts," in *Ghosts: Death's Double and the Phenomena of Theater* (Minneapolis: University of Minnesota Press, 2006), ix–xxxv. Rayner makes this point perhaps most pithily when she writes that "ghosting or haunting is an aspect of theatre as a mode of consciousness in which a fully materialized reality, even a representational reality, is haunted by an appearing not-to-be—that is by its own negation" (xvii).

[37] Lehmann. "Christoph Hein—Chronist und 'historischer Materialist,'" 49.

[38] Hein, *Horns Ende*, 5.

[39] Shakespeare, *Hamlet*, act 1, scene 5, lines 10–13.

[40] The fact that a priest prays for Horn after Horn has committed suicide also creates a contrast between Horn's suicide and that of Werther in Goethe's *Die Leiden des jungen Werther*, since it is explicitly written at the end of the latter novel that no priest prays for Werther.

[41] Hein, "Wir werden es lernen müssen," 52.

[42] Christoph Hein, "Die alten Themen habe ich noch, jetzt kommen neue dazu," interview with Sigrid Löffler, March 1990, in *Christoph Hein: Texte, Daten, Bilder*, ed. Lothar Baier (Frankfurt: Luchterhand, 1990), 38.

[43] Christoph Hein, "Dialog ist das Gegenteil von Belehren," interview with Klaus Hammer (February 1991), in *Chronist ohne Botschaft*, ed. Klaus Hammer (Berlin: Aufbau, 1992), 12–13.

[44] Gordon, *Ghostly Matters*. Similarly, Walter Benjamin defines chronicling as follows: "Der Chronist, welcher die Ereignisse hererzählt, ohne große und kleine zu unterscheiden, trägt damit der Wahrheit Rechnung, daß nichts was sich jemals ereignet hat, für die Geschichte verloren zu geben ist." Benjamin, "Über den Begriff der Geschichte," Thesis III).

[45] Hammer. "*Horns Ende*: Versuch einer Interpretation," 124.

[46] Genette's term is "zero focalization." Genette's concept of focalization is helpful. His term "zero focalization," however is problematic.

[47] In fact, Martinez and Scheffel cite *Horns Ende* as an example of an event that is narrated by multiple narrators. They call this "multiple interne Fokalisierung." As Martinez and Scheffel point out, Franz Stanzel calls this type of perspective "multiperspektivisches Erzählen." Matias Martinez and Michael Scheffel, *Einführung in die Erzähltheorie* (Munich: Beck, 2007), 66.

[48] Gordon, *Ghostly Matters*.

[49] Ibid., 60.

[50] Ibid. Here Gordon is alluding to Jacques Derrida, who writes in *Specters of Marx*, as Gordon cites earlier in her book: "To exorcise not in order to chase away the ghosts, but this time to grant them the right . . . to . . . a hospitable memory . . . out of a concern for justice" (58).

[51] Greenblatt, *Hamlet in Purgatory*, 251.

[52] Robert Shandley, "Hans-Jürgen Syberberg and the State of the Ghost," in *German Studies in the Post-Holocaust Age: The Politics of Memory, Identity, and Ethnicity*, ed. Adrian Del Caro and Janet Ward (Boulder: University Press of Colorado, 2000), 140–47.

[53] Wim Wenders, dir., *Himmel über Berlin* (Road Movies, 1987).

[54] Shandley, "Hans-Jürgen Syberberg and the State of the Ghost," 142.

[55] Gordon, *Ghostly Matters*, 8.

[56] Hein, *Horns Ende*, 99.

[57] Marianne Hirsch, *Family Frames: Photography, Narrative, and Postmemory* (Cambridge, MA: Harvard University Press, 1997), 22.

[58] Hein, *Horns Ende*, 145.

[59] Jacques Derrida, "Force of Law: The Mythical Foundation of Authority," in *Deconstruction and the Possibility of Justice*, ed. Drucilla Cornell, Michel Rosenfeld, and David Gray Carlson (New York: Routledge, 1992), 3–67.

[60] Ibid., *Specters of Marx: The State of the Debt, the Work of Debt, and the New International* (New York: Routledge, 1994).

[61] Ibid., "Force of Law," 244.

[62] Gordon, *Ghostly Matters*, 204.

[63] Greenblatt, *Hamlet in Purgatory*, 251. Michael Douglas Schleihauf Zimmermann—although he more than once imprecisely calls the dialogues between the adult Thomas and the dead Horn "dreamlike dialogues"—comes

close to making Greenblatt's point as he once refers to the posthumous voice of Horn as "personified memory." Zimmermann, "Suicide in the German Novel, 119.

[64] Gordon, *Ghostly Matters*, 8.

[65] Bathrick, *The Powers of Speech*, 220–21.

[66] Hein, "Wir werden es lernen müssen," 59.

[67] Clarke, *"Diese merkwürdige Kleinigkeit einer Vision,"* 94, 312–15.

[68] Ibid., 126.

[69] Christl Kiewitz, *Der stumme Schrei: Krise und Kritik der sozialistischen Intelligenz im Werk Christoph Heins* (Tübingen: Stauffenburg, 1995), 224.

[70] Simon Bevan, "Change and Continuity in the Work of Christoph Hein: A Comparison of *Horns Ende* (1985) and *Von allem Anfang an* (1997)," in *East Germany: Continuity and Change*, German Monitor 46, ed. Paul Cooke and Jonathan Grix (Amsterdam: Rodopi, 2000), 18.

[71] Köhler, *Brückenschläge*, 137–44.

[72] The problem of space was rarely confronted in classical narratology.

[73] Mieke Bal, *Narratology: Introduction to the Theory of Narrative* (Toronto: University of Toronto Press, 1985), 93.

[74] Lubomir Dolezel, *Heterocosmica: Fiction and Possible Worlds* (Baltimore: Johns Hopkins University Press, 2000).

[75] Lotman, *Die Struktur literarischer Texte*, 356.

[76] Hein, *Horns Ende*, 36.

[77] Bärbel Lücke, *Christoph Hein: Horns Ende*, Oldenbourg Interpretationen 72 (Munich: Oldenbourg, 1994), 91.

[78] Clarke, *"Diese merkwürdige Kleinigkeit einer Vision,"* 94.

[79] Christoph Hein, *Der fremde Freund/Drachenblut* (Frankfurt am Main: Suhrkamp, 2005), 171. Originally published in 1982 by Aufbau.

[80] The language of detective fiction here is no accident. At least two of Hein's works that deal with suicide, *In seiner frühen Kindheit ein Garten* and *Frau Paula Trousseau*, may be appropriately deemed detective fiction.

[81] Greenblatt, *Hamlet in Purgatory*, 251.

[82] Lotman, *Culture and Explosion*, 123.

[83] Lotman, *Universe of the Mind*, 272.

Conclusion

Epigraph. Wolf Biermann, "Mich traf ein Mädchen," in *Deutschland im Herbst*, dir. Rainer Werner Fassbinder (Filmverlag der Autoren, 1978). Biermann's song was composed for Fassbinder's film.

[1] Slavoj Žižek, *Welcome to the Desert of the Real* (London: Verso, 2002), 1.

[2] Benjamin Robinson, "Morphine as the Tertium Quid between War and Revolution: Johannes R. Becher," *German Quarterly* 73, no. 4 (2000): 387–400. Sigmund Freud, who was an early proponent of the anesthetic properties of cocaine and became an addict, realized the destructive nature of the drug and quit it already in the fall of 1896.

[3] Levee Blanc, "Georg Lukács: The Antinomies of Melancholy," *Other Voices: The (e)Journal of Cultural Criticism* 1, no. 1 (March 1997), http://other-voices.org/blevee/lukacs.php.

[4] Slavoj Žižek, *Did Somebody Say Totalitarianism: Five Interventions in the (Mis)use of a Notion* (London: Verso, 2002), 88–140.

[5] Florian Maria Georg Christian Graf Henckel von Donnersmarck, dir., *Das Leben der Anderen* (Bayerischer Rundfunk, 2006).

[6] Andreas Dresen, "Der falsche Kino-Osten," *Zeit Online*, April 16, 2009, http://www.zeit.de/2009/17/Dresen.

[7] See, for example Timothy Garton Ash, "The Stasi on Our Minds," *New York Review of Books* 54, no. 9 (May 31, 2007), http://www.nybooks.com/articles/20210; Thomas Lindenberg, "Stasiploitation: Why Not? The Scriptwriter's Historical Creativity in *The Lives of Others*," *German Studies Review* 31, no. 3 (October 2008): 557–66; Jens Gieseke, "Stasi Goes to Hollywood: Donnersmarck's *The Lives of Others* und die Grenzen der Authentizität," *German Studies Review* 31, no. 3 (October 2008): 580–88.

[8] Wendy Westphal, "'Truer than the Real Thing': 'Real' and 'Hyperreal' Representations of the Past in *Das Leben der Anderen*," *German Studies Review* 35, no. 1 (2012): 97–111.

[9] Udo Grashoff, "'The Death of Others': The Myth and Reality of Suicide in the German Democratic Republic," *University College London, School of Slavonic and East European Studies Research Blog*, November 27, 2014, https://blogs.ucl.ac.uk/ssees/2014/11/27/the-death-of-others-the-myth-and-reality-of-suicide-in-the-german-democratic-republic/.

[10] Slavoj Žižek, "The Dreams of Others," *In These Times*, May 18, 2007: http://www.inthesetimes.com/article/3183/.

[11] Ibid.

[12] The song originally appeared in the 1978 West German film *Deutschland im Herbst*, where it functions as a Brechtian commentary on the alleged suicide of Ulrike Meinhof, a leading member of the left-wing terrorist organization Rote Armee Fraktion. Biermann's song asks, What if it emerges that Meinhof did not commit suicide but instead was murdered by the state (the Federal Republic), as many German leftists believe?

Epilogue

[1] This poem, along with an English translation and a brief biography of Kunze, can be found in Charlotte Melin, ed., *German Poetry in Transition, 1945–1990* (Hanover, NH: University Press of New England, 1999), 230–31.

[2] See Jean Améry, *On Suicide: A Discourse on Voluntary Death*, trans. John D. Barlow (Bloomington: Indiana University Press, 1999); Irène Heidelberger-Leonard, *The Philosopher of Auschwitz: Jean Améry and Living with the Holocaust* (London: Tauris, 2010).

[3] Michel Foucault, "The Simplest of Pleasures," in *Foucault Live: Collected Interviews, 1961–1984, ed.* Sylvère Lotringer (New York: Semiotext(e), 1999), 295–97.

[4] Wolf, *Lesen und Schreiben*, 213.

Bibliography

Adorno, Theodor, Walter Benjamin, Ernst Bloch, Bertolt Brecht, and Georg Lukács. *Aesthetics and Politics.* London: Verso, 2007.

Albrecht, Friedrich. *Bemühungen: Arbeiten zum Werk von Anna Seghers.* Bern: Peter Lang, 2005.

Améry, Jean. *On Suicide: A Discourse on Voluntary Death.* Translated by John D. Barlow. Bloomington: Indiana University Press, 1999.

Ankele, Monika. "Begrenzter Raum: Das Bett in der Frauenpsychiatrie um 1900." *Zeitschrift für Kulturwissenschaften* 2 (2008): 61–71.

Ash, Timothy Garton. "The Stasi on Our Minds." *New York Review of Books,* May 31, 2007. http://www.nybooks.com/articles/20210.

Augustine, Dolores L. *Red Prometheus: Engineering and Dictatorship in East Germany, 1945–1990.* Cambridge, MA: MIT Press, 2007.

Bahr, Eberhard. "Unerschlossene Intertextualität: MacPherson's Ossian und Goethe's Werther." *Goethe-Jahrbuch* 124 (2007): 178–88.

Bal, Mieke. *Narratology: Introduction to the Theory of Narrative.* Toronto: University of Toronto Press, 1985.

Bathrick, David. *The Powers of Speech: The Politics of Culture in the GDR.* Lincoln: University of Nebraska Press, 1995.

Becker, Jurek. *Jakob der Lügner.* Frankfurt am Main: Suhrkamp, 1977.

Benjamin, Walter. "Agesilaus Santander." In *Gesammelte Schriften,* 6:520–23.

———. "Der Erzähler: Betrachtungen zum Werk Nikolai Lesskows." In *Gesammelte Schriften,* 2.2:438–65. Frankfurt am Main: Suhrkamp, 1991. In English, "The Storyteller: Reflections of the Works of Nikolai Leskov." In *Illuminations,* translated by Harry Zohn, edited by Hannah Arendt, 83–109. New York: Schocken, 1969.

———. *Gesammelte Schriften.* Frankfurt am Main: Suhrkamp, 1991.

———. "Linke Melancholie." In Benjamin, *Angelus Novus,* 457–61. Frankfurt am Main: Suhrkamp, 1966.

———. "The Storyteller: Reflections of the Works of Nikolai Leskov." In Benjamin, *Illuminations,* translated by Harry Zohn, edited by Hannah Arendt, 83–109. New York: Schocken, 1969.

Berendse, Gerrit-Jan. "'Dank Breton': Surrealismus und kulturelles Gedächtnis in Adolf Endlers Lyrik." In *Schaltstelle: Neue deutsche Lyrik im Dialog,* edited by Karin Leeder, 73–95. Amsterdam: Rodopi, 2007.

Bevan, Simon. "Change and Continuity in the Work of Christoph Hein: A Comparison of *Horns Ende* (1985) and *Von allem Anfang an* (1997)." In *East Germany: Continuity and Change,* edited by Paul Cooke and Jonathan Grix, 15–23. German Monitor 46. Amsterdam: Rodopi, 2000.

Biermann, Wolf. "Mich traf ein Mädchen." In *Deutschland im Herbst*, directed by Rainer Werner Fassbinder. Filmverlag der Autoren, 1978.

Blanc, Levee. "Georg Lukács: The Antinomies of Melancholy." *Other Voices: The (e)Journal of Cultural Criticism* 1, no. 1 (March 1997). http://othervoices.org/blevee/lukacs.php.

Bloch, Ernst. "Philosophische Ansicht des Detektivromans." In Bloch, *Literarische Aufsätze*, vol. 9 of *Werkausgabe*, 242–63. Frankfurt am Main: Suhrkamp, 1965.

———. *Das Prinzip Hoffnung*. Frankfurt am Main: Suhrkamp, 1982.

Bohm, Arnd. "'Klopstock!' Once More: Intertextuality in Werther." *Seminar: A Journal of Germanic Studies* 38, no. 2 (May 2002): 116–33.

Borchert, Wolfgang. *Draußen vor der Tür*. Hamburg: Rowohlt, 1986.

Böschenstein, Bernhard. "Exzentrische Polarität." In *Interpretationen: Thomas Mann; Romane und Erzählungen*, edited by Volkmar Hansen, 89–120. Stuttgart: Reclam, 1993.

Brandes, Ute. "Quotation as Authentication: *No Place on Earth*." In *Responses to Christa Wolf: Critical Essays*, edited by Marilyn Sibley Fries, 326–48. Detroit, MI: Wayne State University Press, 1989.

Braun, Volker. *Unvollendete Geschichte*. Frankfurt am Main: Suhrkamp, 1977. Originally published in *Sinn und Form* in 1975.

Brecht, Bertolt. *Arbeitsjournal*. Frankfurt am Main: Suhrkamp, 1973.

———. "Lob des Kommunismus." In *Gesammelte Werke*, 9.2:463–64. Frankfurt: Suhrkamp, 1968.

Brenner, Peter J. *Plenzdorf's "Neue Leiden des jungen W."* Frankfurt am Main: Suhrkamp, 1982.

Bronner, Stephen Eric. "Political Aesthetics in the 1930s." In Bronner, *Of Critical Theory and Its Theorists*, 116–36. 2nd ed. New York: Routledge, 2002.

Brown, Wendy. "Resisting Left Melancholy." In *Loss*, edited by David L. Eng and David Kazanjian, 458–66. Berkeley: University of California Press, 2003.

Buehler, George. *The Death of Socialist Realism in the Novels of Christa Wolf*. Frankfurt am Main: Peter Lang, 1984.

Clarke, David. *"Diese merkwürdige Kleinigkeit einer Vision": Christoph Hein's Social Critique in Transition*. Amsterdam: Rodopi, 2002.

Cohn, Dorrit. "The Second Author of *Der Tod in Venedig*." In *Probleme der Moderne: Studien zur deutschen Literatur von Nietzsche bis Brecht; Festschrift für Walter Sokel*, edited by Benjamin Bennett, Anton Kaes, and William J. Lillyman, 223–45. Tübingen: Max Niemeyer, 1983.

Cosentino, Christine. Review of *Flucht in die Wolken*. *GDR Bulletin* 9, no. 3 (1983): 10.

"Das Veto der Witwe." *Der Spiegel*, June 10, 1996. http://www.spiegel.de/spiegel/print/d-8933790.html.

"Der neue Werther: Ein Gespräch." *Neue Deutsche Literatur* 21, no. 3 (1973): 139–49.

Derrida, Jacques. "Force of Law: The Mythical Foundation of Authority." In *Deconstruction and the Possibility of Justice*, edited by Drucilla Cornell, Michel Rosenfeld, and David Gray Carlson, 3–67. New York: Routledge, 1992.

———. *Specters of Marx: The State of the Debt, the Work of Debt, and the New International.* New York: Routledge, 1994.

"Deutsche Leiden." *Der Spiegel*, July 26, 1982. http://www.spiegel.de/spiegel/print/d-14341949.html.

Diersen, Inge. *Thomas Mann: Episches Werk, Weltanschauung, Leben.* 3rd ed. Berlin: Aufbau, 1985.

Dolezel, Lubomir. *Heterocosmica: Fiction and Possible Worlds.* Baltimore: Johns Hopkins University Press, 2000.

Donnersmarck, Florian Maria Georg Christian Graf Henckel von, dir. *Das Leben der Anderen.* Film, Bayerischer Rundfunk, 2006.

Dresen, Andreas. "Der falsche Kino-Osten." *Zeit Online*, April 16, 2009. http://www.zeit.de/2009/17/Dresen.

Duncan, Bruce. "'Emilia Galotti lag auf dem Pult aufgeschlagen': Werther as (Mis)Reader." *Goethe Yearbook* 1 (1982): 42–50.

———. *Goethe's Werther and the Critics.* Rochester, NY: Camden House, 2005.

Durkheim, Emile. *Suicide: A Study in Sociology.* Translated by John A. Saulding and George Simpson. Edited by George Simpson. Glencoe, IL: Free Press, 1951.

Emmerich, Wolfgang. "Affirmation—Utopie—Melancholie: Versuch einer Bilanz von vierzig Jahren DDR-Literatur." *German Studies Review* 14, no. 2 (May 1991): 325–44.

———. "Für eine andere Wahrnehmung der DDR-Literatur: Neue Kontexte, neue Paradigmen, ein neuer Kanon." In Goodbody and Tate, *Geist und Macht: Writers and the State in the GDR*, 7–22.

———. "Gleichzeitigkeit: Vormoderne, Moderne und Postmoderne in der Literatur der DDR." In *Bestandsaufnahme Gegenwartsliteratur*, edited by Heinz Ludwig Arnold, 193–211. Munich: Text + Kritik, 1988.

———. *Kleine Literaturgeschichte der DDR*. Berlin: Aufbau, 2000.

———. "Status melancholicus: Zur Transformation der Utopie in der DDR-Literatur." In *Literatur in der DDR: Rückblicke*, edited by Heinz Ludwig Arnold, 232–45. Sonderband. Munich: Text + Kritik, 1991.

Erbe, Günter. *Verfemte Moderne: Die Auseinandersetzung mit dem "Modernismus."* In *Kulturpolitik, Literaturwissenschaft und Literatur der DDR*. Opladen: Westdeutscher Verlag, 1993.

Eybl, Franz M. *Kleist-Lektüren.* Vienna: WUV Facultas (UTB), 2007.

Fallada, Hans. *Jeder stirbt für sich allein.* Berlin: Aufbau, 2012.

Farrelly, Daniel J. *Goethe in East Germany, 1949–1989: Toward a History of Goethe Reception in the GDR*. Rochester, NY: Camden House, 1998.

Fast, Piotr. *Ideology, Aesthetics, Literary History: Socialist Realism and Its Others.* Frankfurt am Main: Peter Lang, 1999.

Fehér, Ferenc. "Lukács in Weimar." In *Lukács Reappraised*, edited by Agnes Heller, 75–106. New York: Columbia University Press, 1983.

Fehervary, Helen. "Autorschaft, Geschlechtsbewusstsein und Öffentlichkeit: Versuch über Heiner Müllers *Die Hamletmaschine* and Christa Wolfs *Kein Ort. Nirgends.*" In *Entwürfe von Frauen in der Literatur des 20. Jahrhunderts*, edited by Irma von der Lühe, 132–53. Berlin: Argument, 1982.

Fischer, Bernd. *Christoph Hein: Drama und Prosa im letzten Jahrzehnt der DDR*. Heidelberg: Winter, 1990.

Foucault, Michel. "Nietzsche, Freud, Marx." In *Aesthetics, Method, and Epistemology*, edited by James D. Faubion, 269–78. New York: New Press, 1998.

———. "The Simplest of Pleasures." In *Foucault Live: Collected Interviews, 1961–1984*, edited by Sylvère Lotringer, 295–97. New York: Semiotext(e), 1999.

Fox, Thomas. *Stated Memory: East Germany and the Holocaust.* Rochester, NY: Camden House, 1999.

Geerdts, Hans Jürgen. "Werner Heiduczek: Tod am Meer." *Weimarer Beiträge: Zeitschrift für Literaturwissenschaft* 24. no. 5 (1978): 143–51.

Genette, Gérard. *The Architext: An Introduction.* 1979. Translated by Jane E. Lewin. Berkeley: University of California Press, 1992.

———. *Narrative Discourse: An Essay in Method.* Translated by Jane E. Lewin. Ithaca, NY: Cornell University Press, 1980. Originally published as "Discours du récit," a portion of *Figures III*, by Genette. Paris: Editions du Seuil, 1972.

———. *Palimpsests: Literature in the Second Degree.* Translated by Channa Newman and Claude Doubinsky. Lincoln: University of Nebraska Press, 1997. Originally published in 1982 by Editions du Seuil.

Getty, J. Arch, and Oleg V. Naumov. *The Road to Terror: Stalin and the Self-Destruction of the Bolsheviks.* New Haven, CT: Yale University Press, 1999.

Gieseke, Jens. "Stasi Goes to Hollywood: Donnersmarck's *The Lives of Others* und die Grenzen der Authentizität." *German Studies Review* 31, no. 3 (October 2008): 580–88.

Görlich, Günter. *Eine Anzeige in der Zeitung*. Berlin: Neues Leben, 1978.

Goethe, Johann Wolfgang von. *Briefe aus der Schweiz.* In *Weimarer Ausgabe*, ser. 1, 19:193–306. In English, *Letters from Switzerland, Letters from Italy.* Translated by A. J. W. Morrison. Edited by Nathan Haskel Dole. Boston: Francis A. Niccolls, 1902.

———. *Die Leiden des jungen Werther.* In *Sämtliche Werke*, edited by Waltraud Wiethölter, section 1, 8:9–267. Frankfurt am Main: Deutscher Klassiker, 1985.

Goldammer, Peter, ed. *Schriftsteller über Kleist: Eine Dokumentation.* Berlin: Aufbau, 1976.

Goodbody, Axel, and Dennis Tate, eds. *Geist und Macht: Writers and the State in the GDR*. German Monitor 29. Amsterdam: Rodopi, 1992.

Gordon, Avery F. *Ghostly Matters: Haunting and the Sociological Imagination*. 2nd ed. Minneapolis: University of Minnesota Press, 2008.

Grashoff, Udo. "'The Death of Others': The Myth and Reality of Suicide in the German Democratic Republic." *University College London, School of Slavonic and East European Studies Research Blog*, November 27, 2014. https://blogs.ucl.ac.uk/ssees/2014/11/27/the-death-of-others-the-myth-and-reality-of-suicide-in-the-german-democratic-republic/.

———. *"In einem Anfall von Depression . . .": Selbsttötungen in der DDR*. Berlin: Christoph Links, 2006.

Greenberg, Martin, ed. "Introduction." In Heinrich von Kleist, *Five Plays*, ix–li. New Haven, CT: Yale University Press, 1988.

Greenblatt, Stephen. *Hamlet in Purgatory*. Princeton, NJ: Princeton University Press, 2001.

Günderrode, Karoline von. *Ich sende Dir ein zärtliches Pfand: Die Briefe der Karoline von Günderrode*. Edited by Birgit Weißenborn. Frankfurt am Main: Insel, 1992.

———. *Der Schatten eines Traumes: Gedichte, Prosa, Briefe, Zeugnisse von Zeitgenossen*. Edited by Christa Wolf. Darmstadt: Luchterhand, 1979.

Hametner, Michael. "Die Literatur von heute wird schnell vorbeigehen." Interview with Werner Heiduczek. *Kunststoff* 3 (2006): 6–9.

Hamilton, Edith. *Mythology*. New York: Mentor, 1969. Originally published in 1940.

Hammer, Klaus. "*Horns Ende*: Versuch einer Interpretation." (1987). In *Chronist ohne Botschaft*, edited by Klaus Hammer. Berlin: Aufbau, 1992.

Heidelberger-Leonard, Irène. *The Philosopher of Auschwitz: Jean Améry and Living with the Holocaust*. London: Tauris, 2010.

Heiduczek, Werner. "Statt eines Vorworts." In *Im gewöhnlichen Stalinismus: Meine unerlaubten Texte*, 7–9. Leipzig: Kiepenheuer, 1991.

———. *Tod am Meer*. Berlin: Aufbau, 1999. Originally published in 1977.

Hein, Christoph. "Die alten Themen habe ich noch, jetzt kommen neue dazu." Interview with Sigrid Löffler, March 1990. In *Christoph Hein: Texte, Daten, Bilder*, edited by Lothar Baier, 37–40. Frankfurt am Main: Luchterhand, 1990.

———. "Dialog ist das Gegenteil von Belehren." Interview with Klaus Hammer, February 1991. In *Chronist ohne Botschaft*, edited by Klaus Hammer, 11–50. Berlin: Aufbau, 1992.

———. *Frau Paula Trousseau*. Frankfurt am Main: Suhrkamp, 2007.

———. *Der fremde Freund/Drachenblut*. Frankfurt am Main: Suhrkamp, 2005. Originally published by Aufbau in 1982.

———. "Hamlet und der Parteisekretär." In *Schlötel oder Was solls: Stücke und Essays*, 177–82. Excerpt from "Christoph Hein antwortet auf Fragen von *Theater der Zeit*." *Theater der Zeit* 7 (1978): 51–52.

———. *Horns Ende*. Darmstadt: Luchterhand, 1985.

———. *In seiner frühen Kindheit ein Garten*. Frankfurt am Main: Suhrkamp, 2005.

———. *Landnahme*. Frankfurt am Main: Suhrkamp, 2004.

———. *Passage. Theater der Zeit* 5 (1987): 50–64.

———. *Schlötel oder Was solls.* In *Schlötel oder Was solls: Stücke und Essays*, 21–85. (Premiered in 1974.)

———. *Schlötel oder Was solls: Stücke und Essays.* Darmstadt: Luchterhand, 1986.

———. *Von allem Anfang an.* Berlin: Aufbau, 1997.

———. *Willenbrock.* Frankfurt am Main: Suhrkamp, 2000.

———. "Wir werden es lernen müssen, mit unserer Vergangenheit zu leben." Interview with Krzysztof Jachimczak, 1986. In *Christoph Hein: Texte, Daten, Bilder*, edited by Lothar Baier, 45–67. Frankfurt am Main: Luchterhand, 1990.

———. "Die Zeit, die nicht vergehen kann oder Das Dilemma des Chronisten: Gedanken zum Historikerstreit anlässlich zweier deutscher vierzigster Jahrestage." In Hein, *Der Ort: Das Jahrhundert*, 140–71. Frankfurt am Main: Suhrkamp, 2003.

Hell, Julia. *Post-Fascist Fantasies.* Durham, NC: Duke University Press, 1997.

Hell, Julia, Loren Kruger, and Katie Trumpener. "Dossier: Socialist Realism and East German Modernism—Another Historians' Debate." *Rethinking Marxism* 7, no. 3 (Fall 1994): 36–79.

Hermlin, Stephan. "Erwiderung auf Friedrich Karl Kaul." *Sinn und Form* 25 (1973): 244.

Hilbk, Andrea. *Von Zirkularbewegungen und kreisenden Utopien: Zur Geschichtsdarstellung in der Epik Christoph Heins.* Augsburg: Berd Wissner, 1998.

Hille, Markus. *Karoline von Günderrode.* Reinbek: Rowohlt, 1999.

Hilzinger, Sonja. *Christa Wolf.* Stuttgart: Metzler, 1986.

Hirsch, Marianne. *Family Frames: Photography, Narrative, and Postmemory.* Cambridge, MA: Harvard University Press, 1997.

Honecker, Erich. Speech given on December 15, 1971. *Neues Deutschland*, December 18, 1971.

Honnef, Theo. *Heinrich von Kleist in der Literatur der DDR.* New York: Peter Lang, 1988.

Hörnigk, Theresa. *Christa Wolf.* Göttingen: Steidl, 1989.

Huyssen, Andreas. "Traces of Ernst Bloch: Reflections on Christa Wolf." In *Responses to Christa Wolf: Critical Essays*, edited by Marilyn Sibley Fries, 233–47. Detroit, MI: Wayne State University Press, 1989.

Johnson, Uwe. *Jahrestage: Aus dem Leben von Gesine Cresspahl.* Frankfurt am Main: Suhrkamp, 2000.

———. *Mutmassungen über Jakob.* Frankfurt am Main: Suhrkamp, 2000.

Joho, Wolfgang. *Der Sohn: Nachrichten aus der Bender Welt.* Berlin: Aufbau, 1974.

Judt, Matthias, ed. *DDR-Geschichte in Dokumenten: Beschlüsse, Berichte, interne Materialien und Alltagszeugnisse.* Berlin: Christoph Links, 1998.

Kadarkay, Arpad. *Georg Lukács: Life, Thought, and Politics.* Cambridge, MA: Blackwell, 1991.

Kalb, Jonathan. *The Theater of Heiner Müller.* Cambridge: Cambridge University Press, 1998.

Kane, Martin. "From Oobliadooh to Prenzlauer Berg: Literature, Alternative Lifestyle and Identity in the GDR." In Goodbody and Tate, *Geist und Macht: Writers and the State in the GDR*, 90–103.

Karasek, Hellmut. "Brecht ist tot." *Der Spiegel*, February 27, 1978, 216–17.

Kaul, Friedrich Karl. Letter. *Sinn und Form* 24 (1972): 219–20.

Kiewitz, Christl. *Der stumme Schrei: Krise und Kritik der sozialistischen Intelligenz im Werk Christoph Heins.* Tübingen: Stauffenburg, 1995.

Kleist, Heinrich von. *Penthesilea: Ein Trauerspiel.* Studienausgabe, edited by Ulrich Port. Stuttgart: Reclam, 2012. In English, *Penthesilea: A Tragic Drama.* Translated by Joel Agee. New York: Harper Collins, 1998.

———. *Sämtliche Briefe.* Edited by Dieter Heimböckel. Stuttgart: Reclam, 1999.

———. "Über das Marionettentheater." In *Sämtliche Werke und Briefe*, vol. 2, ed. Helmut Sembdner, 338–45. Darmstadt: Wissenschaftliche Buchgesellschaft, 1983. In English, "On the Marionette Theatre." Translated by Idris Parry. In the *Times Literary Supplement*, October 20, 1978. Also available at http://www.southerncrossreview.org/9/kleist.htm.

Klopstock, Friedrich Gottlieb. *Werke in einem Band.* Berlin: Bibliothek Deutscher Klassiker, 1971.

Klotz, Günther. "Shakespeare Contemporized: GDR Shakespeare Adaptations from Bertolt Brecht to Heiner Müller." In *Redefining Shakespeare: Literary Theory and Theater Practice in the German Democratic Republic*, edited by J. Lawrence Guntner and Andrew M. McLean, 84–97. Newark: University of Delaware Press, 1998.

Koelb, Clayton. "'The Heavenly Revelation of Her Spirit': Goethe's *The Sorrows of the Young Werther.*" In Koelb, *The Revivifying Word*, 47–67.

———. *The Revivifying Word: Literature, Philosophy, and the Theory of Life in Europe's Romantic Age.* Rochester, NY: Camden House, 2008.

Köhler, Astrid. *Brückenschläge: Autoren vor und nach der Wiedervereinigung.* Göttingen: Vandenhoeck & Ruprecht, 2007.

Kristeva, Julia. *Julia Kristeva, Interviews.* Edited by Ross Mitchell Guberman. New York: Columbia University Press, 1996.

———. "On Yury Lotman." Translated by Martha Noel Evans. *PMLA* 3 (May 1994): 375–76.

———. *Powers of Horror: An Essay on Abjection.* Translated by Leon S. Roudiez. New York: Columbia University Press, 1982.

Kuhn, Anna K. *Christa Wolf's Utopian Vision: From Marxism to Feminism.* Cambridge: Cambridge University Press, 1988.

Kunert, Günter. *Ein anderer K.* Stuttgart: Reclam, 1977.

———. "Pamphlet für K." *Sinn und Form* 27 (1975): 1091–97.

Kurella, Alfred. "Gespräch mit Alfred Kurella." *Sinn und Form* 2 (1975): 221–43.

Kuzniar, Alice, ed. *Outing Goethe and His Age.* Stanford, CA: Stanford University Press, 1996.

Lämmert, Eberhard. *Bauformen des Erzählens*. Stuttgart: Metzler, 1972. Originally published in 1955.

Layne, Priscilla. "The Stranger Within: Black Voices, German Rebels." PhD diss., University of California, Berkeley, 2011.

Lechte, John. *Julia Kristeva*. London: Routledge, 1990.

Leeder, Karin. *Schaltstelle: Neue deutsche Lyrik im Dialog*. Amsterdam: Rodopi, 2007.

Leenaars, Antoon A., ed. *Suicidology: Essays in Honor of Edwin S. Shneidman*. Northvale, NJ: Aronson, 1993.

Lehmann, Joachim. "Christoph Hein—Chronist und 'historischer Materialist.'" *Text + Kritik* 111 (July 1991): 44–56.

Lennox, Sara. "Christa Wolf and the Women Romantics." In *Studies in GDR Culture and Society: 2*, edited by Margy Gerber, Christine Cosentino, Volker Gransow, and Nancy Stephan, 31–44. Washington, DC: University Press of America, 1982.

Lester, David. *Suicide and the Holocaust*. New York: Nova, 2005.

Liersch, Werner. "Wann die Wahrheit." *Neue Deutsche Literatur* 26, no. 3 (1978): 139–44.

Lindenberg, Thomas. "Stasiploitation: Why Not? The Scriptwriter's Historical Creativity in *The Lives of Others*." *German Studies Review* 31, no. 3 (October 2008): 557–66.

Loquai, Franz. *Hamlet und Deutschland: Zur literarischen Shakespeare Reception im 20. Jahrhundert*. Stuttgart: Metzler, 1993.

Lotman, Yuri. *Culture and Explosion*. Edited by Marina Grishakova. Translated by Wilma Clark. Berlin: de Gruyter, 2009. Originally published in 1992.

———. *Die Struktur literarischer Texte*. Translated by Rolf-Dietrich Keil. Munich: Wilhelm Fink, 1993. Originally published in 1972. Translated into English by Ronald Vroon and Gail Vroon as *The Structure of the Artistic Text* (Ann Arbor: University of Michigan Press, 1977).

———. "On the Semiosphere." Translated by Wilma Clark. *Sign Systems Studies* 33, no. 1 (2005): 205–29.

———. *Universe of the Mind: A Semiotic Theory of Culture*. Translated by Ann Shukman. Bloomington: Indiana University Press, 1990.

Low, Anthony. "Hamlet and the Ghost of Purgatory: Forgetting the Dead." *Culture Wars* (June 2000). http://www.culturewars.com/CultureWars/2000/June/hamlet.html.

Lücke, Bärbel. *Christoph Hein: Horns Ende*. Oldenbourg Interpretationen 72. Munich: Oldenbourg, 1994.

Lukács, Georg. "Auf der Suche nach dem Bürger." *Internationale Literatur* 15, nos. 6/7 (1945): 58–75.

———. "Deutsche Literatur im Zeitalter des Imperialismus." 1945. In *Skizze einer Geschichte der neueren deutschen Literatur*, 190. Neuwied: Luchterhand, 1963.

———. "Die deutsche Literatur im Zeitalter des Imperialismus." *Internationale Literatur* 15, no. 3 (1945): 53–65.

———. *Fortschritt und Reaktion in der deutschen Literatur.* Berlin: Aufbau, 1947.

———. "Franz Kafka oder Thomas Mann?" In *Wider den missverstandenen Realismus*, 49–96. Hamburg: Classen, 1958.

———. *Goethe und seine Zeit.* Bern: A. Francke, 1947.

———. *The Historical Novel.* Lincoln: University of Nebraska Press, 1983. Originally published in Russian in 1937.

———. "Das Spielerische und seine Hintergründe." *Aufbau* 11, no. 6 (1955): 501–24.

———. "Die Tragödie der modernen Kunst." In *Thomas Mann*, 49–113. Berlin: Aufbau, 1949.

———. "Über Preußentum." In *Internationale Literatur* 13, no. 5 (1943): 36–47.

———. "Wozu brauchen wir das klassische Erbe?" In *Literaturtheorie und Literaturkritik in der frühsowjetischen Diskussion: Standorte—Programme—Schulen*, edited by Anton Hiersche and Edward Kowalski, 422–27. Bern: Peter Lang, 1993.

———. *Writer and Critic.* London: Merlin, 1970.

———. *Die Zerstörung der Vernunft.* Vol. 9 of *Werke.* Edited by Frank Benseler. Neuwied: Lukács Archiv, 1962.

MacLeod, Catriona. "The 'Third Sex' in an Age of Difference: Androgyny and Homosexuality in Winckelmann, Friedrich Schlegel, and Kleist." In Kuzniar, *Outing Goethe and His Age*, 194–214.

Magenau, Jörg. *Christa Wolf: Eine Biographie.* Berlin: Kindler, 2002.

Mann, Thomas. *Der Tod in Venedig.* Berlin: S. Fischer, 1913.

Marsch, Edgar. *Die Kriminalerzählung: Theorie, Geschichte, Analyse.* Munich: Winkler, 1972.

Martinez, Matias. "Choleratod und regressive Transzendenz: Thomas Mann, *Der Tod in Venedig* (1912)." In Martinez, *Doppelte Welten: Struktur und Sinn zweideutigen Erzählens*, 151–76. Göttingen: Vandenhoeck & Ruprecht, 1996.

Martinez, Matias, and Michael Scheffel. *Einführung in die Erzähltheorie.* Munich: Beck, 2007.

Martinson, Steven D. "'. . . aus dem Schiffbruch des irdischen Lebens': The Literature of Karoline von Günderrode and Early German Romantic and Idealist Philosophy." *German Studies Review* 28, no. 2 (May 2005): 303–26.

Matussek, Matthias. *Das Selbstmord-Tabu: Von der Seelenlosigkeit des SED-Staates.* Reinbek bei Hamburg: Rowohlt, 1992.

McKnight, Phillip. *Understanding Christoph Hein.* Columbia: University of South Carolina Press, 1995.

Melin, Charlotte, ed. *German Poetry in Transition, 1945–1990.* Hanover, NH: University Press of New England, 1999.

Miller, Ann Stamp. *The Cultural Politics of the German Democratic Republic: The Voices of Christa Wolf, Wolf Biermann, and Heiner Müller.* Boca Raton, FL: Brown Walker, 1999.

Mimpriss, Hilary. "'Ohne Hoffnung können wir nicht leben': Christoph Hein's Use of Religious Motifs as an Expression of Resignation and of Hope." In *Christoph Hein in Perspective*, ed. Graham Jackson, 95–114. German Monitor. Amsterdam: Rodopi, 2000.

Minois, Georges. *History of Suicide: Voluntary Death in Western Culture.* Translated by Lydia G. Cochrane. Baltimore: Johns Hopkins University Press, 1999. Originally published in 1995.

Montefiore, Simon Sebag. *Stalin: The Court of the Red Tsar.* London: Phoenix, 2004. Originally published by Weidenfeld & Nicolson in 2003.

Mueller, Magdalene. "Alltagserfahrung? Bemerkungen zur Darstellung des Todes in der neueren DDR-Literatur." *Studies in GDR Culture and Society 8*, edited by Margy Gerber, 127–40. Lanham, MD: University Press of America, 1988.

Müller, Heiner. "Dichter müssen dumm sein." *Die Zeit*, August 14, 1987. http://www.a-e-m-gmbh.com/andremuller/heiner%20mueller.html.

———. *Die Hamletmaschine.* In Heiner Müller, *Werke*, vol. 4, edited by Frank Hörnigk, 543–54. Frankfurt am Main: Suhrkamp, 2001.

———. Interview. *Theater heute* 1 (January 1984): 61–62.

———. *Der Lohndrücker, Philoktet, Die Schlacht: Textausgabe mit Materialien.* Berlin: Klett, 1986.

———. *Rotwelsch.* Berlin: Merve, 1982.

Müller, Peter. *Zeitkritik und Utopie in Goethes "Werther."* Berlin: Rütten & Loening, 1969.

Muthesius, Sibylle. *Flucht in die Wolken.* Berlin: Der Morgen, 1981.

Nafisi, Azar. *Reading* Lolita *in Tehran: A Memoir in Books.* New York: Random House, 2003.

Owen, Ruth J. "Claiming the Body: The Ophelia Myth in the GDR." *Germanic Review* 82, no. 3 (2007): 251–67.

Packalén, Sture. *Zum Hölderlinbild in der Bundesrepublik und der DDR.* Stockholm: Acta Universitatis Upsaliensis, 1986.

Paperno, Irina. *Suicide as a Cultural Institution in Dostoevsky's Russia.* Ithaca, NY: Cornell University Press, 1997.

Paul, Georgina. *Perspectives on Gender in Post-1945 German Literature.* Rochester, NY: Camden House, 2009.

Paulin, Roger. *The Critical Reception of Shakespeare in Germany 1682–1914: Native Literature and Foreign Genius.* Hildesheim: Olms, 2003.

Pearlman, E. *William Shakespeare: The History Plays.* New York: Twayne, 1992.

Pensky, Max. *Melancholy Dialectics: Walter Benjamin and the Play of Mourning.* Amherst: University of Massachusetts Press, 1993.

Pfeiffer, Joachim. "Friendship and Gender: The Aesthetic Construction of Subjectivity in Kleist." Translated by Robert D. Tobin. In Kuzniar, *Outing Goethe and His Age*, 215–27.

Pieck, Wilhelm. *Zur Bildungspolitik der Arbeiterbewegung: Reden und Schriften.* Edited by Rudi Schulze. Berlin: Volk & Wissen, 1981.

Pike, David. *German Writers in Soviet Exile, 1933–1945.* Chapel Hill: University of North Carolina Press, 1982.

———. *The Politics of Culture in Soviet-Occupied Germany, 1945–1949.* Stanford, CA: Stanford University Press, 1992.

Pizer, John. "Staging Violence and Transcendence: Reading Christa Wolf through German Romanticism." *German Studies Review* 33, no. 1 (February 2010): 1–22.

Pizzato, Mark. "Ancient Specters (Prehistoric, Egyptian, Greek, and Roman)." In Pizzato, *Ghosts of Theatre and Cinema in the Brain.* New York: Palgrave MacMillan, 2006.

Plenzdorf, Ulrich. *Die neuen Leiden des jungen W.* West Berlin: Suhrkamp, 1978. Originally published in the journal *Sinn und Form* in 1972 and in Rostock by Hinstorff in 1973.

Quernheim, Mechthild. *Das moralische Ich: Kritische Studien zur Subjektwerdung in der Erzählprosa Christa Wolfs.* Würzburg: Königshausen & Neumann, 1990.

Rabaté, Jean-Michel. *The Ghosts of Modernity.* Gainesville: University Press of Florida, 1996.

Raddatz, Fritz J. "Mein Name sei Tonio K." *Der Spiegel,* June 2, 1969, 153–54. Online at http://www.spiegel.de/spiegel/print/d-45741041.html.

———. "Ulrich Plenzdorfs Flucht nach Innen." *Merkur* 27 (1973): 1174–78.

Rayner, Alice. *Ghosts: Death's Double and the Phenomena of Theatre.* Minneapolis: University of Minnesota Press, 2006.

Reimann, Brigitte, and Christa Wolf. *Sei gegrüßt und lebe: Eine Freundschaft in Briefen, 1964–1973.* Berlin: Aufbau, 1999.

Richardson, Michael D. "Allegories and Ends: Heiner Müller's "Hamletmaschine." *New German Critique* 98 (Summer 2006): 77–100.

Richter, Simon. *Missing the Breast: Gender, Fantasy, and the Body in the German Enlightenment.* Seattle: University of Washington Press, 2006.

Robinson, Benjamin. "Morphine as the Tertium Quid between War and Revolution: Johannes R. Becher." *German Quarterly* 73, no. 4 (2000): 387–400.

———. *The Skin of the System: On Germany's Socialist Modernity.* Stanford, CA: Stanford University Press, 2009.

Robinson, David W. *Deconstructing East Germany: Christoph Hein's Literature of Dissent.* Rochester, NY: Camden House, 1999.

Rohrwasser, Michael. "Das Selbstmordmotiv in der DDR-Literatur." In *Probleme deutscher Identität: Zeitgenössische Autobiographien: Identitätssuche und Zivilisationskritik,* edited by Paul Gerhard Klussman and Heinrich Mohr, 209–32. Bonn: Bouvier, 1983.

Ross, Corey. *The East German Dictatorship: Problems and Perspectives in the Interpretation of the GDR.* London: Arnold, 2002.

———. "The East German Economy: 'Planned miracle,' Victim of Circumstance or Fundamentally Flawed?" In Ross, *The East German Dictatorship,* 69–96.

Sch., Monika. "Der neue Werther: Ein Gespräch." *Neue Deutsche Literatur* 21, no. 3 (1973): 139.

Scharfschwerdt, Jürgen. "Werther in der DDR: Bürgerliches Erbe zwischen sozialistischer Kulturpolitik und gesellschaftlicher Realität." *Jahrbuch der deutschen Schillergesellschaft* 22 (1978): 235–76.

Scherler, Kirsten. *"Wie froh bin ich, dass ich weg bin!": Werther in der deutschen Literatur*. Frankfurt am Main: Peter Lang, 2010.

Schiller, Friedrich. "Nänie." In *Werke und Briefe*, edited by Georg Kurscheidt, 1:182–83. Frankfurt am Main: Deutscher Klassiker, 1992. In English, "Nenia." In *Poetical Works of Friedrich Schiller*, translated by E. P. Arnold-Forster, edited by Nathan Haskell Dole, 253–54. Boston, Francis A. Niccolls, 1902.

Schlenker, Wolfram. *Das "kulturelle Erbe" in der DDR: Gesellschaftliche Entwicklung und Kulturpolitik, 1945–1965*. Metzler-Studienausgabe. Stuttgart: Metzler, 1977.

Schneider, Rolf. "Imagination." In *19 Erzähler der DDR*, edited by Hans-Jürgen Schmitt. Frankfurt am Main: Fischer, 1971.

———. *Die Reise nach Jarosław*. Rostock: Hinstorff, 1974.

Schubbe, Elimar, ed. *Dokumente zur Kunst-, Literatur-, und Kulturpolitik der SED*. Stuttgart: Seewald, 1972.

Seghers, Anna. *Der Ausflug der toten Mädchen: Und andere Erzählungen*. Berlin: Aufbau, 1995.

———. *Das siebte Kreuz*. Hamburg: Rowohlt, 1965. In English, *The Seventh Cross*. Translated by James A. Galston. Jaffrey, NH: Verba Mundi, 2004.

———. *Die toten bleiben jung*. Darmstadt: Luchterhand, 1980.

———. *Transit*. Berlin: Aufbau, 1993.

Sevin, Dieter. *Textstrategien in DDR-Prosawerken zwischen Bau und Durchbruch der Berliner Mauer*. Heidelberg: C. Winter, 1994.

Shakespeare, William. *Hamlet*. New York: Signet Classic, 1963.

Shandley, Robert. "Hans-Jürgen Syberberg and the State of the Ghost." In *German Studies in the Post-Holocaust Age: The Politics of Memory, Identity, and Ethnicity*, edited by Adrian Del Caro and Janet Ward, 140–47. Boulder: University Press of Colorado, 2000.

Sharman, Gundula. *Twentieth-Century Reworkings of German Literature: An Analysis of Six Fictional Reinterpretations from Goethe to Thomas Mann*. Rochester, NY: Camden House, 2002.

Shneidmann, Edwin S. *Definition of Suicide*. New York: Wiley, 1985.

Sontag, Susan. "Under the Sign of Saturn." In *Under the Sign of Saturn*, 109–34. New York: Farrar, Straus, & Giroux, 1980.

Stanzel, Franz Karl. *Typische Formen des Romans*. Göttingen: Vandenhoeck & Ruprecht, 1964.

Stokes, Raymond G. *Constructing Socialism: Technology and Change in East Germany, 1945–1990*. Baltimore: Johns Hopkins University Press, 2000.

Strittmatter, Erwin. *Ole Bienkopp*. Berlin: Aufbau, 1977.

Swales, Martin. *Goethe: The Sorrows of the Young Werther*. Landmarks of World Literature. Cambridge: Cambridge University Press, 1987.

Symons, Julian. *Bloody Murder: From the Detective Story to the Crime Novel: A History.* New York: Viking, 1985.

Teupe, Peter F. *Christa Wolfs "Kein Ort. Nirgends" als Paradigma der DDR-Literatur der siebziger Jahre.* Frankfurt am Main: Peter Lang, 1992.

Titon, Jeff Todd. "Text." In *Eight Words for the Study of Expressive Culture*, edited by Bert Feintuch, 69–98. Champaign: University of Illinois Press, 2003.

Tobol, Carol E. W., and Ida H. Washington. "Werther's Selective Reading of Homer." *MLN* 92, no. 3 (1977): 596–601.

Trebeß, Achim. "Zum Todesmotiv in der DDR-Literatur." *Weimarer Beiträge: Zeitschrift für Literaturwissenschaft* 47, no. 1 (2001): 82–84.

Wallace, Ian. "Andere Lösung Quatsch: Anna Seghers and the Film of *Die toten bleiben jung*." In *Aliens—Uneingebürgerte: German and Austrian Writers in Exile*, edited by Ian Wallace, 71–84. Amsterdam: Rodopi, 1994.

Waniek, Erdmann. "*Werther* lesen und Werther als Leser." *Goethe Yearbook* 1 (1982): 51–92.

Wasserman, Danuta, and Camilla Wasserman, eds. *Oxford Textbook of Suicidology and Suicide Prevention: A Global Perspective.* Oxford: Oxford University Press, 2009.

Wellbery, David, ed. *Positionen der Literaturwissenschaft: Acht Modellanalysen am Beispiel von Kleists "Das Erdbeben in Chili."* Munich: Beck, 1985.

Wenders, Wim, dir. *Himmel über Berlin.* Road Movies, 1987.

Werner, Hans-Georg. "Peter Müller, Zeitkritik und Utopie in Goethes 'Werther.'" *Weimarer Beiträge* 7 (1970): 193–99.

Westphal, Wendy. "'Truer than the Real Thing': 'Real' and 'Hyperreal' Representations of the Past in *Das Leben der Anderen*." *German Studies Review* 35, no. 1 (2012): 97–111.

Wilson, Jean. "Transgression and Identity in Kleist's Penthesilea and Wolf's Cassandra." *Women in German Yearbook: Feminist Studies in German Literature and Culture* 16 (2000): 191–206.

Wittels, Fritz. "Heinrich von Kleist—Prussian Junker and Creative Genius: A Study in Bisexuality." In *Art and Psychoanalysis*, edited by William Phillips, 165–82. New York: World, 1957.

Wolf, Christa. *Der geteilte Himmel.* Munich: Deutscher Taschenbuch Verlag, 1973.

———. *Kassandra.* Frankfurt am Main: Luchterhand, 1983.

———. *Kein Ort. Nirgends.* Darmstadt: Luchterhand, 1979. In English, *No Place on Earth.* New York: Farrar, Straus & Giroux: 1982.

———. *Kindheitsmuster.* Berlin: Aufbau, 1976.

———. "Kleists 'Penthesilea.'" In *Werke*, vol. 8, ed. Sonja Hilzinger, 261–79. Munich: Luchterhand, 2000. Written in August 1982.

———. *Lesen und Schreiben.* Darmstadt: Luchterhand, 1968.

———. *Nachdenken über Christa T.* Halle: Mitteldeutscher Verlag, 1968. In English, *The Quest for Christa T.* Translated by Christopher Middleton. New York: Farrar, Straus & Giroux, 1970.

———. “Projektionsraum Romantik: Gespräch mit Frauke Meyer-Gosau.” 1982. In *Die Dimension des Autors: Essays und Aufsätze; Reden und Gespräche, 1959–1985*, 878–95. Darmstadt: Luchterhand, 1987.

———. “Der Schatten eines Traumes: Karoline von Günderrode—ein Entwurf.” In Karoline von Günderrode, *Der Schatten eines Traumes: Gedichte, Prosa, Briefe, Zeugnisse von Zeitgenossen*, edited by Christa Wolf, 5–52. Darmstadt: Luchterhand, 1979.

Wolf, Christa, and Anna Seghers. *Das dicht besetzte Leben: Briefe, Gespräche und Essays.* Edited by Angela Drescher. Berlin: Aufbau, 2003.

Wurm, Carsten. “‘Uneigennützige Hilfeleistung’: Ein Dokument zu Werner Heiduczeks Roman *Tod am Meer.*” *Neue Deutsche Literatur: Zeitschrift für deutschsprachige Literatur* 44, no. 6 (November–December 1996): 147–51.

Zeckert, Ines. *Poetologie und Prophetie: Heins Prosa und Dramatik im Kontext seiner Walter-Benjamin-Rezeption.* Frankfurt am Main: Lang, 1993.

Zimmer, Dieter E. “Nicht mehr so dogmatisch: Ulrich Plenzdorf, sein neuer Film *Paul und Paula* und sein Werther-Roman als Symptome einer neuen Offenheit.” *Die Zeit*, April 20, 1973.

Zimmermann, Harro. *Freiheit und Geschichte: F. G. Klopstock als historischer Dichter und Denker.* Heidelberg: Carl Winter, 1987.

Zimmermann, Michael Douglas Schleihauf. “Suicide in the German Novel, 1945–1989.” PhD diss., University of Waterloo, 1997.

Žižek, Slavoj. *Did Somebody Say Totalitarianism: Five Interventions in the (Mis)use of a Notion.* London: Verso, 2002.

———. “The Dreams of Others.” *In These Times*, May 18, 2007. http://www.inthesetimes.com/article/3183/.

———. *Welcome to the Desert of the Real.* London: Verso, 2002.

———. “When the Party Commits Suicide.” In Žižek, *Did Somebody Say Totalitarianism: Five Interventions in the (Mis)use of a Notion*, 88–140.

Index